THE UNLIKELY SPY

THE UNLIKELY SPY
PAUL HENDERSON

FORMER MANAGING DIRECTOR OF MATRIX CHURCHILL

AN AUTOBIOGRAPHY

BLOOMSBURY

For Esther

First published in Great Britain 1993
Bloomsbury Publishing Ltd, 2 Soho Square, London W1V 5DE

Copyright © 1993 by Paul Henderson

The moral right of the author has been asserted

A CIP catalogue record for this book
is available from the British Library

ISBN 0 7475 1597 2

Typeset by Hewer Text Composition Services, Edinburgh
Printed by Clays Limited, St Ives plc

Acknowledgements

There are a number of people without whom this book would never have been written.

First, HM Government and HM Customs and Excise, whose naïvety in believing that I would be a willing scapegoat, and spend seven years in prison rather than reveal my links with the intelligence service, led them to attempt prosecution in 'open' court. Had they admitted prior knowledge, there would have been no trial; the thousands of documents proving their knowledge, and my innocence, would never have entered the public domain; allegations of 'cover-up' and 'conspiracy' would not have been made. In short, 'Iraqgate' would never have been.

Secondly, after the trial's collapse in November 1992, it was my solicitor and friend, Kevin Robinson, who persuaded me that there was a story to be told. It was his hard work, arranging meetings with publishers and writers, that set the literary ball rolling.

Thirdly, I would like to thank Doug Frantz who, after many long hours of discussion and clear thinking, helped me produce the manuscript, which Bloomsbury accepted upon first submission.

I would like to thank Nigel Newton and David Reynolds at Bloomsbury. It was owing to their professionalism and enthusiasm that I finally decided to go ahead. The rest of the staff at Bloomsbury also deserve my thanks for all their hard work.

I want to thank all my family for their love and support throughout; in particular, my wife Esther, my son David and his wife Karen and, especially, my daughter Sue, who spent many hours helping me with the manuscript.

I would like to thank John Belgrove, who stood bail for me, and Mark Gutteridge, who not only stood bail, but also revealed his intelligence service links in my defence. Thank you also to all my other friends for your ongoing support. I won't risk missing anyone out by attempting to list all your names. You know who you are. Thanks.

And last, but definitely not least, I want to say thank you again to my brilliant team of legal experts – Geoffrey Robertson, my QC, his co-counsel Ken MacDonald, their legal assistant Peter Weatherby and, of course, my solicitor Kevin Robinson. Without them, this book might have been entitled 'Rough Justice' and written over a seven-year stretch.

Author's Note

The author understood that all names used by intelligence personnel were false; those pseudonyms are used throughout this book.

Prologue

Stepping inside a gracious Georgian house a stone's throw from
Buckingham Palace, I entered the world of espionage. It was half
past ten on a bright, dry morning in late September 1989. I remember
it clearly: the high-ceilinged room with its dull décor; the urgent,
curious voices of my inquisitors; the wall-sized satellite photograph
of Baghdad; the non-stop questions about Iraqi military installations,
munitions factories and secret missile projects. I can recall thinking
to myself, so this is what it's like in their world.

True, I had worked with the British intelligence service for sixteen
years. The KGB had interrogated me; the Romanian secret police
had tried to turn me. I had been told that my information was very
valuable to the government. But most of my intelligence work had
been relatively commonplace; I was not a professional spy – just a
businessman helping his country.

During those years I had carefully noted what I had seen in
factories throughout Eastern Europe, the Soviet Union, China and
the Middle East. I had tried to learn more from the plant managers
and government officials I met, cautiously asking questions until
something told me that my curiosity would remain unsatisfied
and further enquiry would be unwise. Then I had reported my
observations to my controller, usually at a meeting in a hotel
lobby or a pub. It was nothing like the spying portrayed in books
and films.

But that September day in 1989 was different. The stakes were far
higher, though I had no way of knowing it then.

My controller was using the name John Balsom. He was an
intelligent, quiet-spoken man in his mid-thirties, the latest in a
series of contacts assigned to me by MI5 and MI6, the British
intelligence services. It was clear from my dealings with Balsom that

the information I was providing on Iraq was more important to the government than anything I had collected before. So I had agreed to spend a day being fully debriefed by his boss and technical experts in London. We had set up the meeting for 22 September.

By the autumn of 1989 I had risen from apprentice to managing director of Matrix Churchill Limited, a machine-tool manufacturing company in Coventry. The company's majority shareholders were Iraqis, and their government was one of our main customers. My position had given me access to the inner workings of Iraq's major military and commercial installations. For the past year I had been providing Balsom with a steady flow of information about what the Iraqis were doing in their own country and elsewhere in the world.

Matrix Churchill was not alone in selling to Iraq. Hundreds of Western companies were providing technology to Baghdad, with the approval of their governments. Most of the technology was dual-purpose, which meant it could be used for either commercial or military purposes. All of the machine tools that Matrix Churchill had sold to Iraq fell into this category.

This flow of Western technology had begun early in the decade. Britain and the USA had adopted a joint policy of helping Saddam Hussein build a powerful army to counter the fanatical Islamic fundamentalists in neighbouring Iran. The two Middle Eastern countries had been waging a bloody war since 1980, with Iraq depending on aid from Britain and America as well as from the Soviet Union.

When the war ended with a ceasefire in August 1988, the flow of Western goods did not. The governments saw this technology as a useful political lever for dealing with Saddam Hussein. And they saw Iraq as a stabilizing influence to maintain peace in the Middle East. For the manufacturers, the Iraqi market had become too important to lose. This was certainly true for Matrix Churchill.

On that September morning Balsom met me at the station in London and we were driven to a small close off the Mall, near Horse Guards Parade. Our destination in Carlton Gardens appeared to be just another nondescript office building; the ideal 'safe house' for clandestine meetings.

Inside, to the right of the reception, was a large room decorated like a lounge, with settees and comfortable chairs and an antique mahogany dining table. The curtains were drawn. An aerial photograph of Baghdad and the surrounding region covered one wall, and even from a distance it was easy to distinguish the complexes I had visited so often in recent months.

Three men were standing by the sideboard in the room. Two were in their early thirties, not memorable. The other was a grey-haired man in his forties, with a light build. He had the watchful eyes of someone who was in charge and knew what he was doing. There was silence.

The grey-haired man walked over and introduced himself as 'Peter'. He was Balsom's superior. The other two followed suit, using only their first names, Mark and David, as did Balsom and the other intelligence agents I had met. These may or may not have been their real names.

We exchanged pleasantries and sat down at the large table to drink our coffee. Balsom drew a broad outline of the information I had supplied to him about the workings of the Iraqi armaments procurement network and my visits to installations in Iraq.

'Paul has provided extremely valuable information about Iraq's capabilities and intentions,' he said. 'He has also agreed to answer your questions today.'

'Yes, extremely valuable,' agreed Peter, whose nod was duplicated by the other two men. 'Paul, we'll try to jog your memory. It's a simple process of trying to get a few more details from you.'

'I'll do my best,' I replied, watching the three men simultaneously open buff folders in front of them as Balsom retreated to an armchair near the bay window.

The questions were frequent that day in the safe house. Who are the people running the plants? What are they like? Which ones speak English? Are the installations heavily guarded? Is the military there? Is it difficult to get into the plants? What other Western companies are supplying equipment?

The intelligence men were expert on the workings of the Iraqi government led by Saddam Hussein. They also understood the technical issues involved in the manufacture of arms and munitions. It was clear that they had obtained information from other sources. I strained to answer accurately and thoroughly, while they made notes on large pads of paper. The atmosphere was tense.

I described the Iraqi installations, detailed the contracts that Matrix Churchill had signed with them, told them all I knew about the transactions involving other Western companies. I handed over drawings of a mobile-launched rocket for which we were providing machinery to manufacture components, and drawings for Project 210, known as Project Babylon, for a long-range projectile. I tried to recall every detail and by the end of the day I was exhausted.

'This information is extremely useful,' said Peter as he opened the outer door and Balsom and I walked into the late-afternoon chill.

I felt quite satisfied as I left. The world of espionage had not proved so dark after all. I felt I was in control, helping my country without exposing myself to too much danger. They appreciated the risks I took and the information I provided. It was even shared with other governments. Balsom had indicated to me at various stages that my material was being passed on to the CIA.

Only later would I discover the true value of the information I provided to the British and American intelligence services. Only then would I sit in front of the television at my home in Coventry and watch British and American warplanes and missiles lay waste to the very installations I had pointed out on the aerial photograph of Baghdad that day in the safe house. It was a shock: I had helped to provide a road map for the Allied air attacks of Operation Desert Storm.

By then, I had endured many shocks. My life in the world of espionage had ended and I had learned a sad and difficult truth. My trust in the intelligence services was built on an illusion, on the promise that the government will keep faith with you and never betray you. It was a lie and it put at risk everything that was dear to me.

1

Coventry is a West Midlands city of 300,000 that dates back to Saxon times. As every schoolboy learns who grows up there, its most famous citizen was a Saxon woman named Lady Godiva. The statue of the nude woman on horseback stands now in the town centre.

According to the legend, Godiva was the beautiful young wife of Leofric, the Earl of Mercia and founder of a monastery in Coventry in 1043. In exasperation over his wife's endless requests that he reduce Coventry's heavy taxes, Leofric declared that he would do so only if she rode naked through the crowded market-place in the centre of town.

Lady Godiva made the ride, with her long hair covering all of her body except her legs. Legend says the taxes were lowered and the people were happy — with the exception of one unlucky townsman. Lady Godiva had requested that Coventry's male residents remain indoors during her nude ride. One man did not obey and he was struck blind. His name was Peeping Tom.

While the story of Lady Godiva was not part of my Catholic education, I had learned at school that it was the monastery that first brought trade and prosperity to Coventry. By the middle of the fifteenth century the city was an important centre for the wool and textile trade. Later, fine cloth and silk ribbon were manufactured in the town. But the weavers eventually died out and their industry was replaced in the 1860s by bicycle manufacturers, who later turned to the production of motorcycles and eventually motor vehicles. By the beginning of the Second World War, Coventry was a major centre for the motor vehicle, engineering and machine-tool industries.

It was Coventry's industrial power that brought great destruction on the city and provided my first childhood memories. The German air raids of 1940 and 1941 damaged the factories and levelled much of the city. One of my earliest memories is of coming out of our air-raid shelter with my parents and brother the morning after a particularly ferocious bombing raid. Throughout the night we had heard the explosions. When we stepped out of the shelter, we discovered the two houses next to ours had been destroyed. My brother and me were evacuated to my maternal grandmother's home in the Worcestershire town of Malvern. We travelled back and forth between there and Coventry until the blitz stopped.

When the war ended there were celebrations in Coventry, as there were throughout the country. All our neighbours poured into the streets, which were lined with tables filled with food and were the scene of many a celebratory party. On VE Day I was playing in my Uncle Don's garden and fell, gashing my leg quite badly on a piece of metal that was part of the family's bomb shelter. I was taken to hospital, where they stitched the cut. But the doctor, in a fit of patriotic fervour, inserted another cut and turned my gash into a 'V' for victory. I've never forgotten VE Day. I still have the scar.

I was born on 13 August 1938, and my only brother, Peter, four years before me. My father, Henry, was an electrical engineer at the Land Rover Company, predecessor of Range Rover. During the war he was a volunteer in the Home Guard and contracted pneumonia. By the end of the war his condition had turned into tuberculosis and he was quite ill. His lungs suffered severe damage from the disease and he had to leave the factory floor for an office job. I shall never forget his determination to continue working and providing for us.

My mother, Emily, had to go out to work as a shop assistant to help keep us. She worked at the gents' and ladies' outfitters at the end of our road. In those days the small corner shops were very prosperous. It was a difficult time for my mother, looking after us and my father, and working too. We used to have lodgers to provide extra income, but we never had to move house, and my mother still lives there.

I went to the local Catholic school, Christ the King Secondary School in Westhill Road. Academically, it was not very demanding and I was an average pupil. On reflection, the education was not first-class. But I didn't realize this until I left school and started to work. Then I saw how far behind everybody else I was.

In the years after the war Coventry prospered as never before. The industrial boom, more than anything else, seemed to symbolize normality and a return to the way life was before the war, both for the city and the nation.

In the city centre the bulldozers cleared the rubble except for the spire and damaged walls of St Michael's Cathedral, which were left standing as a reminder of the war and its losses. Modern buildings began to spring up in place of the medieval stone structures that had given the city character and charm. I've never cared for the centre of Coventry since. Away from the centre new factories were being built and old ones were expanding. The biggest boom was in the motor vehicle industry, but the prosperity spread to all sorts of suppliers. Among the beneficiaries was the machine-tool industry.

Getting a job in those days was not a problem. You left school and you were sure to be employed. I left school in 1953 at the age of fifteen. My father wanted me to be a toolmaker, for he was an engineer by trade and felt that machine-tool engineering was the best trade for me. Factory work, engineering work – that was the boom industry in those days.

Machine tools are a small part of an industrial society. They are not as visible as huge rolls of steel or cars rolling off the assembly line. The definition of a machine tool is frankly not very interesting: 'an automatic or semiautomatic power-driven tool, as an electric lathe, punch press, drill, or planer'. Yet machine tools are an important part of our economy. They are the machines that make the machines. Every manufactured product is made either by a machine tool or by a machine that was made by one. These little-known machines are the muscle of a healthy manufacturing economy.

Machine tools – lathes, milling, drilling and grinding machines – use power and precision to cut, form and shape metal to specifications measured by the micron – one thousandth of a millimetre. It is machine tools that turn the raw metal from castings and forgings into axles, engine blocks, cam shafts and hundreds of other parts for the finished car. Thread-grinding machines can take a hardened piece of metal and produce a screw by grinding in threads as precise as sixty per inch. Other thread-grinding machines manufacture the components of a gauge that can measure the accuracy of the screw to within half a micron.

In postwar industrial Britain no manual skill was more demanding than that of toolmaking. A master toolmaker could produce any part, requiring any combination of machine operations. And he could make the machines needed to make the parts. It seemed to be an industry where a lad would never be in want of a job.

In 1953 there were three leading toolmaking companies in Coventry. They were Alfred Herbert, the largest and best known, Wickman Machine Tools and Coventry Gauge and Tool Company Limited. The main customer for all three was the automotive industry, where high volume demanded precision machines and components to keep the factories running smoothly and efficiently. Another major customer was the British defence industry, which was rebuilding its munitions and armaments factories from the ashes of the Second World War to face the new Cold War.

I never knew why, but my father preferred Coventry Gauge and Tool. My brother, Peter, had become an apprentice there three years before, so I applied to become an indentured apprentice with the company in August 1953.

The company's 250,000-square-foot brick factory covered almost an entire block in Coventry's Fletchamstead Highway. It had been built in 1936, and during the war its walls had been camouflaged and its windows blacked out so that production could continue without interruption. At the time three-quarters of all the company's products were for the country's defence: from bullets and ammunition to aircraft components. The company's war-time service earned a knighthood from King George VI for its founder, Harry Harley.

Harley, who had risen from apprentice to tool-room chief at Alfred Herbert, founded the Coventry Gauge and Tool Company in 1913. Its first products were accurate jigs and precision measuring equipment. In the 1920s Coventry Gauge and Tool was producing thread-grinding machines and marketing them under the trade name Matrix.

By the 1950s Coventry Gauge and Tool was a profitable, well-regarded manufacturing enterprise. By now run by Stanley Harley, the founder's son, it prided itself on the loyalty of its 600 skilled employees, many of whom had been with the firm for twenty-five years or more. Company-owned houses for workers lined the street on one side of the factory and Coventry Gauge and Tool fielded its own football and cricket teams.

I sat the apprentice toolmaker examination in autumn 1953. It was a simple mathematics test and I qualified to join the next intake of apprentices. It would be a five-year course in the real world, working in the factory during the day and attending technical classes at the local college at night. However, the new intake would not start at the factory until the following March, so I would have several months to wait.

A neighbour of ours was the chief development engineer at the Triumph motorcycle plant in Meriden, about six miles from our home. He suggested that I go to work there, and if I liked the job he would see that I got the chance to take the apprenticeship exam. It was my first job after leaving school. I worked on engine assembly, tightening up nuts on crankcases. We were paid on output, so you had to keep up with the rest of the workers on the track. It was extremely boring and I didn't see a future for myself at Triumph. I doubted I had the qualifications to go into the design and development department, and I had no desire to spend my life on the track. So on 8 March 1954 I was one of thirty young men who made up the engineering apprentice class at Coventry Gauge and Tool. By that time, the plant was a bustling place that employed 2000 people.

The factory itself was one huge machine shop, with high ceilings and a vast, rather frightening expanse of open floor covered with machines. The old belt-driven lathes were whirring and the smell of oil pursued you everywhere. The men used oil to cool the components while they were being machined and it got into everything. A fine mist seemed to hang in the air, and clung to your clothes and hair.

As an indentured apprentice, I was committed to five years of training. My parents and I had signed a paper saying I would not leave. I was the company's property for five years. I would be learning the job, but I would also be paid to *do* the job. In addition, we were required to go to college at night to get our technical qualifications for an engineering certificate. Forty-four hours a week at the factory plus four hours of overtime on Saturdays and two and a half hours a night three times a week at Coventry Technical College – all for two pounds, ten shillings a week.

One of the best engineering qualifications at the time was the Higher National Certificate in Engineering. The course did not deal just with the practical aspects of toolmaking and other engineering jobs, but also with the design aspects and went into material stress, physics and advanced mathematics. It was quite obvious to me early on that my education had not prepared me for this sort of work. Nor did it help that I was off work for two months after an operation to remove a blockage from one of my lungs. Consequently, I fell way behind and failed my first year. It was my first experience of failure and I had to repeat the year. But I tried to meet the set-back the way I would later challenges: with a determination to get it right.

The industry had recently introduced another level of certificate, known as the City and Guilds Certificate in Engineering. This was a more practical course, although there also was a fair amount of maths and theory. I was switched to that course and eventually succeeded in obtaining my certificate.

I had learned the valuable lesson that I was better off in a practical area. I had an instinctive understanding of how machines worked and I would do well to follow that instinct.

As part of the apprenticeship, we spent six to nine months in each different department of the factory: the heat treatment and plating shop, milling machines, turning machines, assembly, and machine test and demonstration. It was structured to provide a very broad experience in manufacturing and design. If I was put into a department, I had to operate a machine and produce components from that machine that met the required tolerances and quality.

There was one supervisor, John Sumner, who had a reputation for being hard on apprentices. If you stopped to talk while you were working and he caught you, he used to give you a bollocking that you never forgot. I know: I got a couple of them. Many years later I realize that he was doing it for the right reasons. He was teaching us the discipline required for the job.

In 1957 I was one of several hundred young workers from throughout Britain who were entered for the annual gauge and toolmakers apprentice competition. We were required to design a gauge or fixture, manufacture it and submit it to the judges. I designed a sine bar, a device for measuring precise angles. I won second prize and attended a dinner at the Savoy Hotel, where the award was presented to me by Sir Stanley Harley.

The following year I was selected to be an apprentice foreman for the new intake of apprentices. I spent nine months guiding them through the first phase of apprentice school, and was beginning to see that I had an ability to deal with people and maybe even manage them.

The apprenticeship and engineering certificate gave me the technical skills to be a toolmaker. The theoretical skills were much harder for me. Yet I did not see myself spending my life operating a machine on the shop floor. It was demanding, highly skilled work and I admired those who did it, but it didn't fit in with my plans.

If my future was on the shop floor, it would be as a manager or foreman.

I finished my apprenticeship in 1960. I had learned the trade and now I had to choose the department where I would develop it. My sights were set on the test department, where all the finished machines were taken to make sure they met the customers' requirements. Part of the job was testing the machines and part was demonstrating them for the customers. This was another clue that I wanted contact with people, and the first sign that I might like a selling role. But first I had to get the job.

Derek Pendleton was the apprentice supervisor, the man who decided which apprentices were assigned to which departments. I had a tremendous battle with Derek, who was a tough-minded bloke. He did not want me to go into the test bay, and when he refused I went to see the foreman of the department, Jack Carnall.

'Mr Carnall, I can do the job,' I told him, filled with the confidence of a young man approaching twenty-two. 'I'm capable of doing it. Give me the chance to prove it.'

He smiled. He said he would have to think about it and talk to Pendleton. A few days later, they told me I could have the job. But there was a price, quite literally. The factory paid its workers on a grading system ranging from A to D. When an apprentice graduated, he usually got a pay level of B or C. They gave me a grade D salary: around £21 a week. Maybe it was because I was too pushy, but I was determined to show them I could do the job.

After completing my apprenticeship, I got married, on 16 July 1960. I had met my bride at a dance at the company's Matrix Hall almost five years before. Coventry had several dance halls in those days, where big bands played and young people gathered on Saturday night. I usually went to Matrix Hall, since that was where most of my mates went.

One evening I had gone to the hall with Alan Doble, who started talking to a girl he knew and ended up asking to see her home. She had come with another girl from her neighbourhood, Esther McVey, and she was worried about Esther walking home alone in the dark.

'Paul, do me a favour, will you?' Alan asked me quietly. 'I want to take this girl home, but her friend needs an escort. She won't go unless I get someone to see Esther home safely.'

'Yeah, all right,' I said.

But Esther was having none of it. 'I'm quite all right,' were the first words she spoke to me. It took some persuading, but finally she agreed to let me see her home.

She was sixteen, the same age as me, and very pretty, with dark brown hair and a lovely smile. She worked as a secretary at Standard Triumph in Coventry. Her parents had moved down from Scotland when she was nine.

We saw each other for a while, but then went our separate ways. During this break, I was quite ill, suffering from a severe case of sunstroke, and one of my friends mentioned it to Esther. She came to visit me at home and after that we started going out together again. We got engaged in 1958 with the promise that we would marry and buy a house when I finished my apprenticeship. We bought our first house, for the princely sum of £2,450, just before we were married.

After finishing my apprenticeship I spent five years working in test and demonstration. They were exciting days, for many new machines were being introduced, and Coventry Gauge and Tool was moving into the manufacture of bigger machines, which meant new products to test and prove to customers. The company was also expanding its export business, particularly in the Soviet Union, and so I was meeting a lot of Russian inspectors from the state buying organizations who were visiting the factory to see a demonstration of the machines that they were buying. This was the height of the Cold War and it was intriguing to deal with the Russians.

We were told many of the machines we were manufacturing for the Soviet Union were for the petroleum industry, which they had recently begun to develop in earnest. Others were for the automotive and aircraft industries. But we never really knew what the machines were used for once they left the factory.

Usually a service engineer from the plant would go to the customer's factory to install the machines. Occasionally I made such trips to Europe, and once went to rural France to install a special grinding machine that ground the teeth of sheep-shearing blades. The Russians, however, never allowed us to supervise the installation of our machines. They came to the factory and saw them in use, and trained their workers to install and operate them. All the machines were accepted by the Russians against our standard test procedure. You never knew the end use of the machines; they just disappeared into that vast country. The only indication we had that the machines were being used was the yearly spares order.

It would be true to say that some Coventry Gauge and Tool machines finished up in the military production industry inside the Soviet Union. After all, 70–80 per cent of the nation's economy was devoted to the defence industry.

While it was unusual for us not to know where the machines were being installed in the Soviet Union, there was nothing extraordinary about using machine tools for military purposes. Some of our biggest customers had always been munitions and armaments factories.

One of the key features of machine tools is versatility. A lathe or a milling machine can be configured to produce parts for a car or a military personnel carrier, parts for a domestic appliance or for a rifle. Even if we had supervised the installation of the machines and set them up to manufacture civilian components in the Soviet Union, any competent engineer could have made the adjustments necessary to turn out military products.

The Soviet Union was not the only communist country buying machine tools from Coventry Gauge and Tool and other British companies. There may have been a Cold War, but the industry and the government were eager for the jobs sustained by exports of machine tools. I got to know a number of officials from the state buying organizations throughout Eastern Europe when they visited our plant at Fletchamstead Highway. I was forming relationships that would be invaluable in the years to come.

With the expansion of overseas sales, in 1965 the company hired a new sales director, Jack Humphries. In May of that year Humphries asked one of my colleagues in testing, Roy Whittaker, if he would like a job in technical sales providing technical advice to Humphries and customers about machines they were considering buying. The job would also involve a considerable amount of overseas travel.

Roy turned the job down, for a combination of reasons, and when Jack Hamphries approached me, as his second choice, I had to think long and hard. Esther and I discussed it long into the night for several days. Apart from the pay being less, we were on the verge of adopting our first child: a boy, born on 3 April 1965. There was a waiting period of eight weeks to give the natural mother a chance to change her mind. If she did not, we would have a son.

I wanted the sales job, despite the imminent adoption and the pay cut. During the past five years I had grown to enjoy the contact with people and the little bit of travel I had done. I told Esther: 'I want to do it. If I haven't made it in two years, if I'm not making a reasonable salary, I'll pack it in and go back to what I'm doing now.'

So, with Esther's agreement, I accepted the job. I was due to start on 1 June. On the evening of 31 May I was sitting on a plane to Stockholm with Jack Humphries. It was the first leg of a trip to China, a journey that would require five separate flights over three days. Once there, we hoped to sell the Chinese some machine tools. For the first time in my working life I was wearing a collar and tie and carrying a briefcase. I had no experience of selling. But I knew about the machines.

2

We landed at Peking airport at seven p.m. on 2 June, after an exhausting but exhilarating journey. From Stockholm we had flown to Moscow and boarded an Aeroflot flight to Omsk in the interior, and from there we had gone on to Irkutsk near the Soviet-Mongolian border. Daylight was so short there that we had seen the sun rise and set over the vast Lake Baikal while waiting for our connection to Peking.

China was a mystery to most Westerners in the 1960s, for few businessmen and even fewer tourists were allowed into the country. The Americans still viewed the Chinese as enemies, while Britain was one of a handful of Western countries with a diplomatic presence in Peking, and our embassy was relatively small. Yet those allowed into the country in those days were treated as honoured guests by the Chinese. It was to be a short-lived relationship, however, for the Cultural Revolution was just around the corner. The following year, 1966, the Red Guard would be turned loose to terrorize Westerners, surrounding the British and Soviet embassies and imprisoning foreigners.

People laughed at me when I told them, but the Chinese actually rolled out a red carpet for us as we got off the plane from Irkutsk. Jack Humphries and I were hurried through customs, ushered into waiting cars and whisked off to the Friendship Hotel. Situated in a walled compound in central Peking, this was a massive stone building, built for the Chinese by the Soviets in the 1950s in the Stalinist style. It was reserved for long-term foreign residents and important visiting businessmen.

Our hosts from the government buying organization were courteous and efficient. They arranged all our meetings, picking us up and taking us to the factories and offices, where we described our machine tools and listened to the Chinese requirements. One day we were driven out of the city to visit the Great Wall. Another day we visited the tombs of the Ming Dynasty, which are located in a valley protected by lovely, gentle hills. We were also shown the lakeside Summer Palace and, by contrast, a commune in the countryside.

Always we had escorts. The reason for our hosts' helpfulness was only part business, as we discovered one night. After our evening meal, Jack suggested a walk around the city. We left the compound and began to wander through the teeming streets, but within minutes we were lost. People stared at us, since Westerners were still an unusual sight. They were courteous, smiling and nodding as we asked directions to the hotel, but no one spoke a word of English; not even a policeman we stopped. Eventually we found our own way back, having learned that without guides there was no chance of finding our way round the huge and ancient city.

We spent two weeks in China. When we left, we had landed a £300,000 contract – a sizeable amount in those days – for a number of thread-grinding machines. We then flew to Canton and took the train to Hong Kong. The Chinese train stopped just before crossing into the British colony, and we got off and carried our bags a hundred yards to the other side of the border, where we boarded another train to continue on to the financial heart of the Far East. In Hong Kong, we stayed at the Mandarin Hotel, a great old place in the finest traditions of the British Empire. This was luxury that I had never seen or even dreamt of. From Hong Kong, it was on to Tokyo for meetings with Japanese manufacturing companies.

By the time I returned home on 28 June, I had been gone nearly a month. It had also been an eventful time at home. Not long after I had left the country, Esther had gone to Father Hudson's Home near Birmingham and collected our adopted son, David. He was nearly three months old the first time his new father saw him.

From that first trip on, I spent half my time overseas on business. My extensive travel created many burdens for Esther, who was left to raise David, and later Sue, largely on her own. But she didn't complain, understanding from the start that I was working as hard as I could to provide for my family and improve our standard of living.

Within a year, I was promoted to technical sales manager. My salary returned to what it had been when I left the testing department. Between 1967 and 1969 I spent many months in the USA, as we had an arrangement with Thompson Grinders of Springfield, Ohio, whereby we manufactured their machines in the UK and they distributed our products in America.

The president of Thompson Grinders, Ralph Baldenhofer, persuaded Jack Humphries to leave me out there for a few weeks to help them promote our products in the USA. A few weeks turned into two years, during which time I was able to return home for a week or two only every few months. In that same period our American business rose from practically nothing to £½ million a year. Exports were becoming a bigger and bigger part of sales at Coventry Gauge and Tool and other British machine-tool companies.

Solely on the basis of a gigantic order for 600 machines placed by the Soviet Union in 1965, the company was restructured. All the space in the main factory at Fletchamstead Highway was turned over to the production of machine tools. The Soviet order was to be delivered over three years, but space was also needed for orders for other customers, so the manufacture of gauges, measuring instruments and cutting tools was moved from the main site to a new location.

This expansion of machine-tool production at the expense of gauges and measuring instruments was a turning-point for Coventry Gauge and Tool. But along with the expansion came increased pressure to keep the order book full and the factory operating at capacity.

Since the British manufacturing base was not expanding at a fast enough rate to keep us busy, I spent more and more time abroad finding new export markets. The most promising were behind the Iron Curtain, where the Russians and their allies were developing their industrial bases. I returned to China only once before the Cultural Revolution virtually closed the world's most populous country, although with Jack Humphries I was making frequent trips to the Soviet Union, Poland, Hungary and Czechoslovakia.

By the late sixties, Coventry Gauge and Tool was exporting 70–80 per cent of its output. Eastern Europe and the Soviet Union had become absolutely vital markets for us, particularly since their governments had access to loans from Western governments that guaranteed payment on our contracts. It was good business, and the other British toolmakers were competing for the same sales. But it also meant that the machine-tool industry in Britain had become dependent on foreign markets for the first time in its history.

My big test as a salesman came in July 1968. At that time the managing director of Coventry Gauge and Tool was John Everest, with whom I got on all right, although we never really clicked. I wasn't his type of person, since I was more practical than theoretical and he was a theoretical person with a good education. I know little about his background, but I was sure he hadn't started out as a fifteen-year-old apprentice on the shop floor.

Jack Humphries was trying to promote me to head of export sales. But I learned from him that Everest had doubts about whether I was the man for the job, and wanted to bring in somebody else.

Jack and I had a trip planned to the Soviet Union in May. The order for the 600 machines was coming to an end, and another sale of that size was extremely unlikely. Yet we needed to land some new contracts. We had an opportunity to sell fifteen machines to Stankoimport, the state buying organization for engineering products, and so we were off to Moscow. However, just before we were due to leave, Jack became ill and had to pull out. I had been to the Soviet Union on business many times, but never alone. Now, if I wanted the export manager's job, I had to prove that I could do it myself.

'Everest will be watching you. Whatever you do, you have to come back with an order,' Jack warned me. 'Not only do you have to come back with it. You've got to get better prices than we've ever had before.'

Jack set the prices for me in each machine category. The idea of my first solo selling trip was troubling enough. He didn't make things easier with his parting words: 'Don't come back without the order.'

Like most foreign businessmen, I stayed at Moscow's National Hotel. Built early this century, it reflects the grace and style of pre-Revolutionary Russia, with its antique-filled rooms and waiters formally attired in black. Many of the rooms overlook the Kremlin.

Doing business in Moscow was difficult at the best of times. The Russians would invite you to discuss a contract, but they would not give you a specific time to meet them. When you arrived in your hotel, you would get on the telephone to make an appointment. But the people you needed to see were never available.

I spent a couple of days trying to set up appointments and getting nowhere. Finally I got an appointment and saw the people at Stankoimport, but only for an hour. Leaving with the promise 'We'll call you' ringing in my ears, I went back to my room and spent hours going over the quotation and the prices on a proposed contract. There is a limit to how many times you can review a quotation, so I bought an English edition of the metro system map and spent hours exploring Moscow. Just to kill time, I used to get on the metro and see how far I could go for the modest sum of five kopeks. It was a long way. Although I did not know it at the time, it was information that was to prove invaluable at a later date.

This pattern continued for almost three weeks. I would visit the Stankoimport offices in one of those hideously ornate buildings built after the First World War. The translator would be there, a Russian girl named Nelly, and I would argue with the Russians over prices. Most of the negotiations were with Victor Dianov, who was a tough bastard. After an hour or two, I would be dismissed and go back to my hotel.

By Wednesday of the third week, we had reached a stalemate. I was angry; the Russian tactics were ridiculous. I was not going to sell any machines for the prices Jack had set. As I was not going to get the order there was no point in sitting around any longer, so I booked my trip home on the British Airways flight leaving Moscow on the Friday.

Those were the days when you couldn't breathe without the Russians knowing what you were doing, and within an hour of booking my flight I had a telephone call inviting me to another meeting at the Stankoimport offices immediately. But we just repeated the same pattern, and the next day it was the same story all over again.

Finally I told them: 'Let's forget it. I've booked my flight and I am going home tomorrow. We can't agree. You'll have to go over my head with the company back in Coventry. That's it. To go below this price is going to need a board decision.'

'Make a phone call,' Dianov urged me. 'Get permission to lower your prices.'

'There is no point in making a call. I know what is going to happen. They are going to tell me no. The board will have to take it up. There is absolutely no point.'

On Friday, an hour before I was to leave for the airport, Dianov and two other men from Stankoimport walked into my room at the National. Dianov had brought the contracts typed and signed. The prices were what I had demanded.

Over the years, I learned this was not an unusual occurrence. They put you under tremendous pressure to squeeze out the last possible kopek. You are in a strange country, you don't speak the language and you are on your own. But you don't want to leave without a contract.

In fact, for the contract I could have gone below the prices set by Jack Humphries. But I had to prove that I was a tough negotiator, otherwise I was never going to get a good price. I was determined to prove myself both to the Russians and John Everest.

It required the same determination to get a table in a good restaurant when you were alone in Moscow. I used to go into a place and ask the head waiter for a table for one. 'Nyet.' I'd wait and wait and no table. Then I discovered a system that never failed: I used to stand where there was the most waiter traffic, right in their way. In the end, they would get fed up with me and give me a seat.

The food in Russia was not brilliant in those days. My staple diet used to be black bread, caviar and vodka, which turned out to be good preparation for my dealings in Eastern Europe.

After my success, even though I was promoted to export sales manager I soon learned that John Everest was still not a fan of mine.

Later in 1968, Jack Humphries died, leaving vacant the position of general sales manager. It was a big step up for a young man of just thirty, but I believed I had earned the job. One day Everest called me into his office and we had a bit of a dust-up about it. 'Paul, I just don't think you can handle this job,' he told me. 'You're a strong technical engineer, but a general sales manager needs different talents. I think I'm going to give the job to someone else. I hope that you'll remain in export sales.'

I was angry. 'I've earned this job. I've worked all my life for this company. Sales are going extremely well. I know I can do the sales manager's job.'

'All right,' he said. 'If you think you're that good, we'll send you down to a consultant. We'll get an objective consultant to give us a view of your capabilities.'

This struck me as just the response of a theoretical man. But what choice did I have? A few days later I took the train to London to the consultants, Urwick Orr. They kept me waiting half an hour, the whole purpose of the delay clearly to unsettle me and see how I reacted.

When they came to get me, I went into an office where a man introduced himself as John Addy. We chatted across his desk for

16

about an hour. He was fiddling with a cigarette lighter, which he then slid across the desk to me.

'If you're a salesman,' Addy said, 'sell me that.'

I sat for a few seconds thinking, what am I going to do? A lighter? I don't know anything about selling bloody lighters. My job is technical: quality machine tools. How do I respond to this?

I guess it was more anger than anything else. An instinct perhaps. I slid the lighter back and said, 'I don't sell rubbish.'

'Thank you, Mr Henderson. That will be all.'

I walked out of there believing I'd blown it.

Addy phoned me a few days later: 'I thought you might like to know that I am recommending you for the job. You did exactly the right thing. If you had tried to sell me the lighter, it would have been the biggest mistake you could have made.'

A few days later Everest sent for me. He tried to convince me that the consultants had said I was not the man for the job.

'That's not true. Absolutely not true. They told me they would recommend me for the position,' I protested.

I insisted that we telephone John Addy so that I could hear for myself what he had to say. I had nothing to lose. If Everest was going to appoint somebody else, I would be left with no alternative but to leave the company. Everest backed down and I was promoted to general sales manager in late 1968; it was a turning-point in my career.

The following summer I was away with my family on holiday in Mallorca. By this time Esther and I had adopted Suzanne, who was born on 24 July 1967. As with David, I had been abroad when Sue was brought home from the orphanage. I was sitting on the beach reading the newspaper when I saw something that made me stop: a Birmingham company called Tube Investments had taken over Coventry Gauge and Tool. I was shocked and I silently handed the newspaper to Esther, pointing to the story.

'I may not have a job when I go back,' I warned her as she read the article.

But I wasn't worried about finding another job, because, as my father had told me, there was always work for a man with a trade. Also, the experience I had gained in recent years in export sales was highly marketable. Even so, because Coventry Gauge and Tool was the only place I had ever worked, the thought of losing my job was unsettling.

17

Tube Investments Group, which was generally known as TI, was a diversified engineering company. With 68,000 employees in seventy companies, it had interests in manufacturing steel tubes, automotive parts and a range of consumer products. It was structured along the lines of the American conglomerates, which acquired a wide range of companies and often found themselves spread too thin when it came to running such a diverse business.

The machine-tool industry was expanding, although it had never been a very profitable industry. Sales were growing through exports and the technology was advancing with the introduction of computer-controlled machines. The previous year TI had purchased Charles Churchill Gear Machines Ltd and with the purchase of Coventry Gauge and Tool formed the TI Machine Tools Division.

Everest remained as managing director. I believe I was retained, along with the chief designer, Ray Palmer, because of the position I had obtained in late 1968 and because of my sales skills. I had a lot to thank Jack Humphries for.

During the first year under new ownership, I became friends with Walter Lees, the divisional director responsible for machine-tool manufacturing. As Jack had done earlier, Walter became my mentor and guided me through difficult stages in my career.

In early 1971 TI was still making many changes. By this time, Everest had left the company and new managers were being brought in from other TI companies. It was a very unsettling period and I considered leaving to set up my own consultancy. One day, Walter Lees took me to one side, saying: 'Never rush into anything. Don't be impetuous. You never know what's around the corner.'

Towards the end of the year TI formed a centralized export selling company called Matrix Churchill International Limited. This was the brand name under which Coventry Gauge and Tool machines were marketed. Churchill was another respected British machine-tool company that TI Group had purchased in 1968. It was the first time the names Matrix and Churchill, two of the best in the industry, had come together.

In the field of machine tools, Churchill was a respected company. An American named Charles Churchill had emigrated to England in 1837 and started a wire-braiding plant for crinoline dress frames in London's East End. Over the next century, the company had grown into one of Europe's foremost manufacturers of machine tools, with its headquarters in Birmingham and large factories in Halifax and Blaydon on Tyne in Durham.

When TI bought Churchill, its main customers were the automotive and munitions industries. In fact, the company was the largest supplier of machine tools to the British government's Royal Ordnance factories.

Churchill specialized in the manufacture of copy or tracer lathes, the forerunner of today's computer-controlled lathes. Copy lathes were used heavily in the armaments industry. A template would be produced to the shape of the circular part the machine was designed to make. The machine would then turn a piece of metal to the required shape, such as the tapered cylindrical shape of a 155mm artillery shell. The process would then be repeated over and over, providing accurate components at a high rate of production. Copy lathes were classed as 'dedicated' machines.

Matrix Churchill was set up as the sales and marketing company to handle all overseas sales for TI Machine Tools Division. The managing director was Edward Weston, below whom were three sales directors. Charles Tearne was in charge of Australia, the USA and South Africa. David Walder was director for Western Europe. I was sales director for Eastern Europe, the Middle East, Asia, the Far East, Japan, China and Russia. Gordon Cooper, a friend of mine and another former apprentice, went to Cleveland, Ohio, to work for Matrix Churchill Corporation, our sales outlet in the USA.

This was a major step forward in my career. I had been given the difficult markets in which to sell not only Matrix equipment but also the Churchill range of machines. This would involve me much more with the defence industry, and it would also mean spending more time away from home.

By this time I had been selling in the Soviet Union and Eastern Europe for several years, and I liked many of the people I met there, for they were talented engineers and clever people. I learned not to judge them by their standard of living or the way they dressed, but treated them with respect and recognized them for what they were.

One of my favourites was Madame Vera Czerkawska, who always appeared to be better dressed and better mannered than the average bureaucrat. She was a tough senior official who drove a hard bargain for Metalexport, the Polish state buying organization. But she offered a human side, too. She taught me manners and the correct way to deal with her associates. For example, one day she took me aside after a meeting and said: 'In Poland, when you speak to a lady, you never put your hands in your pockets. It is impolite.'

Socializing with government officials in the early seventies in countries such as Poland, the Soviet Union and Czechoslovakia was quite difficult. Officially they were not allowed to mix with Westerners and were supposed to report all conversations to the authorities. Even after a contract had been signed, we had to apply for permission to take our counterparts to dinner, and even then a Communist Party member from some ominous ministry would attend as well. And when they visited the UK they always had a party member in tow to make a full report when they returned home.

In spite of the restrictions I developed friendships with people I did business with. Selling in that part of the world was very personal. You had to have a quality product; they wouldn't buy anything that wasn't going to do the job. But if there was a choice between you and a competitor with a technically equal product, they would go with the people they trusted, even if it meant paying a slightly higher price. The key to our success was that salesmen like John Belgrove, Mark Gutteridge and Jim Chapman were able to develop this trust with the customers. It was a personal relationship even if it wasn't a friendship, but the mutual respect took many years to develop.

Despite Western stereotypes, officials in Eastern Europe often had a wonderful sense of humour. Once John Belgrove, Jim Chapman and I were trying to close the sale of two grinding machines at Metalexport in Poland. We had reached a stalemate on price with Narcyza Barczak, the principal negotiator. Suddenly Jim left the room and returned a few minutes later holding a single red rose. He went down on one knee and presented it to Narcyza, begging her to break the deadlock. Everybody fell about laughing, because in Poland giving a single red rose to someone means that you love that person. But we ended up with the price we needed to do the deal.

Accustomed as I became to working in those countries, I never escaped the feeling of being trapped once I crossed the border into Poland or Czechoslovakia or, in particular, the Soviet Union. If you did anything wrong, getting out of the country without their knowledge would be virtually impossible. Cross a border somewhere? No chance. You always assumed your room was bugged and your conversations overheard in restaurants and other public places. It was oppressive and intimidating, but so far I had no reason to be afraid.

Poland's buying operation was run like the Soviet Union's. Because of the state-imposed secrecy, you did not go to the customer's factory, but instead the factory sent representatives to Metalexport and you met them there. The initial negotiations would take place in a large reception room at Metalexport's offices. Scattered around the room would be all of your competitors: Americans, Germans, Swiss, and in later years the Japanese. The Polish negotiators would move from one group to another, playing us off against each other to push the prices down. It was their way of putting pressure on you.

Once a tentative deal was reached, the talks would move up a gear to involve people such as Marek Piotrowski, a senior director of Metalexport, whom I first met in 1966 when he was attached to the Polish embassy in London. Piotrowski would always ask for a further discount. I soon realized that he had to get a better deal to justify his senior position, and I learned to keep something in reserve during the initial round of talks. It was a game, but it had to be played.

From the start Piotrowski struck me as coming from a different background from most of the bureaucrats in Warsaw. He was a little bit better dressed, a tall, good-looking man who spoke very good English. Eventually I learned that he came from an aristocratic family, and that he wanted more money and a better standard of living than the average communist bureaucrat and was determined to get it.

My job played hell with my personal life. Esther was left on her own with the children while I was away for five or six weeks at a time. If a company driver was at the airport waiting for me when I returned home on a Friday night, I knew that I would be off again for Prague or Moscow on Sunday night. I never hesitated, since I was progressing, and providing a better standard of living for my family. And Esther never complained.

It was during this time that I formed friendships with John Belgrove and Mark Gutteridge. It was normal to travel in pairs when on business in Eastern Europe. Like me, John and Mark were technical men who had learned the commercial side through experience. I always believed it was easier for a technician to learn the commercial aspects of business, rather than the other way round.

We were usually restricted to the capital cities: Moscow, Prague, Warsaw, Budapest. Since the people we dealt with were not allowed to socialize with foreigners, we spent many evenings dining and drinking our way across Eastern Europe. John and Mark were good companions and, like me, developed a taste for caviar and vodka. And yet there was a sense of isolation, since we were cut off from our families. The glamour wore off quickly and it became a hard job. But over those years, I developed a friendship with John and Mark that would last a lifetime – and one day prove invaluable to me.

It was in the early seventies that the Japanese started to market their machine tools in Europe, at prices much lower than ours. TI Machine Tools really needed to expand its product range to include smaller, less expensive grinding machines to avoid losing business to them. Designing and manufacturing a competitive range of machines would take too long. At the time we were selling a few machines to the Japanese, but the market there in machine tools – as in other products – was restricted for foreign companies. However, I began spending more time in Japan.

In 1972 I began working on a joint venture with the Japanese machine-tool company Okuma, which was located in the major industrial city of Nagoya. By the spring of 1973 the two companies were ready to sign an agreement that would allow us to sell Okuma's range of cylindrical grinding machines in the UK and Eastern Europe. Okuma would manufacture and market our range of thread-grinding machines in Japan.

Walter Lees and I travelled to Japan to finalize the contract details with Okuma in Nagoya. Once we were satisfied with the contract, Arthur Turner, our deputy managing director, and some other directors of TI Machine Tools, would fly over for the signing ceremony.

While Walter and I were in Japan, we learned that Eddie Weston had abruptly left Matrix Churchill International, so that the managing director's position was vacant. I was pretty ambitious at that stage of my career, and as far as I was concerned there was only one person who should be the new managing director. But I was young for the position. The most obvious candidate was Charles Tearne, another of the sales directors, who was older than me. I expressed these feelings to Walter. 'Screw it,' I said angrily, standing up from my chair in the office we were using at Okuma. 'I think that job should be mine. If Charlie Tearne gets it, I'm leaving.'

Walter sat me down, saying: 'Look, don't be hasty. Wait until Arthur arrives and see what happens. I have to tell you, I don't believe you will become managing director. It's nothing to do with your ability. It's your age. TI may consider you too young to be a managing director.'

I put the thought of being managing director to the back of my mind. The most important thing at the moment was concluding the deal with Okuma, and once that was over I could sit down and decide what to do if I didn't get the job.

A few days later, we went to Tokyo to meet Arthur Turner and the other directors who had flown over. The following day, we all travelled to Nagoya by train. During the journey Arthur asked Walter if he could have a word with him. On returning to his seat next to me, Walter said: 'I think you're in for a surprise.' When we arrived in Nagoya, Arthur Turner suggested that we all meet in his suite for drinks at six-thirty. 'Paul, can you come fifteen minutes early?' he added.

When I got to his suite, he offered me the job. The others came in shortly after and we opened some champagne. The next day we signed the agreement with Okuma.

As part of the management change, Walter Lees took on more responsibility within the division, and I become the new managing director of Matrix Churchill International Limited, the worldwide sales organization for the division. Just short of my thirty-fifth birthday, I was the youngest managing director in the British machine-tool industry.

3

I've read that the perfect spy is nursed on deceit and schooled in betrayal. These are doubtless good qualities in an intelligence agent, but the essential nature of this clandestine business is access to information, the true currency of the intelligence trade.

Britain's intelligence service is divided into two branches. These are often confused in the public's mind, because the government tries to maintain an absolute secrecy about their operations and that lends itself to misinformation, if not disinformation. I read a little about the subject when I realized it was going to become part of my life, and picked up further insights from my various controllers over the years.

Our tradition of maintaining a secret service dates back to the reign of Henry VII, although the first modern agency was established in 1909 to conduct espionage and counterintelligence activities in all British territories. Originally known as Military Intelligence, Department 5, it is better known today as MI5. As the empire has shrunk, MI5's jurisdiction has been reduced accordingly, and it is now deployed mainly in Britain as a counterintelligence agency, its primary responsibility being to protect the state from espionage, terrorism and subversion. MI5 often works with Scotland Yard's Special Branch, but its agents are also alert to potentially subversive activities originating abroad.

Two years after the creation of MI5, the government set up what is now known as MI6 or the Secret Intelligence Service (SIS). Its responsibility is to gather intelligence abroad through spies and officially approved exchanges of information with other governments.

Both branches of the intelligence service often use British business-men to gather information because they have access to places where

24

government officials are not allowed. We can, by the nature of our job, ask questions about a wide variety of matters. In short, we have access. We make unlikely spies.

Sometimes such activities have disastrous effects for the businessmen, as in the case of Greville Wynne. He was attending a trade fair in Budapest on 2 November 1962 when he was arrested at a cocktail party on charges of smuggling information out of the Soviet Union. Wynne was taken to Moscow and put on trial for four days in front of the world's press. After the trial, his Soviet accomplice was sentenced to death and executed, Wynne having received an eight-year prison sentence. Eleven months later Wynne was exchanged in Berlin for a Soviet spy arrested in London.

When Esther and I saw Wynne released from prison on television, she said to me: 'Paul, that poor man. He looks terrible, all grey and thin. You'd never do that, would you?' I had assured her I would not, but at that time I had no idea that I would break the promise a decade later.

A few weeks after my promotion to managing director of Matrix Churchill International in the late spring of 1973, the sales staff who travelled in Eastern Europe and the Soviet Union were called to a meeting in the boardroom next to Arthur Turner's office in the main factory in Coventry. Apart from me, John Belgrove and Mark Gutteridge, several others were there too. We were introduced to three grey men who were identified only as government officials. I suspected they were from the Ministry of Defence. I don't recall whether any reason was given for the meeting, but the topic turned out to be how British businessmen should conduct themselves in communist countries. The government men were concerned that those of us doing business in those countries should not put ourselves in positions where we could be blackmailed or bribed to work for them.

The visitors spent a couple of hours of going through the dos and don'ts. Don't get involved with women, they warned us. Be careful what you say in your hotel room because it will be bugged. Don't go to anyone's home. Eastern Europeans and Russians are told that they must not mix with foreigners. Obviously, if you are invited to someone's home, you can be sure that person is working for their intelligence service. Watch what you say in restaurants. Never put yourself in a compromising position.

John, Mark and I had spent several years living and working in those places. Christ, it was a bit late to tell us now. We chuckled to ourselves when the officials described what that they called 'the seven deadly sins', which were a summary of their two-hour talk. The only specific sin I remember was that it was illegal to give venereal disease to a Soviet citizen.

A couple of weeks later I received a telephone call from a man who had not been at the meeting but referred to it and asked if I had any objection to talking with him about helping the government. I said that I had no objection to a meeting, and we arranged to meet in London.

He introduced himself as Mr Kilby and said he was from the Ministry of Defence. I ended up meeting him briefly on three occasions: 15 May, 31 May and 5 July. He described how the government would like me to pass on information that I picked up on my travels. I sensed he was assessing both my willingness and my ability to help.

By the third meeting Kilby was repeating himself and I couldn't tell if he had a handle on how this game was supposed to be played. I was not sure if I wanted to get involved, and he must have sensed this because he said he wanted me to meet someone else, someone who would become my contact with the government.

It was 12.30 on the afternoon of 31 July 1973 when I arrived at the pub, as arranged. I didn't see Kilby as I scanned the room, but within a couple of minutes a woman walked up to me.

'You're Mr Henderson, aren't you?' she asked.

'Yes,' I said.

She flashed an identification card. 'I'm Miss Eyles, a colleague of Mr Kilby's.'

Later I learnt Miss Eyles worked for MI5. She was not what I expected. Around thirty years old, she was attractive, with shoulder-length brown hair, and was about five foot six and of medium build. She was dressed smartly and spoke in a soft but firm voice. She was earnest and formal, and in fact I never knew her first name. She could have been one of the bright, university-educated businesswomen working in the City. Instead she was my first controller.

Miss Eyles told me in detail what the government would like me to do. She made it sound safe, routine, free of risk; she also made it sound important, a way to help my country. 'Obviously we have the Cold War situation,' she said. 'It is very important for this country to monitor what is happening in Eastern Europe and the Soviet Union, particularly since those countries are so close to home.'

The intelligence service's main concern was the developing munitions and military industries behind the Iron Curtain. They were interested in what sort of equipment was being bought and what use it was being put to.

'Is anybody selling them equipment that they should not be selling?' she wanted to know. 'Which technology going into those countries is outside the export restrictions?'

Miss Eyles also wanted to know about the senior people in the industrial and state buying organizations. Her employers were especially keen to know when some of these officials would be visiting Britain. Where did they stay? Who did they talk to? What were their lifestyles?

Although British intelligence had people in embassies around the world, she explained, the only way they could really obtain first-hand information about foreign officials was by having people on the ground; for example, businessmen who were prepared to keep their eyes and ears open and feed back information.

'Would you be prepared to be one of those people on the ground?' she asked me in a steady, earnest voice.

I didn't see any risk or problems in helping intelligence, so I said I'd give it a try. She then made a surprising admission. As events unravelled in later years, I would find out that such candour was extremely rare among intelligence people. 'We approached your employer and asked permission to talk to you about this,' she told me. 'They refused. They said they thought the risks were too great and they didn't want one of their employees doing this sort of work. We thought about it and decided to approach you directly.'

'This is my decision,' I replied. 'Just as well they don't know, I suppose.'

Then the MI5 woman told me what I had to do. Observe the types of machines and products in the factories I visited. Listen carefully to the conversations around me. Ask questions, but never attract attention to myself by pressing too hard. Learn to use public transport as much as possible, since it makes you harder to follow and allows you to blend in.

There were more 'nevers' too. Never take notes until I was safely back in Britain. Even then, just jot down a phrase or at most a line to help me remember what I had learned until I was debriefed. Never record my contacts with her in my diary. Even more importantly, never tell anyone what I was doing. Not my employers. Not my colleagues. Not even my wife.

'If you tell someone and somehow it leaks back to one of these countries that you are doing work for the British intelligence service, then you are putting yourself at risk,' she said sternly, placing both hands flat on the table for emphasis.

She gave me a telephone number where I could reach her, although she wouldn't answer herself, and if she were unavailable I should leave a message. I should call before making a trip abroad and, on my return, to set up a meeting where I could be debriefed. I should also let her know when someone was coming over, perhaps to visit the factory in Coventry or as part of a trade delegation.

That was it. I didn't sign the Official Secrets Act or anything else; I received no further instruction in what the spies call tradecraft; and I knew I wasn't going to be paid. I agreed to work for the intelligence service for two reasons. As I was fairly young, the first was the glamour. This was, after all, the James Bond era. The second was simply, if I could help my country, why not? But in all honesty, at that stage the glamour aspect was more attractive to me than the patriotism.

When you stop to think about it, however, it sounds crazy, since working for the intelligence service was only glamorous if I could tell somebody. Yet I reasoned there is also an appeal in knowing a secret that you can't tell anybody. Not even your wife. It was one of the very few secrets I ever kept from Esther, and it never made me feel good that I couldn't share it with her. Indeed it was part of the problem we would later experience in our marriage.

At first I didn't take my role as an intelligence service informant very seriously. I'd telephone Miss Eyles and meet her for half an hour before going overseas. Then I'd meet her again when I returned and tell her what I had seen. She was always interested in where I was going, who I was seeing. She might say: 'If you go to this plant, could you find out what they are making, what type of machines they are using?' And she wanted to know who the competitors were in contract negotiations and what type of machines they were offering. She also asked questions about the financing of these deals.

The information I was supplying helped the intelligence people form a picture of the economic and technological situation in the Soviet Union, Poland, Hungary and Czechoslovakia, and then assess the capabilities of these countries. Over the years it became obvious that they had a number of contacts to gather information and that they used each of us to verify what the others had told them.

During the Cold War the West wanted to know how the Comecon countries of Eastern Europe were being restructured. I provided details on the companies that I visited, such as the product being produced; the management structure; how many people were employed; salary levels; turnover; profit levels; what equipment they were using; where they were buying it from; the level of technology; whether any Western countries were evading the COCOM regulations; how the imports were being financed; whether the factory was efficient and what the quality of the product was like.

During the second half of the seventies the emphasis of my activities moved towards details of the people that I met, particularly those that had access to travel or life in the West. I had many contacts within the Comecon countries at all levels, from ministerial down to the man who operated our machines. The intelligence service's main interest was in the higher-ranking officials, so I would keep the intelligence people informed of their overseas travel arrangements, when I would be meeting them, which hotels they were staying at and the restaurants we would be eating at.

This arrangement later developed into providing more personal information, such as what those officials' likes and dislikes were – drinking, gambling, women, for example – the purpose being to set up compromising situations which would leave them with no choice but to work for British intelligence. My other main task was to identify persons who would voluntarily provide information in exchange for political asylum.

I had started to work for MI5 at a good time. It was becoming a little easier to move about in Eastern Europe, and I could travel out of the capital cities and visit factories. Driving through small towns and touring the plants, it wasn't difficult to assess what the economy and standard of living were like. The information was all there – if you had access.

We were also receiving more communist bloc visitors at our factory, and relationships which had developed over the years were turning into friendships. I was spending more time entertaining in Eastern European countries, eating and drinking long into the night.

Collecting information for the intelligence service became a regular part of my life, but it was also necessarily a secret part of it. This caused some problems at work, since as an employee of the company I couldn't simply take off and meet Miss Eyles in London. Instead I would see her after work. I'd drive down to London about five o'clock and it would be ten or later when I got home. Sometimes, she would come to Coventry and we'd meet in a local pub, although rarely at the same place twice. I always assumed this was for security reasons.

Because of the intensity of my work and the need to travel, Esther accepted my absences. When it wasn't intelligence people, I was entertaining people for business and looking after visitors frequently in the evenings, so often I was out five nights a week and part of the weekend. But when it was an intelligence meeting, I'd have to tell Esther a lie, saying that I had been meeting a customer or somebody from an embassy in London or having dinner with a business contact. It was leading to tension between us, although the problem only really emerged in the early eighties.

Even though I was managing director, I was spending a lot of my time in the field. I valued technical skills in the salesmen who worked for me and I thought of myself as a hands-on manager.

There was a lot of infighting within the company, and I learned from friends that I was the target. Maybe some people thought I'd moved up too fast, but I wasn't there to defend myself and it really didn't worry me too much. As long as I was selling, I was successful, for if we didn't get the orders, there was no company. So I spent more time in the field than in the office, particularly in Poland.

TI Machine Tools was doing excellent business in Poland, supplying lathes, grinding and thread-grinding machines in large quantities to Metalexport and the equivalent buying organization for the agriculture industry, Agromet. We were spending so much time there that we had rented a three-bedroom flat in Ulitza Smolenskiego Bielany, in Warsaw.

With the relaxation of travel rules in Poland, we were no longer restricted to visiting the buying organization offices in the capital. We visited factories along bumpy roads two or three hours outside Warsaw, touring plants where our machines were to be installed and eventually having our service engineers install the machines.

Agromet was buying large numbers of our chucking automatics. Apart from being able to produce agricultural components, these machines were used heavily in the munitions industry. Agromet bought a large number of the biggest chucking machines, which could be easily converted to munitions production. They were going to a large factory a couple of hours outside Warsaw where a multitude of products were being manufactured.

I was suspicious that these machines were being used for more than agricultural production, and tried to find out a lot more about the company and the plant. I asked many questions when I visited the factory and attempted to get into restricted areas where they weren't interested in taking me. I never really got the answer that I was looking for, and I told Miss Eyles this.

After each of these trips, I would telephone the number she had given me and arrange to meet her at a quiet pub or hotel bar somewhere in London. These meetings occurred every month or so and we formed an easy, if distant relationship. I would describe where I had gone, what I had seen, who I had talked to, while she took notes and asked questions. Her questions reinforced my original impression that she was an economist. She seemed particularly concerned with the economic infrastructure of Poland, the Soviet Union and the other countries where I was doing business.

I continued to meet Miss Eyles during the rest of 1973 and throughout 1974, during which time I became more serious about my intelligence work, for I was beginning to realize that I had better keep my eyes open, not only with regard to what I was watching but about who might be watching me. At the same time, I was getting more brazen. When you are gathering sensitive information you have to be able to openly ask a person a difficult question and hope to get an answer without alarming them. You also have to ask to see things that normally they wouldn't show you.

I would be walking around a factory in Poland and say: 'How about showing me what's going on over there?' or 'What have you got in that section?' People would take me into those areas because they trusted me. We had developed personal and business relationships over the years that were proving to be extremely important in my other life.

Not everything of significance was reported to Miss Eyles, however. In Poland and some of the other countries during the seventies, there was a thriving black market in currency. Anywhere we went, someone was sure to recognize us as Westerners and try to exchange their currency for sterling or dollars. The rate would be four or five times the government exchange rate, so we would change our money and live well on caviar and vodka.

The streets and hotels were filled with people offering to change money. We developed a safe circle of people and dealt only with them. It cut down on the risks, because we could have been jailed if we were caught. In Poznań, the city in western Poland where the country held its trade fairs, our money-changer was a senior police official.

On one occasion John Belgrove and I took a couple of new guys on their first trip to Poland to the trade exhibition in Poznań. We picked them up at the airport and drove them to the hotel. We had a meeting to go to and said that we would be back in a couple of hours.

'Whatever you do, don't change any money,' John warned them. 'If anybody approaches you, forget it. You'll either get arrested or ripped off.'

The two of them went down to the bar and had a couple of drinks. Two attractive women came up to them and started chatting, and talked them into changing money at a rate of ten to one. You could get stupid rates, but you ran the risk that you were being set up or that you wouldn't get real currency, since there was a lot of counterfeit money and outdated currency floating around these countries.

They each exchanged a hundred pounds and the girls disappeared. We were late getting back from our meeting and they had decided to pay the bar bill and go back to their rooms. When they tried to give the bartender the new money he laughed at them: they each had a worthless stack of old Polish war bonds.

But even experienced hands sometimes found themselves in awkward situations. I often drove my Ford Granada to Eastern Europe, particularly when I was going to more than one country. It was easier than catching the national airlines, which were notoriously unreliable, and also I had to carry a lot of catalogues and other material.

One night a group of us decided to drive about fifty kilometres west of Warsaw to a restaurant called the Wiczek in the village of Sochaczew which had been recommended by our representative in Poland, Konrad Rymaszewski. John Belgrove and Jim Chapman were with me, along with a couple of other people. When John had phoned to book a table there had been a moment of silence at the other end of the line before the man took his name.

The Wiczek looked like a transport café: dark, with a few small tables and groups of men noisily drinking and talking – hardly the sort of place where you booked a table. A man in a green apron walked over to us and we explained that we had a reservation.

'Ah, yes, the Britishers, the Britishers,' he exclaimed, attracting the attention of the others in the restaurant. With a flourish, he took us through an opening in the back wall that looked like it led to the kitchen but in fact opened into another, larger and better decorated private room where stuffed deer and antelope heads lined the walls. He ushered us to the table and quickly brought a bottle of vodka.

As we were ordering caviar and other dishes, the proprietor began to realize that we were prepared to spend a good deal of money. 'You want to exchange money?' he enquired, tilting his head slightly and smiling conspiratorially. 'Give you good deal.'

We agreed and the man disappeared. He was gone long enough to make us begin to worry. Had we been set up? Was he going for the militia? When he came back, however, he was carrying wads of zlotys. He had gone round the village, gathering up all of the money he could find to exchange it for our dollars.

Suddenly someone rushed into the back room from the front of the restaurant, shouting and gesturing wildly. We all knew enough Polish to recognize that the police were coming. The little man's trip around the village had clearly aroused official suspicion. Scooping up his money, he grabbed me by the arm and hurried the three of us out through a side door to our car. Gesturing for us to leave quickly, he ran to the front of the car.

'Follow me. Follow me,' he shouted as he ran down the narrow cobblestone alleyway as fast as he could. Quickly he came to a set of large wooden gates. He threw them open and motioned us through, his arms windmilling in panic. The car jumped off the cobblestones and hit the road. I jerked the wheel to the right and took off at top speed until we were clear of the village.

A narrow escape, tinged with humour. Fuelled by adrenalin and vodka, we couldn't stop laughing. Next time, I wouldn't be so lucky.

There were five or six mandatory trade exhibitions a year: East Germany, Poland, the Soviet Union, Hungary, Czechoslovakia and Romania. We regularly attended all these, spending a considerable amount of money at them. The exhibitions were an opportunity for manufacturers to display their products to customers and their peers alike. Manufacturers from around the world competed for attention at stands lined up in the huge exhibition halls.

As well as raising the corporate flag, a company was virtually assured of selling the machines it exhibited. Because of the business culture in the host countries and their desire to promote the exhibition, the government arranged for foreign currency to be made available to purchase machines on display. There was almost never a return freight bill to Coventry.

Any company that failed to attend exhibitions could find itself on a virtual blacklist, for officials in the host country would feel that it was not investing in its market, and make it difficult for its salesman to get appointments.

The trade fairs were also one of the few places where Western businessmen could mix socially with the government officials who were buying their machines, and this contact was very valuable. But the effort was killing, and if a salesman had a couple of hours' sleep he was lucky. These people expected to be entertained, and companies would throw lavish parties in restaurants where thirty or more people would gather around a table, drinking champagne and vodka, sometimes until dawn.

The first Moscow trade fair that I attended was back in 1967 with Jack Humphries. We had signed a contract with the Russians and they invited us to dinner. It was a rare social occasion, and marked my introduction to vodka, which I was merrily drinking, ignoring Jack's warnings and the laughter of the Russians. When I stepped out of the restaurant, however, my legs collapsed under me. I don't even remember getting back to my hotel room.

That was my first lesson in vodka, after which I learned to pace myself, and not get drawn into matching the Russians drink for drink. But over the years I seemed to live on vodka and no sleep during the trade fairs. Perhaps it was lack of sleep that made me careless when I was in Moscow in 1975, attending the machine-tool exhibition and staying at the National Hotel. I was there on my own as the managing director of Matrix Churchill International Limited.

Every year, we hired the same interpeter, a woman named Ljuba Kudriavtseva. She would work at our stand throughout the day, translating questions from customers and our replies. I got to know her quite well over the years, learning, among other things, that her husband Vladimir worked for *Pravda*, the Communist Party newspaper. By this time, I was becoming a more active seeker of information for Miss Eyles, and Vladimir seemed to be a promising source of information.

Of the communist countries the Soviet Unions was the strictest about contact between its citizens and Westerners. About the only time that I could associate socially with Russians was during an exhibition. I couldn't pick up the phone and suggest dinner, since they were prohibited by law from having Westerners in their homes. So the exhibition became an excuse for getting to talk to Vladimir.

On one of the last nights of the exhibition I asked Ljuba if she would like to have a meal. She said yes, but she was concerned about going to one of the big hotels, being in her early thirties and reasonably attractive, for prostitutes hung around the hotels and if she were seen with a Westerner there she might well be branded as one. Instead we walked to a fish restaurant just off Red Square.

After the meal I offered to see her home.

'No. No. I'll go on the metro,' Ljuba replied.

'The least I can do is see you home. I'll get a taxi.'

'A taxi is too expensive. You can come on the metro with me.'

So we took the metro to her block of flats, which was very close to the British embassy club, in a pleasant part of the city. There was a short walk from the metro station. It was November and pretty cold, so I was wearing the customary heavy coat and fur hat. Wrapped up like this, I didn't stand out quite so much as someone in Western clothes would have done.

Ljuba invited me in and Vladimir was there. It was a one-room apartment that they shared with their thirteen-year-old daughter, who had a small alcove as her room.

Once you got a Russian to talk, you learned that all except the most hard-line communists were dissatisfied with their lifestyle and standard of living. We had a drink and we talked, with me asking questions about the economic and political situation for about an hour. Vladimir was a very easy guy to talk to. The journalist expressed some dissatisfaction as he talked about the economic situation and compared his system and mine. He also talked about the impossibility of making progress or improving one's standard of living.

It was about eleven-thirty when I left, so the metro was closed and getting a taxi was difficult. But the National Hotel wasn't far away, and I decided to walk back along the Moscow River. I had to cross a bridge near the British embassy and so down Kalinina Prospekt, onto Marxa Prospekt, which ran all the way back to Red Square and the hotel. I had just reached the top of the steps leading to the bridge when someone tapped me on the shoulder.

'Mr Henderson, may I have a word with you?' said a voice in good English.

I was near the British embassy club, so I assumed it was one of the exhibitors who had been to the club, which was frequented by Englishmen. Most likely he had seen me and decided to walk back with me. I turned around and smiled, thinking I would know the man. But I didn't recognize him at all.

'Who are you?' I asked, angry and frightened. Even in the dark, his eyes were so cold they chilled my blood.

'We are Russian officials.'

It was then that I saw the second man standing in the shadows. I was frightened. I was suddenly out of breath, and felt sick. I was in grave danger. So were Ljuba and Vladimir; and their danger might have been even greater. They had clearly violated the law by having a foreigner in their home, and if the authorities began to question them about me, what might they deduce? I had probed about some sensitive political matters. What would Ljuba and Vladimir say to protect themselves? I would not blame them if they told the truth.

In that part of the world, you do not argue with government officials. I walked down the steps between the two bulky men and was pushed into the back of a black car. The Russians sat either side of me during the short drive to Dzerzhinsky Square, where the KGB and the Lubyanka prison were situated.

I was locked in a room the size of a prison cell, though it was not one. I sat in silence in the only chair, beneath a bare light bulb, for about half an hour. I measured the room: six feet wide, nine feet long.

What had gone wrong? How much did they know? Greville Wynne popped into my mind. The government had swapped him for a Soviet agent named Lonsdale, but he looked terrible after nearly a year in a Russian prison. Esther remarked on the weight he had lost when we saw him on television. Was I important enough to MI5 to be exchanged?

I was worried but I did not panic. I was just desperate to analyse the situation as clearly as possible. OK, I've been out to dinner with a Russian woman, I told myself, but that's easily explainable: she is my interpreter. It was a way of saying thank you for the help. Then I walked her home. The only thing that they could hit me for was going into the flat. Or, it suddenly occurred to me, could the questions I had asked Vladimir be construed as spying?

If they knew I had been in the flat, then they would question Vladimir and Ljuba, who would both be in trouble for certain, and I might find myself in deeper, too. So I was trying to decide whether to tell the officials the truth about going into the flat or not mention it. The danger in keeping quiet was that they already knew that I had been there and had questioned Ljuba and Vladimir. Lying would increase the suspicion hanging over me. But if they already knew I'd been inside the flat, I was in trouble anyway. I decided to risk lying.

I was taken to another, larger room. The wooden floor was painted dark red and there was a table. The man with the cold eyes was there, and another I had not seen before. I was told to sit down. While a light shone directly into my eyes, they started to ask me questions. I was scared.

'What are you doing in Moscow? Where have you been? What have you been doing this evening? Why were you out so late? It is unusual for foreigners to be out so late. Who did you meet?'

'I took my interpreter to dinner to thank her for the work she had done at the exhibition,' I answered. 'After dinner I walked her home. I left her at her door.'

I was gambling that Ljuba and her husband would not dare to admit that I had been in their home, for that simple fact could have cost Vladimir his job and prevented Ljuba ever working again as an interpreter. They could be sent away from Moscow.

'You left the restaurant at ten o'clock. Ninety minutes later we stopped you on the bridge. Where did you go?'

Suddenly I sensed that my interrogators really didn't know I had been inside the flat. They knew I had had dinner with a Russian woman, and that we had left together, but then they had lost us on the metro.

'We took the metro back to her flat,' I said. 'I walked her home and left her at the door. Then I went to the club at the British embassy for a drink. I decided to get some air and walk back to my hotel.'

I knew they couldn't check whether I had actually gone to the club at the embassy. A Russian policeman was stationed at the door to the club – to keep Russians out, not to monitor Westerners going in. They never checked a passport or recorded a name.

Again and again they asked me the same questions and got the same answers. Finally they seemed to tire of the stand-off and I was returned to the small, cell-like room, having been told that they didn't believe me.

At about three in the morning I was taken back to the larger room and asked the same questions again. This procedure was repeated twice more at intervals of a few hours. I was given nothing to eat or drink. Clearly the KGB men were set on breaking me.

Finally, at about four in the afternoon the day after I had been taken into custody, the two men who had stopped me on the bridge came and escorted me to a car. They drove me towards the National Hotel, which stood in the shadow of the Kremlin. Again I was wedged between the two of them in the back seat. A third man was driving. One of the men, not the one with the cold eyes, suddenly said: 'We followed you and the woman to the restaurant and then into the metro. We lost you on the metro.'

I hadn't tried to shake off anyone by using the metro. In fact, I had wanted to take a taxi, but this would have been a mistake, and it was only Ljuba's frugality that had spared me from making it. Had we taken a taxi, the KGB would have known I had been inside her apartment between 10.30 and 11.30 p.m. They obviously thought I had lost them on purpose.

The entrance of the National Hotel was lit up as the government car pulled into the drive and up to the steps. The one with the cold eyes slid out so that I could leave the car. As I started to walk away he smiled tightly and said: 'Be careful in the future, Mr Henderson.'

The gamble had paid off this time.

4

'You've made a mistake. We never asked you to take that sort of risk. You chose to do it. You needn't have. You mustn't do it again.'

We were at a corner table in the Bell, a pub near my home. Miss Eyles had always been persistent in her questioning of me. Occasionally she had suggested ways that I could discover more information that the service wanted, although she was never pushy or stern. But that evening I got a glimpse of the steel behind the smart clothes and pleasant smile.

I had described what happened in Moscow the week before. I had also told her what Ljuba had said to me at the exhibition the day after my detention by the KGB. They had gone to her flat while I was being interrogated. They had demanded that she describe the evening. Had I visited her home? What had we talked about? She and Vladimir had both said that I had only walked her to the door before leaving, and that our conversation had been innocent.

I was proud of my quick thinking under the KGB's questioning, pleased that I'd predicted the reactions of Ljuba and Vladimir. Perhaps Miss Eyles had sensed a dangerous boasting in my tone. Her stern reaction dispelled any James Bond fantasies I might still have had.

'You left yourself open to being caught in the flat,' she upbraided me, her knuckles whitening as she gripped the table edge. 'It was a mistake that must not be repeated. Especially in the Soviet Union. You must be far more careful in the future. They are much more serious about such violations there. And being detained for something like that might lead to more serious enquiries by the authorities.'

Well done. Great performance, Miss Eyles, I thought. Not a word of what she had said was the truth. It was exactly what the intelligence service wanted me to do. How else could I obtain valuable and

39

accurate information? The only way was to create relationships, cultivate friendships and develop trust so that people would talk more openly. What she was really doing was warning me: 'get into trouble and we'll disown you.'

Yet it was a warning that reminded of the nature of what I was doing. Working for the intelligence service may have started as a glamorous game, but Miss Eyles had re-emphasized the very real dangers, especially in the Soviet Union.

The style of business was starting to change in some countries of Eastern Europe, particularly Poland, Czechoslovakia and Romania. Many members of the state buying organizations were travelling more, looking at what was available in the West and how the people they did business with were living. And in their own countries, the governments were opening hard-currency shops where people could shop for a better class of goods, although only with foreign money. These officials, who were not paid much, saw businessmen visiting their countries and signing large contracts, and also saw what was on offer in the West and in their own foreign-currency shops. To them, here was an opportunity to make money on the side to improve their own standard of living.

The men and women from the state buying organizations had tremendous influence in deciding who was awarded the contract. The end user, the factory representatives, had to pick three companies who were acceptable, and unless you had a major advantage over your competitors, the organization could decide who got the contract. So when someone suggested that a few pounds or dollars might influence a contract, I was willing to pay up. I was not paying large sums of money – perhaps £500 or £1000 per order – and I paid only after we had got the order. There was never any money up front.

Around this time, the mid-seventies, the Americans were in the middle of a scandal over paying bribes to foreign governments and officials. Lockheed, the big aircraft manufacturer, had been convicted of paying hundreds of thousands of dollars in bribes in the Middle East. New rules were approved in the USA to eliminate the bribing of foreign governments, and they had started to influence British companies, especially large corporations such as TI Group.

George Ashton was the managing director of the TI machine-tool division at this time. I tried to convince him that it was necessary to pay these small amounts to get business. It was as much a part of doing business in those countries as showing our catalogues. 'I don't want to know about it,' he said. 'I'll leave it to you. You do what you have to do.'

I was fortunate to have a person like Ashton as a boss. I kept putting the payments down as expenses when I filled out my accounts, and I told the people who worked for me to do the same. The expenditure was thus all contained within Matrix Churchill International, of which I was managing director.

Ultimately, if there was an investigation it would have been me who would have been on the receiving end. But what we did was a necessary way of doing business in Poland and Czechoslovakia. I could have stopped it, but we would have forfeited the business, and jobs would have been lost at the factory.

Controls on these payments were much stricter in the Soviet Union, East Germany, Hungary and Bulgaria. In any case, personal relationships still counted for a lot there.

At Technoimpex, the Hungarian state buying organization in Budapest, the receptionist was a woman named Clara Moldavani. She was a big woman, in her middle forties at that time. Everyone at Matrix Churchill knew and liked her. In addition, the company had a special relationship with Hungary because we had signed an agreement in the mid-sixties with a company called Czepel for them to manufacture a range of Matrix thread-grinding machines.

I got along particularly well with Clara, who said to me one day: 'My son is writing a book about an Englishman.'

'Oh, really,' I said.

'I hope you don't mind, but he is using your name, Paul Henderson. You're going to feature in the book.'

It didn't bother me. I was mildly flattered. Clara told me that the book was for the Hungarian market, and that her son was very excited about its prospects.

About six months later we were chatting again and I remembered the book.

'Hey, did your son ever publish his book?' I asked.

Clara smiled broadly, pleased that I had remembered. 'Oh yes,' she said.

'And did I feature in it?'

'Yes. You were the British businessman.'

'Well, what was the book about?'

'Oh, it was about a British businessman who was a spy.'

I did my best to smile. Clara was smiling, too. Fortunately I saw nothing but a mother's pride in her face.

Along with the Swiss and Germans, our main competitors in these markets by this time were the Japanese, who were becoming quite strong in new computerized lathes.

It was back in the mid-sixties that machine tools had first been linked directly to an advanced computer. This was a major technological advance and these machines eventually came to be known as computer-numerical controlled, or CNC, machines. Within a decade CNC lathes were becoming popular around the world. Copy lathes relied on templates to produce the required shape and they had to be altered for each new operation. Now, an operator could programme the machine by himself for a variety of operations controlled by the computer. It was more flexible, faster and more precise, allowing the machines to carry out a number of different operations at a higher production rate.

The first Japanese CNC lathes sold in Britain and Eastern Europe were based on inexpensive, flat-bed machines. British toolmakers tended to diminish the potential of these machines, saying they were cheap and would never take serious business away from us.

But I realized that the Japanese would eventually improve their machines and would become a serious competitor throughout the world. However, it seemed to me that it would be some time before CNC machines would be sold in any numbers in Eastern Europe, because those countries tended to lag behind us technologically. In addition, there were export restrictions that would prohibit them from buying machines controlled by advanced computers.

Matrix Churchill was marketing TI machines around the world, and the company's Churchill division was developing its own line of CNC lathes. These would be larger machines, with a slant-bed design that would make them stronger and more rigid. It would be three or four years before the improved models were available, and in the meantime the company needed a low-cost range to sell. We had to find someone who already manufactured a lathe that could be equipped with computer controls to get us into the market quickly.

We had a strong commercial relationship with Poland, including plans to set up a joint venture with Metalexport that would allow Matrix Churchill to sell Polish machine tools in British. One of the Polish companies we would represent was Ponar Wrocław, which manufactured a flat-bed lathe that would be ideal for the new project. An agreement was negotiated with Metalexport and Wrocław whereby the Polish machines would be fitted in Britain with computer controls and sold through Matrix Churchill International. It was to be signed at the Poznań trade exhibition in 1976, and two TI officials, Derek Greenway and Brian Hodgson, were coming out for the signing. A major deal for Poland, it was one of that country's first joint ventures in machine tools with a Western company. John Belgrove, Jim Chapman and I were feeling quite pleased with ourselves.

Twenty-four hours before Greenway and Hodgson were to arrive, the Metalexport directors called me to a meeting at their offices in the exhibition hall.

'We're going to change the terms of the contract,' said Andrej Dyszy, the export director of Metalexport. 'My people have gone through the contract and we want to change it.'

This was not unusual: there were often last-minute attempts to obtain a better deal. I remained calm. 'What sort of changes do you want?' I asked.

Dyszy started to run through a long list of demands. They wanted us to pay more for the machines and to increase the number that we would guarantee to purchase.

'Let's forget it,' I interrupted. 'You and I did a deal. We shook hands. As far as I'm concerned, a deal is a deal. And it's a good deal for both companies. We're both going to make a lot of money. If you start applying these terms and conditions and raising the price of the machines, we will not achieve the objective of volume sales.'

We argued back and forth. But I would not budge. They wanted to go too far. At the price they were demanding, the machines would not be competitive with the Japanese. Finally Dyszy, a little guy who could be quite charming, said: 'Well then, we don't have a deal unless we can get these changes.'

'Fine,' I said, getting up from my chair and walking out.

Later that day I got a telephone call. Dyszy said it would probably be all right. He asked me to go ahead and bring the others to the Metalexport office in the morning for the signing. But when we arrived, the contract was not ready to be signed. We spent much of the morning swapping stories. I could see what was happening. Greenway and Hodgson were not senior to me, but as directors they were authorized to sign the contract, and Dyszy thought that they might pressure me to do the deal the Poles wanted since they had travelled all the way to Poznań.

About 12.30, Dyszy suggested that we go to lunch at the nearby Metropol Hotel. We were greeted by a big spread of food and vodka and lots of Metalexport staff, male and female. The drinking started and it looked as though it was going to be a heavy session.

'Come on, Paul, we can change this price a bit,' Dyszy said to me. 'You can be flexible.'

Realizing what he was up to, I stood my ground. 'I am not talking about this during lunch. We can discuss it tomorrow morning,' I told him.

After lunch we left the hotel and got in cars. As the exhibition was nearby, it occurred to me that we were not going there. No, our hosts explained, we're going out to the lake and our villas. We drove out to a beautiful wooded area beside a lake outside the town. There were a couple of small log cabins, furnished very nicely. Our hosts had laid it on again, for there were more drinks and girls. I wasn't sure they were Metalexport girls this time. John Belgrove and I were chaperoning and took the other two to one side and told them: 'No matter what you do, fellas, under no circumstances will we conduct any business today.'

The party went on until about four o'clock in the afternoon. Afterwards we all got into the cars again and headed back to the exhibition. John and I were in one car, but Greenway and Hodgson had been put in a second vehicle. When we got back to our stand at the exhibition: no Greenway and Hodgson. After a while I asked John to go to the Metalexport office to find them.

'Not there,' he said when he returned.

Another half an hour passed and I was getting a little concerned. So John and I went back to Metalexport.

'Have you seen Andrej Dyszy?' I asked the receptionist.

'He's tied up in a meeting.'

'Are Mr Greenway and Mr Hodgson here?'

'No. No. No.'

Suddenly we heard Greenway's voice and I started towards a door. The receptionist told me that I couldn't go into the room, but we walked in anyway. Brian and Derek were in there discussing the contract. Dyszy was a crafty sod. He had deliberately separated us and was trying to get the deal done his way. We had to drag Greenway and Hodgson out. In fairness to Dyszy, he realized then that he had lost the battle. The following day the contracts were signed as originally negotiated. And the deal worked out well for both companies.

I had been in sales for more than a decade by this time, and realized that if I wanted to become managing director of the TI machine-tool division I needed to get more experience on the manufacturing side of the business. George Ashton was the managing director then and I approached him about a transfer. I explained that I enjoyed selling, but that my real ambition was to take over his job when he decided to move on to better things.

Ashton was sympathetic and discussed my request with several other senior people in the company. Later he called me back to his office and said they had decided my skills were in the marketing field. They didn't want me to move out because they thought that would hurt the business as a whole. He went so far as to assure me in writing that my relative lack of manufacturing experience would not be an obstacle when it came to choosing a new managing director at some point in the future.

But it wasn't long before I discovered that the promise wasn't worth the paper it was written on. In early 1977 I was called into the boardroom at Coventry along with the other directors. Then Ashton walked in with another man. 'This is Tony Weddle,' he said. 'He is going to be the new managing director.'

I sat there completely flabbergasted. I was upset that I hadn't got the job, but I was even more upset that Ashton did not have the courtesy to tell us before he brought Weddle in. None of us had any warning, and I wasn't the only one in that room who had had an eye on the managing director's job.

Weddle sat down and said that he would like us to go around the table introducing ourselves and saying a bit about our jobs. I was fuming by the time it was my turn. 'My name is Paul Henderson and you're sitting in my chair,' was all I said.

In fairness to Tony Weddle he didn't push it, but just moved on to the next director. It was the wrong thing to have done, but I always said what I felt.

Weddle called me afterward and asked me to go to his office. 'Look, I know how you feel,' he said. 'But I hope you can set those feelings aside and work with me. The company needs both of us.'

I never really accepted Weddle as my boss. While that was my problem, I never thought he had much respect for me. He was a theoretical person, a great one for marketing surveys and consultants. I didn't like his strategy for the business: he was moving away from the machines that were our bread and butter and developing new products in fields where we had no experience. I was worried, and in the back of my mind I felt it wouldn't be long before I left Matrix Churchill.

Walter Lees had left the company earlier to become managing director of Alfred Herbert Limited in Coventry. Once one of Europe's largest machine-tool companies and our long-time competitor, Alfred Herbert had fallen on hard times and was now a state-owned company. Walter was the managing director and, with government backing, had developed a comprehensive and competitive line of CNC lathes.

I discussed the situation with Walter, who told me: 'When you've decided you're leaving, give me a call. I don't want to poach you, so I'm not prepared to offer you anything right now. But when you have decided to leave, pick up the phone. I've got a job for you.'

In early 1978 I was trying to set up a deal with Polamco, a Polish machine tool marketing company based in Chicago. Polamco was to sell the CNC lathe that we were manufacturing jointly with Ponar Wrocław. Polamco planned to sell a hundred machines a year in the USA. It was a two-year contract after which Wrocław would manufacture the machines and market them direct through Polamco. Matrix Churchill and TI were scheduled to have a competitive range of CNC machines ready for the market later in 1978, so the Polish machines would have been phased out anyway.

Early in May I was in Chicago. We were within a couple of days of signing on the dotted line with Polamco. TI Group was a great believer in holding annual conferences, but I thought they were an utter waste of time and money. This trip had enabled me to avoid another one.

Late one evening I was in my room at the Marriott, a substantial businessmen's hotel in Michigan Avenue, just a couple of blocks from the Chicago River. Anne Bailey, my secretary, called me. It was the middle of the night in Coventry, but she hadn't been able to get me before because I had been in meetings.

'Tony Weddle told me to reach you,' Anne began. 'He says that you have to come back and attend the machine-tool division conference. All of the directors have to be there.'

'You can tell Tony that I'm just about to sign this contract,' I told Anne. 'There's no way I'm walking away from an order like this to attend a damn conference.'

Doing deals is an unpredictable business. Timing is important, and if you walk away from the bargaining table without a good reason, all kinds of things can happen. I was not about to leave Chicago without this order, which would produce both profit and jobs for the company.

Then it was my turn to be up in the middle of the night. As soon as Anne got to work the next morning and delivered my message to Weddle, albeit in more polite terms, she was back on the phone to me.

'Weddle says to tell you that you must come home,' she said. 'You have no choice.'

We had a couple more telephone conversations before I finally told Anne to tell the managing director that I would return for the bloody conference on one condition. 'I want a written instruction, signed by him, ordering me back,' I said. 'I want him fully aware of what he is forfeiting. If this deal falls through, it won't be my responsibility.'

Sure enough, I got a telex at the hotel from Weddle instructing me to be on the first plane home.

The annual conference was at Harrogate, in Yorkshire. I would be landing at Heathrow Airport about seven in the morning and still have about 250 miles to travel, so I wouldn't get there until lunchtime on Friday, the last day of the conference. Therefore I flew back first class and insisted that the company send a chauffeur to meet me.

At the conference Weddle walked up to me, all friendly and smiling, thanking me for being there. 'I hope you realize my returning has most likely blown our chances of signing the contract,' I said. 'It was absolute nonsense to bring me back to attend a bloody conference for a couple of hours.'

The managing director just looked at me and decided I was best left alone. Then I discovered why he had insisted that I return.

During the session after lunch Weddle announced that Matrix Churchill International, the sales and marketing organization I headed, was going to be reduced in size. The manufacturing companies within TI Machine Tools would get more responsibility for selling their own products. Matrix Churchill would become a coordinating operation. When he had finished, Weddle asked if there were any questions. No one said anything; the room was completely silent. I had the feeling the other directors were all looking at me.

'Well, Paul, how does it sound to you? What do you have to say?' asked Weddle.

I was very angry, as much with myself as with Weddle. While I had been out selling, trying to do what I thought was my job, spending my time in hotel rooms to keep the order book filled, I had had my operation pulled out from under me.

'Is the conference over?' I asked.

'Yes,' Weddle replied.

'Thanks. I'll go home now.'

I walked out of the room, got into the chauffeur-driven car and was taken to Coventry. Back home I told Esther what had happened. She was as stunned as I was, and equally adamant about what I should do. 'It's all over as far as I'm concerned,' I told her. 'I can't continue to work with people who are not straightforward and honest. They've gone behind my back. They are going to destroy the company.'

'They'll destroy it without you then,' said Esther. 'You should call Walter Lees.'

I was terribly committed to Matrix Churchill. I had worked there for twenty-four years, more than half my life, rising from apprentice to managing director of a division. My family had suffered from my commitment. I spent months at a time on the road selling machine tools. Esther had been left to bring up the children, to take all the responsibilities that come with being a parent.

At the weekend I called Walter Lees and told him what had happened. I said that I was going to tell Weddle on Monday morning that I was resigning.

'OK, get it over with and then come and see me,' said Walter. 'We'll work something out.'

I had calmed down by Monday. I took what I thought was a sensible approach with Weddle, telling him that I thought Matrix Churchill International was effectively going to disappear. I said I saw no room in the new organization for me.

'You've made me redundant. My job has disappeared.'

'No, no,' Weddle protested. 'You'll still have your job.'

'It's a lesser job, lesser responsibilities. I am not prepared to take a lesser job.'

George Ashton, who was still working for the machine-tool division, came to see me the following morning. I explained my feelings to him about what had happened to Matrix Churchill, about the overall direction of the company.

'Well, what will you do?' he asked.

'More than likely, I'll apply and see if I can get a job with Alfred Herbert.'

'You're bound to get one,' he said. 'But they're our competitors.'

Then Ashton asked me what I thought of setting up my own business. I said that I had considered it, but that I did not have the money to finance it. Esther and I were comfortable by then, and although we still had a mortgage on our house, we had no other debts. But we didn't have a lot in the bank.

Ashton went away and when he came back a few hours later he had had David Smith, the personnel manager, put together a package that was designed to keep me from joining the competition. The proposal was that I start my own company and represent TI Machine Tools in Eastern Europe. I would still get my redundancy pay, about £21,000. In addition, they would give me a £15,000-a-year consultancy for two years, an amount about equal to my salary at Matrix Churchill. I would also get a commission of 1½ per cent on sales in Poland and 6 per cent on sales in the remainder of Eastern Europe. And they would pay for the furnishing of an office for my new company.

It was enticing. But I didn't want to go it alone. The business would require two people if it was to operate properly. I asked Anne Bailey if she would be prepared to join me as office manager and she agreed. Then I approached John Belgrove, one of my closest friends and a good salesman. He agreed to come in with me as a partner. In this way Hi-Tek Export Consultants Limited was born in the summer of 1978. I held 51 per cent of the stock and John Belgrove held the remainder.

My last action as an employee of Matrix Churchill was a formal resignation meeting with the personnel director, P.M. Roberts. We went over my redundancy package and he wished me well. He also handed me a written analysis of my career with the company that he had prepared for Weddle. I was flattered by one entry: 'It is a success story.'

I wondered if the same would be said of my new venture. It was a hell of a risk, even with the financial assurances provided by TI Machine Tools. I had worked for a salary all my life, bringing financial security to my family and improving our lifestyle. Our children were attending private schools. Esther supported the move, as she had backed me at every significant point in my career.

Together we went to the Midland Bank branch in Tile Hill and presented them with a business plan. They provided us with an overdraft facility of £25,000 to cover travel expenses and other start-up costs, but we had to put up the house as surety.

Weddle asked me to stay with Matrix Churchill until the end of June. He wanted me to represent the company at the Poznań exhibition in Poland that month. Then I would start at Hi-Tek.

Now, I had been talking with a Polish company in Katowice that manufactured mining equipment about a sizeable order for the new large CNC lathes that Churchill was now producing. The deal was worth about £2 million. During the exhibition in June the transaction started to gel. I was still employed by Matrix Churchill, so if we signed the deal during the exhibition there would be no commission, and that meant I would lose £30,000.

I couldn't turn away from the deal. Timing was everything, as I'd seen with the Polamco deal. A few days after Weddle had ordered me back from Chicago, Polamco had decided not to go ahead. So I continued to negotiate with the mining company during the exhibition. It was Tony Weddle who came to my rescue. Towards the end of the trade fair Esther telephoned me, saying he had called her and said he wanted to throw a farewell party for me. He wanted me back in the next few days.

I wasn't going to fight this one. I knew the customer well enough to say that I had to return urgently to Britain. When I asked for a delay in signing the contract, he agreed on one condition. 'You'll be back personally to sign, all right? And it must be no later than 1 July.'

The day after flying back to London I took the train to Coventry, where a party was held for me in the directors' dining room. Anne Bailey had asked Esther what I wanted as a gift.

'Maybe you ought to buy him a clock,' my wife had said. 'He has no idea what time is. He says he's coming home at six o'clock and he comes home at eight o'clock the next day.'

My consultancy contract was signed and came into effect on 1 July 1978. I immediately caught a plane back to Poznań to sign the contract for the £2 million order. On 3 July we signed the order. Tony Weddle had given me a bit more than a clock as a farewell gift.

*　　*　　*

Eighteen months earlier, in November 1976, MI5 had changed my controller. My debriefings now were conducted by a woman who called herself Miss Lambett. Again, no first name. In fact, she was quite similar to Miss Eyles: fairly attractive, quite bright, all business. Probably an economist or something similar, but definitely not a technical person. She would ask many questions whenever I described anything to do with engineering or manufacturing, taking page after page of notes.

The glamour of working for the intelligence service was gone by now. Suddenly you step back and see that you're not just collecting a bit of information. You see a pattern in which you are trading on long-standing relationships with people in Poland, Czechoslovakia and other Eastern bloc countries.

Miss Eyles and Miss Lambett had both pushed me to identify trusted employees of foreign companies and state organizations who could be turned. I began to wonder what would happen if they actually turned someone I had suggested. Are they going to expect me to run the man? Am I going to be his contact? Will I have to take his information in Warsaw or Prague and bring it back to Britain?

Three other events caused me grave doubts about my service to the government and the risks it entailed. In 1977 I had engineered a joint venture with a Polish machine tool company called Polmach. A new firm, TI-Polmach, had been created, with an office in Warsaw to sell Matrix Churchill and other British machine tools, and an office in Coventry to market Polish machine tools in Britain. I was chairman of the board, but there were several Polish directors.

Kris Warokomski was an absolutely superb technical man. The Polish government had sent him to Britain as the technical director of TI-Polmach and he was living with his wife and young daughter and son in a nice house in Kenilworth, a lovely town just outside Coventry and only a few minutes from the factory. I had spent a good deal of time with Kris and liked him very much. He was quiet, gentle and easygoing.

One day in 1978, just before I resigned from Matrix Churchill, I got a call in my office. Kris had been found hanging by a rope from the banisters in his home. I was stunned. How could this likeable, outgoing guy kill himself?

Kris's death was kept very quiet in the press, all handled very gently by the British and Polish authorities. The coroner's court ruled his death a suicide and his family returned to Warsaw, where I attended his funeral.

I could not come to terms with Kris's death. I couldn't understand why he had committed suicide. If he committed suicide. In the back of my mind was the intelligence service. I had never given them his name as a candidate for turning, but I would have discussed in general terms his work with us at Coventry. I just couldn't understand why he would want to kill himself. Then again, often the reasons for suicide are not clear-cut.

The second factor that influenced my movement away from the intelligence service was Hi-Tek. I had my own business, and my income, and the security of my family, depended on my ability to get orders. If I had been arrested while working for TI, the company probably would have looked after Esther and continued to pay my salary. If it happened now, there was no one else to turn to. It was unlikely that John Belgrove would be able to do enough to support both of us.

The first thing that brought home the risk to me of my intelligence-gathering activity occurred in late 1979. Marek Piotrowski, my aristocratic friend from Metalexport, had been placed in charge of the TI-Polmach operation in Britain by the Polish government. Marek had once worked for the Polish embassy in London and he was very glad to be living in the West again, mainly because he could educate his daughter in Britain.

When I formed Hi-Tek, Marek was irritated that I would be selling Matrix Churchill and other TI machines in Poland. Clearly he had seen my resignation as an opportunity to get more territory for himself and ensure his place in the company – and in the West.

'Why not sell your tools through Polmach in Poland?' Marek had asked Weddle at one of the meetings I attended. 'Why do you need Paul Henderson? Why are you paying him a commission? At the end of the day, it is our customer who is paying for that commission.'

But Polmach could not handle the sales of TI machine tools. Without me the company would have had to send sales directors and technical people to Poland regularly. The whole basis for the reorganization of Matrix Churchill had been to reduce its size, and having me and John Belgrove handle Poland and the remainder of Eastern Europe had helped them to do so.

During this running battle with Marek came an intriguing incident. His sister-in-law was married to a Polish television journalist who was working in London. In late 1979 there was a scandal related to the disappearance of a large sum of money from the TV company's account. Then Marek and his family were suddenly recalled to Warsaw at very short notice. It appeared that he had returned under a bit of a cloud.

I didn't believe that the journalist did anything wrong. Certainly Marek had not. But it must have been a black mark for him. He wound up back at Metalexport, but with a job of lesser importance.

Then one day when I was about to fly out to Poland I received a telephone call from Marek. 'You shouldn't return to Poland,' he told me. He sounded very ominous, whispering into the telephone and clearing his throat repeatedly.

'Why?' I asked.

'Well, you've got problems. You're under suspicion.'

'Suspicion for what?'

'To do with bribery and corruption. Some of your competitors have been talking about you.'

This was twenty-four hours before I was due to go back to Poland. I sat back and thought about it. This could be a real warning. Or it could be some of Marek's mischief. It was unlikely, however, that he would have been able to make that call without permission.

My concern was simple. If I didn't return, Hi-Tek would lose its biggest market for machine tools. Word might also spread to other Eastern European countries, for they were all connected through their intelligence services. If I didn't go back and face whatever this was, Hi-Tek could be finished. In the end I decided I had no choice. I would go to Poland as scheduled.

That night, as I packed for my trip the following morning, I told Esther about Marek's call. I explained that I had decided to go anyway and that the business depended on my ability to work there. I did not mention the intelligence work, although it weighed on my mind that this could somehow be involved.

Esther was very uncomfortable. Perhaps she suspected what I had been up to for the government. But more likely she was simply frightened about me disappearing behind the Iron Curtain.

I got on the plane and was in Warsaw the following day. I was a popular person at Metalexport. I knew the receptionists and other employees, calling them by their first names, and they in turn were friendly to me. The minute I walked in this time I knew something was wrong. I asked for the senior person with whom I had an appointment and Sonia, the receptionist, said that I had to see Mr Jung.

Aleksander Jung was the director general of Metalexport. We had been involved in several deals, including the joint production of the CNC lathes and the setting up of TI-Polmach.

'What's this all about?' I asked Sonia, trying to sound calm, and to conceal the hollowness in the pit of my stomach.

'We can't tell you,' she said.

Of course, it had something to do with the warning from Marek. Perhaps my old friend had indeed tried to help me. I was taken up to the top floor, where Jung occupied a larger corner office. He was pleasant enough but cool as he greeted me and motioned me to a chair in front of his desk.

'We have a problem,' he said.

'Really. What's the problem?'

'It has been made known to us that you are offering bribes to get business. You are offering bribes to Metalexport employees in order to obtain orders.'

'Oh really!' was all I could muster. Unless he was playing out some strategy, it did not appear that this was related to my intelligence work. And I had stopped paying bribes in 1978 with the formation of Hi-Tek. It was a risk that I didn't feel I could take with my own company. However, I had given small amounts of money to employees of Metalexport and other state organizations in the past when I was with Matrix Churchill. There was no way I could admit that. I would have been arrested immediately.

'Rubbish,' I said. 'That is the last thing I would do. I haven't given a bribe to any of your employees. What do you call a bribe? Is a bottle of Scotch a bribe? Is a bottle of perfume? Is it a bribe to take someone to dinner or give them a calendar? 'If those are bribes, then I'm guilty. But so are you, Mr Jung. I have brought you bottles of Scotch on many occasions. You have accepted them.'

'No, no,' he said hurriedly, waving both hands as if to ward off flies. 'We are not talking about that sort of thing.'

'Then what are we talking about? That is all I have done.'

'We have heard otherwise.'

'I'd like to know where these lies come from. Who has told you that Paul Henderson has given bribes to your people?'

He thought for a minute, staring down at his desk and shuffling some papers.

'Your competition.'

'That's a laugh, isn't it? It's the competition jealous of our success.'

'It's a little more serious than that.'

'It's not Marek Piotrowski, is it?'

He refused to answer. He did not deny it was Piotrowski who had made the charges against me. Instead, he tried to deflect me.

'I'm sure you're aware, Paul, that you have to be careful what you say in restaurants.'

'I've travelled enough in this part of the world to know that people that work in hotels probably work in the intelligence service, too. But I have nothing to hide.'

'Well, your conversation was overhead and taped at the Victoria Hotel while you were having dinner with some people.'

I had never talked about anything sensitive at the Victoria or any other hotel. Even if my business instincts had not prevented it, my experience in intelligence work would have.

'That's absolute rubbish,' I said. 'If you have a tape, play it back for me.'

We played this game of cat and mouse for nearly three hours. Finally Jung said: 'OK, Paul, I believe you.' He did not apologize for the accusation. That would have been expecting too much. He reached into his desk and pulled out a bottle of vodka. We had a drink and talked about machine-tool orders. As I left, the director general wished me good luck.

Clearly someone had tried to discredit me. Was it one of my competitors? The Germans or the Swiss? Was it Marek Piotrowski, embittered at his forced return and intent on running Polmach once more?

There was no way of knowing. That was the most frightening aspect of the incident. If someone was out to get me, where would it stop? And how much did it increase the dangers of working for the intelligence service? Was it related to my detention in Moscow?

On the way home a few days later, these questions were swirling in my mind. Coupled with the rigours of operating my own business and the death of Kris Warokomski, the new encounter was unsettling. I decided it was time to ease out of my relationship with the government. I had served my country, taken chances and provided valuable information. I had to be concerned with my own security now, and that of my family. But would the intelligence service simply let me go?

5

Hi-Tek was a moneymaker in the beginning. John Belgrove and I were earning more than ever before from commissions on the sales of machines for Matrix Churchill and other British companies. We bought ourselves a couple of flash cars, on the company. Mine was a canary-yellow Jaguar XJS with a black interior and twelve-cylinder engine. John got the same model XJS, but in air force blue.

The cars were a mistake; a bit too loud a signal of our success. They created envy among some people at Matrix Churchill and the other companies we represented. The guys at Matrix Churchill nicknamed mine the 'flying daffodil'. But the cars must have made them wonder if they were paying too much in commissions.

John and I justified the Jaguars to ourselves because we were working so hard. I was spending more time on the road than ever before. With Matrix Churchill, my management responsibilities had kept me at home a certain amount of time to entertain visiting customers or to work out personnel problems, but now my job was pure selling, which resulted in trips of two months or more through a string of Eastern European countries.

Although I was spending a great deal of time in Bulgaria, Romania and other communist states, my work for the intelligence service had dwindled to nothing. There had been no formal separation; no farewell clock as with Matrix Churchill. But I had slowly pulled away, calling Miss Lambett less and less with my reports. The switch seemed to suit the professionals. In 1979 Miss Lambett had asked me for the names of people still working at Matrix Churchill who might be willing to help the government. Because she was MI5 and her primary responsibilities were for counterespionage in Britain, she had always been particularly interested in Eastern bloc officials visiting the country. Since I was no longer at Matrix Churchill, and often travelling abroad, I did not always know who was coming to the plant or visiting other parts of Britain.

I gave Miss Lambett the names of two people. First, Mark Gutteridge, who was one of my oldest friends at the company. We had spent a lot of time together in the Soviet Union and Eastern Europe. The other, Jim Chapman, was also a friend and salesman who travelled and worked extensively abroad.

I learned that the intelligence service approached both men. Once Miss Lambett indicated that intelligence might be working with Mark. But she never confirmed it and I didn't ask her. It would be a couple of years before I asked Mark.

I kept the phone number for the intelligence service, which was lucky, because I needed it.

Often in those days, I would drive my car on business trips. As well as making it easier to carry the many catalogues and the other material that I needed, it was cheaper than flying. But there was another advantage to driving. I could fill the boot with the small gifts that were part of doing business in Eastern Europe: girlie calendars, bottles of Scotch, lighters, pens and, in Romania especially, Kent cigarettes. I don't know why the Romanians preferred this particular brand. Perhaps they had done a good advertising job. But Kents were our passport in Romania. Into the country with a cursory customs check; out of a speeding ticket with a sly smile.

The value of Kents was illustrated for my son, David, in the summer of 1981. He had just turned sixteen and I decided to take him on a month-long business trip. We had driven into Hungary and stayed at the Geliert Hotel, a lovely place in the old part of Budapest. The following morning we drove towards Romania. We intended to go to Bucharest, then cross into Bulgaria and wind up at the Black Sea port of Varna. As we approached the Romanian border I could see a long line of cars waiting at the checkpoint. It was at least a four-hour wait. 'We've caught the holiday traffic,' I said to David. 'We're going to be here ages.'

The Romanian border guards used to walk up and down the lines of the cars, peering in and, I suppose, keeping an eye out for anyone or anything suspicious. Because I drove through these border points often, one of the guards recognized the silver Granada that I used for travelling in Europe. He looked in at me, nodded and walked over to David's side. Opening the door, he stood on the edge of the car and ordered me to pull into the diplomatic lane. I drove cautiously to the front of the queue and we were cleared through customs in a matter of minutes. Later, when we opened the boot, the carton of Kents I had placed on top of our luggage was gone.

In the autumn of that year I drove to Leipzig for the annual machine-tool trade fair. Mark Gutteridge was there from Matrix Churchill, along with Tom Atkins. As business had picked up at Hi-Tek, John Belgrove and I had brought in Tom, who was also ex-Matrix Churchill, as a third salesman.

One night we entertained a large party of East Germans at a restaurant in town, and there was a lot of eating and drinking. The East Germans were very strict on drinking and driving. One drink and you were not supposed to drive. In fact, all Eastern Europeans were strict. Fines were a way to generate hard currency from foolish Westerners. When we walked out of the restaurant to my car at about two o'clock in the morning, I refused to drive.

'I've had too much to drink,' I said.

'So have I,' chimed in Mark.

'Well,' said Tom, 'I've had as much as you two. But I'll drive. One condition though: if I get stopped, we split the fine.'

We agreed. Driving very carefully, Tom manoeuvred through several checkpoints and was within a hundred yards of the private house where we were staying when a policeman stepped out of the shadows and stuck up his hand. The street lighting was poor, but we could just make out the police car.

I was sitting in the back seat and Mark was in the passenger seat. The policeman walked over to Mark's side of the car and motioned for him to get out. He walked Mark over to the police car, took his driving licence and passport and breathalysed him.

Mark tested positive, of course, and he was fined 200 Deutschmarks, then about £50. The policeman sent him back to the car and told him not to drive. Mark started to get back into the passenger seat, but the policeman called out something in German and waved him over to the other side. Only when the policeman walked a little closer to the car did he realize that the Granada was not a left-hand-drive German model, but a right-hand-drive British car. Mark hadn't been driving at all. The policeman smiled. He had been paid, so he just waved us on and Tom drove the hundred yards or so to where we were staying.

The next morning Mark demanded that we give him our share of the fine, but Tom and I protested. The arrangement had been to share the fine for the driver; nothing had been said about the passengers.

Adding insult to injury, the policeman had given Mark the small phial containing the results of his breathalyzer test as a souvenir. However, he had put it in the pocket of his Burberry raincoat and forgotten it, and some days later in Prague he pulled the coat from the boot, the phial smashed and the acid burned a hole in the coat.

By now I was spending a fair amount of time in Bucharest, working with Romania's state buying organization, Machinoexportimport. Mark was the Matrix Churchill salesman who covered the country and we often worked as a team.

The standard of living in Romania was a lot lower than in the other countries of Eastern Europe. Also, it was a police state where the people were strictly controlled. It was the law that any citizen who had contact with a Westerner had to report it to the police. While the atmosphere wasn't exactly unpleasant, you could see that people were frightened.

Even in the early eighties, when other countries had relaxed their attitudes somewhat, it was very difficult to get Romanians to come out to dinner. When you signed a contract, you had to go through the protocol office to invite someone to dinner to celebrate. Then, if you got permission, someone from that office would come along, sitting there taking notes and watching everything in silence.

There was one person who stood out in this impoverished, rather bland setting. Dorian Furnica was six feet tall, heavily built and had an ingratiating smile. He was always immaculately dressed. In a country where a government official might wear the same frayed shirt for a week, Furnica had a different Western suit and a clean shirt every day. I sensed he was more than someone who negotiated contracts at Machinoexportimport.

When we were in Bucharest, Mark and I stayed at the Park Hotel, a small place on the outskirts of the city. Furnica would often call on us there, which was very unusual. The receptionists at all the hotels had to report to the police, so his presence set off alarm bells. Here was a guy who was more than he appeared.

Once in the room, Furnica always insisted on talking to us in the bathroom, with all the taps running and the toilet flushing. It all seemed a bit daft: three grown men jammed into a steamy bathroom, talking about machine-tool contracts.

I was in Bucharest on my own one clear, sunny autumn day in 1981, eating lunch in an outdoor restaurant at the Flora Hotel, close to the Park Hotel, when Furnica approached.

'Mind if I sit down?' he asked in his fluent English.

'Not at all,' I said, motioning him to the empty chair facing me.

'I'd like you to meet somebody, a very senior person in the ministry. It can be very helpful to you,' he said

'Business – related?'

'Of course,' Furnica assured me. 'I will pick you up tomorrow evening at five o'clock outside the hotel. We will have dinner.'

What did I have to lose? I didn't know which ministry, but I assumed it had to do with machine tools. Furnica always had my alarm bells ringing, but no more so this time than any other time.

The following afternoon I was waiting in the reception area of the hotel when a huge black Zil limousine pulled up. Nobody but high government officials used those cars. Furnica stepped out of the back and, with a great smile and a tip of his head, shouted to me: 'Shall we go?'

We drove into the centre of Bucharest and stopped outside a small, elegant building. There were no signs or a menu in the window, and the curtains were drawn, so I couldn't see in. As we stepped inside I realized that this was one of the special places reserved for senior Communist Party officials. It was beautifully adorned with antiques and oriental rugs. We walked up three broad flights of stairs and into a small dining room where, sitting alone at a table, was a small man in a business suit.

'This is Mr Henderson,' said Furnica, pulling out a chair.

The man responded with only a nod of his head, ignoring my outstretched hand. 'You are doing a lot of business here in Romania,' he said in English. 'It is good for you and good for our country. But there are limits to what we can accomplish under the current arrangement. We would like to improve our own machine-tool industry. To make our products more attractive to sell in the West.'

I didn't respond and I don't think he expected me to. He was right: unlike Poland and the Soviet Union, Romania had little in the way of machine tools to offer countries with hard currency.

Nothing was asked of me; it was simply a general discussion of the machine-tool business and what would be required for Romania to develop production. The purpose of the meeting, however, seemed clear. I expected that, at some point, the ministry man would ask my help in obtaining Western technology. Perhaps it was as innocent as arranging a licensing agreement or joint venture in which Romania would produce machines for Matrix Churchill or another British company. Perhaps it was less innocent.

On my next trip to Bucharest Furnica again invited me to dinner. This time, as the Zil pulled up outside the hotel, Doina, the girl at the reception desk, said to me: 'What are you doing with the Romanian secret police?'

'The secret police?'

'Oh yes, that car belongs to the secret police.'

The chances of a joint-venture agreement seemed remote, and this soon became clear when Furnica and I arrived at the same anonymous restaurant for a second meeting with the man whose name I had never learned.

'We need certain, ah, technology,' said the man. 'We are interested in specific items and it has been suggested that you might be able to help us.'

What he wanted, the ministry man explained, was for me to provide him with technical designs of Western machine-tool technology. His particular interest was in cylindrical grinding machines. There was no mention of paying me – it was something that I could do to help the Romanian government.

When I returned to Coventry I phoned the intelligence service. When Miss Lambett rang back. I explained briefly what had occurred and she said that she would meet me the following day.

I was concerned that the Romanians had learned I had worked for British intelligence. I knew that the Eastern European nations and the Soviets exchanged intelligence. Greville Wynne had been arrested in Hungary after a tip-off from the Russians and sent to Moscow for his show trial. Were the Romanians going to confront me and then pressure me to be a double agent?

Miss Lambett was dubious of that scenario as we talked quietly at the Malt Shovel, a pub in Stonebridge, about six miles north of Coventry, that was managed by my brother and his wife. She thought it best for me to play along and see what the Romanians wanted. If necessary, she said, I could give them some general drawings, nothing useful, just enough to keep the game going. But I must be certain not to provide them with anything that could be considered detrimental to the British machine-tool industry.

Over the course of several trips in the following weeks I provided

Furnica with general drawings of machine-tool designs and some production processes. There was nothing that would have helped them to manufacture the machines.

Things were becoming very unsettled in Eastern Europe about that time. In mid-December 1981 I was in Warsaw when martial law was declared in Poland. It happened overnight and when people woke up the next day it was quite eerie. Tanks and soldiers were on the streets and there were no radio or television broadcasts. By the end of the day, special flights had been arranged for foreigners and I was out of the country.

A few days later, still unsettled by what I'd seen in Poland, I had another disturbing experience. I was flying from London to Bucharest and had stopped in British Airways' executive club lounge to have a drink before boarding the plane. Later, as my plane began its descent into Bucharest, the flight attendants handed out customs forms. When I reached for my passport to get the details, it was missing. Thirty minutes from Bucharest I realized I had left my passport, wallet and other documents at Heathrow.

I alerted the flight attendant and she told the pilot, who radioed ahead to the Romanian authorities for guidance and was told that I would have to remain on board and get off only with an escort to identify my luggage. The bags and I would return to London, where British Airways personnel had located my documents.

The plane landed and after everyone else had disembarked and I had identified my luggage, the pilot invited me to sit in the cockpit with the crew while we waited for the return flight.

I was angry with myself, because I was going to lose a week. It was a Monday and there was no return flight to Bucharest until Friday. While I was sitting there the pilot radioed my name and occupation to Romanian officials. It was just a formality, he told me. Half an hour later an officer in military uniform came aboard. He stepped into the cockpit and said: 'Mr Henderson, will you come with me, please?'

I asked why, what had I done wrong, but he told me not to worry. We walked off the plane and down the gangway to where my suitcase was now standing. I identified it and the man called over a baggage handler to take it to Customs.

'Do you have any identification with you?' he then asked.

All I had was my driving licence – nothing with a photograph. I handed it to him and he walked off. About half an hour later he returned and handed me my licence and a slip of white paper, saying: 'You can go through customs. Enjoy your stay.'

I was confused. A British Airways staff member came over and explained it to me. This was most unusual, even unheard of. But for some reason the authorities had decided to allow me into the country without my passport. The white slip of paper would serve as my documents for the trip. British Airways would lend me some money and then fly my passport and wallet in on the Friday flight.

In the middle of the week Furnica contacted me and arranged another meeting over dinner with the man from the ministry. I had brought another set of drawings and this time I took them to the meeting and handed them to the man, who seemed really satisfied with the inconsequential material I was providing.

When I stood to leave after dinner, he put an envelope on the table and thanked me. Then he gestured to me and I picked up the envelope and tucked it into the inside pocket of my suit jacket.

Back at the hotel, safe in my locked but probably bugged room, I opened the envelope. It contained the equivalent of £1000 in dollars.

When I described the episode and the cash to Miss Lambett, she just smiled. She wasn't bothered by the money, so I kept it. It was the only time I was ever paid for intelligence work.

I was getting nervous about this relationship with the Romanians. Sooner or later they were going to want material of genuine substance. That would leave me in a tight spot. But the economy came to my rescue, even as it threatened to drive me into bankruptcy.

By this time business was drying up across Eastern Europe. For years Western governments had guaranteed low-interest loans to those countries so that they could buy Western products. But the loans were not being repaid and indeed several countries had stopped paying interest on their foreign debts. In response, the West had done the natural thing: the cashier's window was slammed down.

Machine tools are extremely expensive machines, nowadays costing £50,000 or more each. Hi-Tek and the manufacturers we represented had thrived on these loan guarantees. When they vanished, so did our business, for our communist bloc customers no longer had the hard currency to pay for the expensive machinery.

On the bright side, this meant my trips to Romania stopped. To be honest, I would have preferred to try to work things out with Dorian Furnica and his friend to losing Eastern Europe as a market. When sales there dried up, it almost pushed me into receivership.

On New Year's Day 1982 I woke up and lay in bed trying to figure out how I was going to avoid bankruptcy. Hi-Tek was deep in debt to the bank. John Belgrove and I faced losing the homes we had put up as surety. Shortly before Christmas we had decided we'd have to let Tom Atkins go, since the business wasn't even supporting the two of us. Fortunately Tom had seen what was happening to the company and had already been offered a new job in the Philippines before we had to tell him.

So I lay in bed that morning counting pennies. Hi-Tek had started business in 1978 with a £25,000 overdraft facility at Midland Bank. As the business had expanded, the overdraft had risen to £100,000. But it was almost used up, and we were £70,000 in debt. As far as I could see, we would not be able to generate enough in commissions selling machine tools to pay it off.

A few days later I ran into Jim Bartholomew, an old friend who ran his own company, Renata Engineering. He too had been selling in Eastern Europe, although he sold different equipment. He was in the same financial situation as Hi-Tek, but he had the chance of two big contracts in Poland. All he needed was someone to help finance them. He asked if Hi-Tek was interested.

We had always worked on a commission basis: our principal would sign the contract and pay us a commission when he was paid. But this deal with Jim would be different. We would be the contractor, which meant we had to buy the goods before we were paid, a big risk considering our financial position.

Nevertheless, John and I went to the Midland Bank and they were extremely helpful. We had told them earlier about Hi-Tek's troubles. This time we asked them for a £100,000 letter of credit to finance the contracts. We would then earn a nice profit and move into a new line of business that might see us through the difficult years.

It was a risk, for us and for the bank. If it didn't work, we could find ourselves so deep in debt we'd be finished. But the pay-off was good, too. John and I figured that if we could work with Jim on similar deals we might see our way through the problems.

The bank agreed and fortunately the transaction went smoothly. Throughout 1982 we arranged similar deals and sold a few machine tools here and there. We managed to keep the company afloat and eventually to pay off the £70,000 debt. But the cost was high. We sold the Jaguars. One day John and I had driven them to a dealer in Leicester and in one last fling we drove side by side along the M6, racing at over a hundred miles an hour.

More importantly, the pressure of the work created personal problems for me. The strain on Esther and the children was difficult, too. For a lengthy period, I moved out to live on my own.

But by the end of 1982 my marriage was steady again and John and I could see ourselves coming out of the doldrums. We realized that Hi-Tek could survive. What it could not do, however, was support two fairly expensive people, so one of us would have to find another job. It was decided that John would look for a job and I'd stay on at Hi-Tek. Once the market turned around, he would come back.

Earlier in 1982 we'd had to let Anne Bailey go and Esther had come in to help out in the office. Anne had been dating David Smith, a former personnel director at TI Machine Tools Division, who was now in the same position with a company called Lancer Boss in Leighton Buzzard, a market town about forty miles south of Coventry on the road to London. Anne had mentioned the troubles at Hi-Tek to David and just before Christmas he rang me up. Lancer Boss had an opening for an export director. Was I interested?

Lancer Boss manufactured fork-lift trucks, from small electric models to forty-tonners that unloaded container ships. It was owned and run by two brothers, Neville and Trevor Bowman-Shaw. I didn't know anything about fork-lift trucks, but I knew selling. I went down for an interview. The job would cover Europe, Eastern Europe and Scandinavia. In addition, the export director had responsibility for subsidiary companies in West Germany, France and Ireland.

Neville Bowman-Shaw was the chairman and Trevor was the vice chairman. David Smith had cautioned me that they ran a disciplined company. Indeed I quickly learned from others I met there that the previous export director had not lasted long because the brothers were so demanding. Yet the job was attractive and when it was offered to me, I was inclined to accept. John and I discussed it and agreed that he would remain with Hi-Tek and I would give Lancer Boss a try. I joined the firm on 2 January 1983, and although I never thought of Lancer Boss as a permanent home, I was determined to do a good job.

As I had with machine tools as a young apprentice, I had to learn the anatomy of fork-lift trucks before I could sell them. The selling itself was more aggressive and I dealt more with the distributors than with the customers. And working for the Bowman-Shaws was far different from anything I had ever experienced. They were extremely demanding people, whom you had to address as chairman and vice chairman. They demanded long hours and total availability. As part of the job, I was supposed to move my family to Leighton Buzzard, but I wanted to put that off as long as possible. However, the hours were so long and irregular that I moved into a company house during the week.

I always thought that I had a fairly good way with people, and that I could get the best out of them. But I began to realize that I was probably too easy in my management style. At Lancer Boss I learned that being a little bit harder, being able to recognize a person's weaknesses as well as abilities, were also necessary skills in a manager.

There was an element of unpredictability in working for the Bowman-Shaws. They could come into your office and give you a dressing-down you never forgot. But I came to like both men, and to understand what they were trying to do. I didn't always agree with the way they treated people, but I learned a tremendous amount about management and about people.

It was a challenge. The atmosphere was demanding. But I was determined to survive. When I left, it would be on my own terms. I wasn't going to get thrown out on my ear. I don't like losing to anybody. That's part of my character.

During 1983 I was contacted again by the intelligence service. They had kept tabs on me and were interested in what I was learning in my new job. I was travelling to different cities now and meeting different people.

One day a man who called himself Richard Stanbury phoned me at work. I agreed to meet him, but I told him that he would have to come to Leighton Buzzard, because the demands on my time were too strict for me to slip into London.

We met one evening in the Cock at Wing, a small village a few miles from Leighton Buzzard. It is an old pub, with low, beamed ceilings and several fireplaces surrounded by comfortable chairs and small round tables. Stanbury, a stocky, nondescript fellow, said the intelligence service was interested in the people I was meeting at the state buying organizations and the people who were coming to Britain as part of trade delegations.

I fell into the same pattern as during the seventies. Only Stanbury had to come to Leighton Buzzard or a nearby village. I met him several times during 1983 and 1984. He was particularly interested in what I heard and saw during my travels in the Soviet Union, and we spent much of our time discussing that country. He was also interested in a joint venture between Lancer Boss and Balkancar, a Bulgarian firm, and a particular Polish official, Ryszard Heleszko, with whom I dealt regularly.

There was a lot more freedom of travel in the communist bloc by this time. When I was visiting a dockyard or factory I developed a technique of dropping back, pretending to inspect some machine or other. The person assigned to me would walk over to where I was standing. These were good occasions to strike up a conversation about the factory or what sorts of material were moving in and out of the port.

By late 1984 I had had enough of Lancer Boss and fork-lifts. I wanted to get back into machine tools. After twenty-four years at Coventry Gauge and Tool, TI and Matrix Churchill and another five years selling their products, I couldn't get machine tools out of my system.

It took a measure of humility, but I wrote a letter to Tony Weddle, who was still the managing director of TI Machine Tools. I was still in touch with old friends there and I had picked up a rumor that Weddle might be leaving the division soon. I had also heard that the sales director's job might be coming vacant, as Charles Tearne, who had taken the position when I quit, was nearing retirement.

Weddle agreed to meet me for dinner one evening, but after that I never heard from him again. I later decided it was because he knew he would be leaving soon, not out of any spite towards me.

I applied for two other jobs. One was as export director at a company in Halifax that manufactured textile machinery, and the other was a similar post with a machine-tool maker in the same city.

I was still being considered by both companies when I received a phone call from Michael Downes, the personnel director at TI Machine Tools Limited, as the machine-tool division was now called. John Wareing, the new managing director, wanted to meet me and talk about a possible job as sales director.

Wareing was commuting to Coventry from a town near Leighton Buzzard, so it was easy enough to meet for dinner one evening. He described his plans for restructuring the company, his desire to return to the basic machines that had once made it strong. He stressed the need for a top sales director to help get the business out of the continuing slump. Rather than simply deal with export sales, as I had done with Matrix Churchill, I would also handle Britain. It was a bigger job than the one I had left.

I was short-listed for the sales job along with one other candidate. In the meantime, I was offered both of the other jobs. In fact, Esther and I were to meet the chairman of the textile-machinery manufacturer on a Saturday as a final formality before I was offered the position. What I really wanted, however, was the TI job. I knew the industry and, more important perhaps, I knew and respected the company and the men who worked there.

The Wednesday before I was to meet with the chairman of the textile-machinery firm, I was interviewed by the personnel director of the TI Group. It surprised me that someone from the parent company was involved in a hiring decision at this level, but it turned out there was some concern about whether I was the man for the job.

'Paul, how do you think you've changed as a manager since you left us?' he asked me.

It was a good question. My experience at Lancer Boss had taught me a lot about managing people. I tried to explain it.

'I used to think that managing people meant being one of the lads, out in the field doing it yourself. I've learned that it isn't always a question of being one of the lads. It is a matter of organization, managing your people and making sure the job is done the right way. I don't see the sales director's job as always being out there doing it yourself.'

The next day I got another call from Mike Downes. Could I be in John Wareing's office in Coventry on Friday afternoon? Wareing offered me the job and I accepted on the spot. Officially I would become the sales and marketing director of TI Machine Tools Limited.

I telephoned the textile company and the other machine-tool firm and told them I was going to TI Machine Tools Limited. The textile people were left out on a limb. They had no other candidate, and asked if I knew anyone who might be right for the job. I gave them the name of one of my fellow sales directors at Lancer Boss and he eventually took the job.

The Bowman-Shaws tried to persuade me to stay. They offered me a better salary than I would be earning at Matrix Churchill, but my heart was in machine tools. Then they insisted that I work my three months' notice, after which Esther and I took a short holiday in Spain.

Finally, in May 1985, seven years after leaving in anger, I once again walked into the factory at Fletchamstead Highway.

6

In the spring of 1985 TI Machine Tools Limited was not a healthy company. The order book was far from full, with only two or three months' work in sight instead of the year to eighteen months that had been standard seven years ago. In part the decline was the consequence of the overall economic situation and the increased competition from imported Japanese machine tools.

The British automotive industry, once the largest customer for the nation's toolmakers, was in a steep decline. The remainder of the country's manufacturing sector was also doing poorly. As far as export business was concerned, the Japanese were producing high-quality machine tools at good prices. They were making it tough not only on the British companies, but also on the Germans, Swiss and Americans. Every British manufacturer was suffering. But TI Machine Tools seemed harder hit than the rest.

The company had languished without proper attention from the parent company or its own management. During boom times a business can survive with little direction. But slumping sales and economic lethargy are not kind to a company that is adrift. The machine-tool division, never a big profit centre even at its peak, was losing in the region of £2 million a year on a turnover of £20 million on average, and had been for several years.

The business still had a good reputation for quality, engineering and service. But its market had shrunk dramatically. The British base had declined from 200 customers to about forty. A similar decline had occurred in exports, with markets declining to a fraction of what they once were. If the company was going to survive, sales would have to increase quickly.

The whole purpose of John Wareing taking over as managing director was to turn the business around. He had even come up with a name for the restructuring. It was called the 'Profit Improvement Plan', or PIP. Fat would be trimmed, operations centralized and sales turnover increased.

What I learned within weeks of my return was that the goal was not simply to return the company to financial health. TI Group wanted to put the machine-tool division back on its feet and turn the red ink to black for a different purpose. They wanted to make the division attractive for somebody to buy.

The sales operation was a hodgepodge, symptomatic of the lack of an overall company focus. Matrix Churchill International, the division I had left seven years before, had been reduced to executing contract details on export sales. A separate commercial office handled British sales. The two manufacturing companies within the division – Matrix and Churchill – had taken over the technical sales operation. Separate salesmen represented each company, which was not only costly but ineffective.

For example, Mark Gutteridge was assigned to export sales for Matrix equipment at the Coventry plant. Ron Ash, another experienced salesman and a favourite of John Wareing, was working for Churchill at Blaydon on Tyne.

With John Wareing's approval, sales for both companies were centralized in Coventry. Matrix Churchill International's functions also were merged into the new operation. Then, with a single sales and marketing set-up once again, we began to concentrate on filling the order book.

During this period I had a difficult decision to make in the matter of restructuring. There were two export managers in the company, Mark Gutteridge and Ken Southwell, and I had to select one of them to run the consolidated operation. Mark was a close friend of mine, someone with whom I had spent a great deal of time on the road and whom I respected. But I thought that Southwell was the better man for the job. He had broader experience. Mark, although he had travelled extensively, had concentrated on Eastern Europe and Russia.

This dilemma would have been more difficult to cope with before my two years with Lancer Boss. It was still a tough decision because it involved a personal friend. But I made the choice I thought was best for the company and selected Southwell. Mark was unhappy and there was a risk that he would leave the company. I tried to explain my reasoning to him, but I could only hope that he would remain.

John Wareing confronted a more painful restructuring. The business was smaller and showed little hope for enough growth to support two major manufacturing plants, the Matrix one at Coventry and the Churchill one at Blaydon on Tyne. On top of that, the mandate from TI Group was to get the company into saleable shape as quickly as possible. One of the factories was going to have to be closed down so that production could be centralized.

The Churchill factory was physically the better plant. Its operations were more modern, mainly because it was using the latest technology to produce CNC lathes. Although the Coventry factory was larger, it was older and some of its production methods were out of date. The machines manufactured there, such as thread-grinders and machining centres, were not produced in large quantities.

The logical choice was to close the Fletchamstead Highway factory and move the operation to the Newcastle area. However, there was concern about whether enough Coventry workers would be willing to transfer more than 200 miles north. There is an art to manufacturing thread-grinding machines; it requires a lot of skill and experience. Without skilled workers, delays in gearing up to produce these machines would be lengthy and costly. Given the division's financial condition, it might be fatal.

Of course, there is skill involved in the manufacture of lathes as well. But there was an experienced workforce in Coventry to replace any Churchill workers who chose not to move south. TI had bought the manufacturing rights to Alfred Herbert Limited's lathes when the company went into receivership in the early eighties, and moved the production to the Churchill plant. A fair number of the Coventry men who worked at Alfred Herbert were still in the area.

It was decided that the thread-grinding operation could not be moved as smoothly as the lathe production. So the decision was taken in early 1986 to close the Churchill factory at Blaydon on Tyne. It was a sad turn of events. About 500 skilled manufacturing and administrative jobs were lost at a factory that, in my opinion, could have been kept open with proper direction in previous years. Most of the Churchill workers decided not to move to Coventry.

For the Midlands, there was a bright side. About 300 new jobs were created in the Coventry plant to take up the manufacture of CNC lathes. It brought total employment at the Coventry plant to about 850 – a far cry from the 2000 employees of the postwar boom, but enough to make the company one of the area's largest employers.

Business was picking up by 1986. The selling operation had been consolidated in refurbished offices alongside the Coventry factory. Indeed sales were going so well that I was worried the disruption caused by the transfer of the lathe operation to Coventry would leave me without enough machines to fill orders. So I took a gamble.

Normally machine tools were so expensive that we only built a limited number to keep in stock. But I convinced the board of directors that Churchill should build fifty machines for stock. They would be available to me during the months it would take to get the new operation up and running. It was risky. Had we been left holding those machines, it would have represented a costly inventory.

The actual change-over in the factories went far better than expected and the sales force were pushed hard and sold the fifty machines in stock several months sooner than anticipated.

Once the manufacturing operations were consolidated, sales also picked up. Exports increased and the company was recovering its customer base in Britain. It then became clear that TI Group were intent on selling the division as soon as possible.

Near the middle of 1986 Ben Simon, the managing director of Ketlon, approached TI about the possibility of buying TI Machine Tools. Ketlon owned Wickman Bennett, a machine-tool maker in Banner Lane in Coventry, about half a mile from the TI Machine Tools plant. Both companies were part of the Berisford Group, a major public company best known for its trade in commodities.

Rather as Wareing had moved to put our company on a stronger footing through consolidation, Simon had convinced Berisford that Wickman Bennett would show a better bottom line by acquiring TI Machine Tools. The manufacturing would be consolidated on a single site and the result would be a superb, well-positioned machine-tool company.

The negotiations progressed quickly. Simon interviewed the directors at TI Machine Tools and selected which would stay with the new company. He wanted me to become the sales director of the new company.

The contracts were drawn up. The purchase price was in the region of £9 million. A date was set in September to sign the deal. Wareing and some of the executives from TI Group were on hand at the appointed hour at TI's head office in Curzon Street, London. Simon never showed up.

I later learned that Berisford had had doubts at the last minute.

They were not sure that they wanted to invest more money in a troubled industry that was so far removed from their central business interests. Later Simon actually purchased Wickman Bennett from the parent group and ran it himself.

While the deal had fallen through, it was clear to the executives at TI Machine Tools that the company was up for grabs. The turnaround was complete, and the resulting business was strong enough to attract at least one buyer. Further confirmation would come at the end of 1986, when the company broke even, its first year without a loss since the mid-seventies.

In last quarter of 1986 the management of the machine-tool division decided that we should consider buying the company. I was eager to become an owner, as were John Wareing and several other members of the board of directors.

The group began talking to venture-capital organizations about putting up the money for the management buy-out. There was interest from the moneymen, particularly since the entire management team had agreed to invest in the deal and stay with the company. Towards the end of the year, however, John Stride, our financial director, started to express reservations. It soon became clear that he was not willing to invest in the new deal. I was for pushing on, but the venture capitalists become quite nervous once the company's own financial man said he had doubts. The proposal collapsed, and we were left to wait for another suitor.

In March 1987 I was sitting in my office when Mark Gutteridge telephoned from London. Mark had remained with the company and was now the export sales manager. He had been meeting two businessmen who represented Iraqi government officials interested in purchasing a major quantity of machine tools.

'A delegation is coming over from Baghdad and they are going to visit a number of companies in the UK,' said Mark. 'Wickmans. Cincinnati Milacron. Some others.'

'We've not done any real business with Iraq, have we?' I asked.

'Not really, no. But it's worth a try. These could be large orders. This could be very big business for us. These people are talking about spending millions and millions of pounds. I'm going to make arrangements to bring the delegation to our plant. I'll take care of everything.'

'Fine, Mark. Bring 'em up.'

At this stage I didn't expect any business to materialize from Iraq.

TI Machine Tools had exhibited at a trade fair in Baghdad in 1982 and it had been a complete waste of time. The Iraqis had concentrated on buying Swiss and German machine tools. I felt it would take a lot of effort to obtain business from Iraq. I was later proved wrong.

I am enough of a history buff to know bits and pieces about how civilization began in the land now known as Iraq. The Sumerians, who inhabited the Mesopotamian plain south of present-day Iraq's capital, Baghdad, in the third millennium BC, developed the world's first system for writing and its first urban culture.

Baghdad was designed in the shape of a circle in the eighth century. But the modern state of Iraq owes its borders to the British, who carved out the country from the ashes of the defeated Ottoman Empire in 1916. While the result was a unified Iraqi state, the final map deprived the country of its traditional access to the Persian Gulf through what is known today as Kuwait. It was that omission that sowed the seeds for so much later trouble.

From 1916 until the late 1950s the British played a major role in Iraqi affairs, particularly in the matter of oil. Iraq sits atop the second-largest oil reserves in the Middle East, after only Saudi Arabia. The British were supplanted by the Soviet influence in Iraq in the 1960s, but by 1987 the country had swung back towards the West. At the time it was in the seventh year of its bloody conflict with neighbouring Iran.

Saddam Hussein was a poor boy from a peasant family that lived in the village of al-Auja on the River Tigris, a hundred miles north of Baghdad. He had risen through the ranks of the Ba'ath Party to become the undisputed leader of Iraq.

Soon after becoming president in 1979 Saddam began taking steps to make his country the dominant military and political power in the Arab world. In less than a year his ambitions led him to attack Iran, which was run by the Ayatollah Khomeini and his radical followers. Saddam had been led to believe it would be an easy victory, but the result was a stalemated conflict that was claiming thousands of lives on both sides.

In the early 1980s Margaret Thatcher and Ronald Reagan united in a policy of assisting Saddam and his armed forces as a means of containing the spread of Islamic fundamentalism. They saw the Ayatollah's brand of religion as a threat to stability in the oil-rich region. Both governments extended millions of pounds' worth of loan guarantees to the Iraqi regime and, equally important, permitted it to buy technology.

The access to technology was done quietly in both countries, because each had taken the public posture of not providing aid to either side in the war. Sir Geoffrey Howe, then Britain's Foreign Secretary, had promised Parliament in October of 1985 that the government was 'doing everything possible to see this tragic conflict brought to the earliest possible end'. As a result, he said, a policy had been adopted to prohibit sales to Iraq or Iran of 'defence equipment which, in our view, would significantly enhance the capability of either side to prolong or exacerbate the conflict'.

But, as I was going to find out the hard way, it was a policy subject to frequent reinterpretation by various governments. In fact, the British government and their American counterparts were willing to licence the sale to Iraq of technology with both civilian and military uses as a key part of their backing for Saddam Hussein. So were the French, the Germans, the Swiss and many other Western nations. They just didn't want it to be widely known.

As a result of this policy, billions in Iraqi oil revenue and loans from the country's Arab neighbours flowed to the West, while sophisticated technology flowed back, including computers, nuclear technology, missile components and other defence products that were turning Iraq into a regional power. And all this with the blessing of Western governments.

In late March 1987 Mark Gutteridge brought the delegation of Iraqi engineers and purchasing officials to Coventry to tour the plant. The group was led by Safa al-Habobi, an engineer and the director general of the Nassr State Enterprise for Mechanical Industries, a major manufacturing facility north of Baghdad. With him and the technical people was a middleman brokering the Iraqi purchases, an Iraqi by the name of Anees Wadi, who had a partner called Roy Ricks, a British security expert.

Mark is a good salesman, capable of evaluating an opportunity and developing a strategy to seize it. The Iraqis had bought a lot of German and Swiss machine tools, but they told Mark that they now wanted to broaden their purchasing channels. The Germans and Swiss were also supplying Iran, which meant delivery was slow from their very busy factories. The Iraqis were looking for faster delivery, perhaps at better prices.

Mark took them on a tour of the factory, stopping in the various departments to have a machine demonstrated and explain the advanced technology available from the company. After they had gone, he stopped by my office to brief me.

'Guess what they liked best,' he said, smiling broadly as he eased his six-foot frame into a chair across the desk from me and lit a cigarette. He couldn't wait for my speculation. 'Ron Ash's shop,' he said.

Ron Ash's office was cluttered with models of artillery shells, cartridge cases and the like. He was our defence projects engineer, the man who supervised orders for machines to manufacture munitions and other military equipment. On the shop floor the Iraqis had also been shown lathes being manufactured to fill a large order for a munitions factory in Helwan, Egypt, called Factory 99.

'They are definitely interested in munitions products. And their interests could run into the millions of pounds,' said Mark, who smelled a big order.

There was nothing alarming or unusual about an interest in machines to manufacture munitions components. With its Churchill heritage, TI Machine Tools was a major supplier to Britain's Royal Ordnance factories. The company also filled substantial orders of machines for munitions production from such places as the USA, France, Belgium, Pakistan and India.

One of the reasons John Wareing had wanted me to bring Ash down to Coventry from Churchill was to develop and extend the munitions side of the business. And anyway, they were all basically the same tools. Someone could set up a lathe or a grinding machine to manufacture components for an artillery shell or parts for a family car.

The Iraqis had been relying on Soviet-manufactured artillery in their war with Iran. Now, they were tired of depending on the Russians for weapons and munitions. They had decided to manufacture their own.

Even after the Iraqis began to flood the company with enquiries about machines and component drawings, I had my doubts that anything would come of the visit. But I had to take a decision, for these were potentially very big orders, running into millions of pounds. If we got the contracts they would keep the factory humming and workers employed for many months. But responding to them meant tying up the technical sales department to prepare nothing but technical quotations for Iraq for several weeks. I was reluctant to do this because of what I saw as the slim chance of actually getting a contract.

In the machine-tool business a company does not just quote a price on a machine from a brochure. The customer provides drawings of the components that the machine is supposed to manufacture. The technical staff must then select the machine or series of machines required to produce the component and work out a production process. There are numerous variables in the equation, and ultimately the quotation for each type of machine is a book of its own, complete with production times, layouts, tooling and prices.

I had not yet met the Iraqis, but Mark was beginning to convince me that there was good business in prospect. So we decided to prepare presentations on several of the packages. About 90 per cent of the technical staff were tied up getting the quotations ready. The UK salesmen were complaining because they couldn't get their quotes out to customers because of the volume of Iraqi enquiries.

The first quotation was for machines to manufacture parts for 60mm and 80mm artillery shells. Ron Ash and Mark were supervising the whole job, Ron coordinating the technical side and Mark overseeing the commercial aspects. Because of the size of the prospective order, the final prices would require approval from John Wareing and me, but Mark would know the price range when he went to London to negotiate with the Iraqis and their representatives, Wadi and Ricks.

Early in the summer of 1987 the company had bought tickets in a hospitality suite at Twickenham for an England–Wales rugby match. We were entertaining people from Rolls-Royce engines division in the hope of selling them some machines. John Harris, the UK sales director, and I were driving down to the match on a Saturday morning when John's beeper went off. It was Mark.

We stopped at a telephone box at the side of the road and telephoned the number he had left, which was that of the London office of Wadi and Ricks, where he was deep in negotiations with the Iraqis.

'I've got problems,' said Mark. 'Wickman Bennett has come in with a better package than ours. I'm afraid I'm going to lose the deal.'

We discussed prices and commercial terms, finding some room to reduce the prices in the quotation. But TI Machine Tools was not prepared to sell machine tools just for the sake of getting a large order. It had to be profitable business. It was one of the strategies that were helping to turn around the company in those days.

Wickman Bennett got the contract. The price of the company's package was lower and they had included in their offer multi-spindle machines which were non-CNC and could be used in higher-volume production. What really swung the order its way, however, was that Wickman Bennett agreed to supply the Iraqis with a computer manufactured by the American firm Hewlett Packard. It had nothing to do with the machine tools. The Iraqis had wanted it for other reasons and asked Wickman Bennett to supply it. There had been no mention of a computer to us, and I don't think we would have done it anyway.

The following week I was tempted to say 'I told you so' to Mark. We had devoted a lot of hours and expense to preparing those quotations and nothing had come of it. But I held my tongue.

'Don't worry, Paul,' he assured me. 'We'll get some good business out of these Iraqis. Some profitable business.'

7

Anees Wadi was a man of medium height and build who might have passed for any age between thirty and fifty, although he was actually forty-two. He dressed smartly and expensively, had a confident manner and was very intelligent. 'Suave' always seemed the right word to describe Wadi.

'We can arrange for you to get these contracts,' he said one May morning in 1987 as I sat in his London office. 'If you get orders, you make money. If you make money, obviously I make money. It's fair, yes?'

'Yes, it's fair,' I responded. 'But I'm not willing to pay 10 per cent. That's a bit more than fair.'

Wadi and his British partner, Roy Ricks, had taken a floor of offices in a small, smart building at 37 Duke Street, just off Oxford Street in central London. The space seemed far larger than they needed, like everything about Wadi. Their company was called MEED International and they specialized in Iraq.

Ricks, who was short, slim and bald, had worked in security systems of some sort. I always suspected he had something to do with British intelligence, but I never knew it for a fact. He said he met Wadi in Kuwait and they had done a few deals together before coming to London to set up MEED.

Wadi was clearly the boss. He said he had earned a fortune selling air-conditioning equipment in the Middle East. Much as he would like to, he said he couldn't return to his native Iraq. He led us to believe that he had left under a bit of a cloud and could never go back. Something about a government execution, he said. It lent him an air of mystery.

There was no mystery about Wadi's resolve to earn another fortune in commissions on the transactions he was arranging on behalf of

Iraq. He and Ricks wanted 10 per cent of the price on any sales they arranged for Western manufacturers. Commissions are normal in business, and Hi-Tek had worked on a commission basis selling equipment for Matrix Churchill and a number of other machine-tool manufacturers. But Wadi's cut bordered on extortion, particularly given the size of the deal on the table that morning.

After losing out to Wickman Bennett on the first order, Mark Gutteridge had convinced me to go ahead with a second proposal. This was to be a far larger transaction, covering three separate orders. All of them involved machines, primarily CNC lathes, to manufacture parts for artillery shells. One was for 155mm shells, a second for 122mm shells and the third covered the manufacture of thin-walled tubes, presumably for a small rocket. The total price was likely to reach £19 million. Thus Wadi's share would be £1.9 million.

Mark and I had driven to London for a meeting with Wadi and Ricks to get ready for a big negotiating session with the Iraqis. Safa al-Habobi and the other Iraqi engineers, based in Bonn, had scheduled negotiations on the three orders for later in May. The competition was going to be tough, with proposals likely from German, Italian and Swiss firms as well as other British machine-tool manufacturers. We wanted to have as many details worked out as possible in advance, including the support of Wadi.

'I can't make a competitive bid if you take 10 per cent off the top,' I explained to him. 'This is a big order, but we have to make a profit. Mark and I have to be able to offer the best possible price to get the contract.' Wadi said he understood. He expected this to be the first of many contracts that TI Machine Tools would receive from Iraq – with his help, of course. So he agreed to take a smaller fee. We haggled a bit and ended up at £600,000 for the whole package. Wadi insisted on celebrating with a long lunch at an expensive Chinese restaurant. I paid the bill.

After losing the first order, Mark, Ron Ash and I had sat down to go over what had happened. We could do nothing about Wickman Bennett supplying the Hewlett Packard computer. In fact, Wadi was saying Wickman Bennett was having difficulty getting an export licence for the computer because it was American-made and required permission from the USA too. Our CNC lathes were better than Wickman Bennett's machines. But they offered a non-CNC lathe, a multi-spindle chucking automatic, that we did not produce.

A spindle is the powered shaft that rotates the part being machined on a lathe. A multi-spindle automatic rotates six or eight parts simultaneously, each on a separate spindle. It is not as flexible as a CNC lathe because its movements cannot be varied as easily or as quickly once it is set up. However, for high-volume production of a single item, such as munitions components, it is reliable and fast. The Iraqis were accustomed to using these machines, particularly models from the German firm Gildemeister AG.

While we were preparing our next package for the Iraqis, I took a chance and approached Keith Bailey, the managing director of a smaller machine-tool manufacturer called BSA. Once known as British Small Arms and more famous as a maker of motorcycles, the company manufactured a line of multi-spindle automatics. I told Bailey we wanted to quote our CNC lathes and his automatics for two major contracts with Iraq.

The risk was that BSA also made CNC lathes. The Iraqis had not yet visited the firm, so I was opening the door for another competitor by mentioning the potential orders to Bailey, who could put together his own package. But I counted on being able to trust him.

Mark and Ron were travelling regularly to Bonn to work out the technical and commercial aspects of the contract. Mark telephoned me from Bonn and suggested it would be a good idea for me to meet him and Ron in Milan.

'One of the Iraqi engineers is discussing transactions there with an Italian firm run by two Iraqi brothers,' Mark explained. 'It might be wise for you to meet him in Milan. He is the decision maker on the 155mm contract. He is staying at the Leonardo da Vinci Hotel. Ask for Mr Talat. We'll be there as well.'

The next afternoon I touched down in Milan on board a British Airways jet. Mark and Ron had already arrived. We met Mr Talat in the hotel lobby shortly before dinner. Also present were the Abbas brothers, Hussein and Kassim, who owned Euromac Italy and were doing much the same thing as Wadi and Ricks on behalf of Italian machine-tool manufacturers.

Apart from Wadi, who, I would learn, was far from typical, Talat was the first Iraqi I could recall meeting. As would occur with many of his countrymen, I was never to learn his full name. When we corresponded with him, the letters were addressed to 'Engineer Talat' or simply 'Eng. Talat'. His came back signed in the same manner.

Talat was a rather short, scruffy man: he needed a shave and his shoes were unpolished. Although we were going to dinner at a fairly smart restaurant, he wore khaki trousers and an open-neck white shirt without a jacket.

It was after midnight when we returned to the hotel. Throughout the meal and drinking, we had discussed our proposals for the various Iraqi orders. Talat, in poor English, had made a few noncommittal noises and nodded his head a lot. When we sat down in the hotel bar for a drink afterwards, we found him ready to discuss prices and delivery dates for the largest of the three contracts, the one to manufacture components for 155mm shells.

Sometime after 1 a.m. we shook hands around the table. We had reached an agreement and Talat said that he would relay the terms to Safa and the others in Bonn the following morning. But we weren't done yet.

'Now we have a deal,' said Talat, 'I want a present.'

I looked at Mark and Ron, who were as surprised as I was. None of us understood what Talat was talking about. Finally, after an awkward pause, I asked him: 'What do you mean, a present?'

'Not for me. I assure you of that. A present for the contract. For the deal.'

'What exactly are you looking for?'

'Well, we want a shell-banding press.'

Banding presses are the machines that place a copper band around the back end of a munitions shell. The parts for the 155mm shell we were to produce called for such a band, but TI Machine Tools did not manufacture a banding press and the subject had never arisen during the discussions on the contract. It was an item that the Iraqis were responsible for providing, for our machines were to produce components for the shells, but it was up to the customer to build the assembly line and acquire the other machines necessary to produce the shells.

Talat said he had received quotations for banding presses from a British company called Fletcher Stewart. But he wanted us to buy three of the machines and supply one free of charge. We were talking about equipment costing a few hundred thousand pounds, which came as a bit of a shock when we had already negotiated a price. We had done relatively well on the price with Talat, but we had not built in this cost. This, I would learn, was a typical Iraqi negotiating technique.

We left it that we had a contract and that we'd look at the banding presses and see what they cost and what we could afford. There was no way we'd say yes to buying these presses. When we got back to Coventry we obtained quotations for the presses. The three were going to cost us about £200,000.

Fortunately Talat did not have a quotation, only a catalogue. So we decided to mark up the prices and make a profit on the deal. We would sell the Iraqis three machines for £250,000, telling them that was the price for two machines and we were throwing in the third for free, as a present. But effectively, we would make a good profit.

We still had to go to Bonn, since we hadn't discussed with Talat any of the payment terms and commercial conditions of the contract. All we had done was negotiated a price. At least I thought we'd negotiated a price.

It was the last week of May when the three of us and Talat met in Bonn at the Iraqi embassy, which was in a residential area outside the centre of Bonn. It struck me as a large residential property that had been converted into an embassy. Numerous security cameras were on the external part of the building, which was surrounded by a high wall topped by very tall iron railings. There were big metal gates, where you had to ring a bell. The staff never released the gates, but always came to see who you were before allowing you in.

That day we were taken into a large conference room and for the first time I met Dr Safa al-Habobi, the director general of the Nassr establishment, a huge engineering complex about forty kilometres north of Baghdad.

Dr Safa, or just Safa, as I came to call him, never struck me as a director general. He was a heavy man, quite overweight, and perhaps five foot nine tall. He didn't speak much English, and would mainly talk through Wadi or one of the others. Most of the time he wore short-sleeved shirts, and when we went out in the evening he would wear casual trousers, an open-neck shirt and a leather jacket. Apart from their generally very casual look, what struck me about Safa and the other Iraqis was their shoes. Except for Wadi, their shoes never looked as though they had been polished.

But Safa was a good engineer. Very straight and intelligent, and certainly no fool. He would not have been director general of Nassr if he had not had a lot of ability. I would learn that in Iraq, more than in Eastern Europe, people got to the top on their ability to do a job, not their rank in the Party – in Iraq's case, the Ba'ath Party. These were clever people and, as I was to discover shortly, shrewd negotiators.

I was introduced to the other Iraqis in the room: Ali Ali, the commercial counsellor at the embassy and two engineers who worked at Nassr, Hana P. Jon and Yass Abbas. (The latter was not related to the owners of Euromac.) Ali was better dressed than the others. Since he worked and lived in Germany, he had adopted a Western style of dress. Abbas spoke good English and told me that he had been educated at Liverpool University.

We thought we had concluded a deal with Talat, but we were nowhere near the end of the discussions. They had just got us on the hook and that day we began the negotiations almost all over again. We were talking about more than just the 155mm order, since there were also the 122mm shells and the thin-walled tubes, which we called the 'ABC contract'.

A couple of days later I was taking a breather from the talks in the Iraqi embassy garden when I saw Keith Bailey and his sales director, David Blizzard, walking around the garden too. I was surprised.

Bailey was not particularly forthcoming about what he was doing. But Mark and Ron Ash were reasonably well in with the Iraqis by this time, so they were able to find out what Bailey was up to. He was negotiating against us on the 122mm and 155mm contracts. So were Wickman Bennett, an Italian firm and possibly a German company.

About this time I was introduced to Club 56. Mark and I had gone to dinner with Wadi. As always, Wadi chose the restaurant, an expensive Italian place. There, he had introduced me to Pinot Grigio, of which we'd had several bottles by the time the restaurant began to close. Wadi suggested we find a club. Somehow he'd lined up a Bangladeshi taxi driver who seemed to be at Wadi's beck and call when he was in Bonn. So the driver was waiting and we climbed into his taxi, asked if he knew a club that might still be open and took off.

'I know where to go. No worry,' said the taxi driver.

The first place he found was closed. No worry, he said. He drove for about twenty-five minutes to a building in what looked like an industrial area. The Bangladeshi got out of the cab and walked up to the door. There was no window in the door – just a little shutter, which slid open. The Bangladeshi said something, the door was opened and we all went into Club 56.

It wasn't much brighter in the club than it had been outside. As my eyes adjusted I could make out a large, U-shaped bar and several groupings of settees and comfortable armchairs around the large, open area. There was no dance floor, but I saw a number of topless women, some working as waitresses, others mingling with the handful of customers. We had a couple of drinks and then left.

Not long after that night, Mark, Ron Ash and I were back in Bonn for another negotiating session. We decided to take Ron out for dinner because it was his birthday, 25 May. Safa and Wadi came along. So did Hana Jon and Yass Abbas and Ali Ali from the embassy. The Iraqis had been pulling our legs about Club 56 after Wadi described it to them, and after dinner they said they wanted to go there.

Now Ron was in his sixties, and a very nice, very straight guy. When we got to the club he was very uncomfortable with what he saw. We ordered a drink and he went over and sat down alone on one of the settees. Mark and I had a chat with a couple of the topless girls and got them to go and sit either side of Ron. Poor Ron just sat there not knowing where to look. Finally he just got up and said he was going back to the hotel. I don't suppose he ever told his wife. But then again, he is so straight that he probably did tell her.

Mark and I stayed with the Iraqis. They were in and out of the rooms at the back of the club with the women. One of the women said there were saunas in the back. There was a lot of activity going on. I could only guess what was happening. Mark and I sat at the bar with Wadi and had some drinks and talked to a few of the girls.

It must have been five in the morning when the barmaid finally brought over the bill. I looked at it and nearly had a heart attack.

'What the hell is this?' I said to her, pointing to the total. 'What the bloody hell did we have worth £12,000?'

The manageress came over and assured me the bill was correct. I complained about it, said there was no way we'd drunk enough Scotch and champagne for a £12,000 bill.

'Come on, let's get it paid and get out of there,' Wadi told me. 'We don't want any problems.'

'But Anees, they're ripping us off,' I told him. 'I don't care how much the champagne cost.'

'Paul, there were, er, other activities. Not the sort they itemize.'

I put two and two together. Disappearances into the back rooms. Saunas, my arse.

The barmaid refused to put the entire bill on my American Express Gold Card – it was too much for one card, she insisted – so I used my personal credit card as well and Mark used two of his cards. In the end we spread the night's bill over four credit cards and spent the next several months putting it through our expense accounts.

I flew home later that day, leaving Mark to finalize the commercial aspects of the contract. When he had got the details worked out he was to ring me, then John Wareing, and I would fly to Bonn for the signing. Wareing had insisted on attending the signing because of the magnitude of the deal.

Near the end of the following week I returned to Bonn. The contracts were almost complete. Mark needed my approval for some minor, last-minute changes. We negotiated a little more, but reached an agreement.

The contract was a complicated, lengthy document about an inch thick. It set forth the technical specifications for the machines, price quotations, delivery dates, performance guarantees, payment schedules and a lot of other commercial data. The Iraqis had agreed to use our standard contract and in the end we had reached what looked like a mutually acceptable agreement.

Mark, Ron and I were pleased. These were large orders, 150 machines with a total price of £18.9 million – enough work to occupy two-thirds of the factory's capacity for the next eighteen months. The timing was perfect, because machine-tool orders from other customers were fading and the first half of 1988 had been looking bleak. These orders could turn 1988 into the first profitable year in a decade at TI Machine Tools.

The largest contract was the one for the machines to make the 155mm shells, which was worth £11.5 million. The machines would be set up at the Al Hutteen factory about fifty kilometres south-west of Baghdad on the road to the legendary Hanging Gardens of Babylon. The smaller number of machines to manufacture the 122mm parts was also going to Al Hutteen, while the ABC contract was destined for Nassr itself.

Safa, Ali Ali and I shook hands on the deal. It was a Friday night when I telephoned John Wareing to come to Bonn the next day, 6 June. All he was supposed to do was rubber-stamp the contract. Mark and I picked up John at the airport and took him to the hotel. The signing ceremony was scheduled for eight that night in the hotel, rather than at the embassy. We had hired a room and the three of us were waiting there shortly before the appointed time.

The Iraqi delegation didn't show up. We waited and waited. We telephoned Wadi but there was no answer. The same happened when I tried to call their embassy. Eventually the Iraqis turned up at about ten o'clock.

After the niceties, completely out of the blue, the Iraqis said: 'OK, we have an agreement. There's our contract.' They tossed a totally new document onto the table. Mark and I looked at one another. We'd brought the managing director of the division out here. We'd told him that we'd struck a deal and dragged him out to Bonn to be presented with a contract that we'd never even seen.

The three of us read over the new contract. Everything we'd agreed on had been changed. The Iraqis were not paying as big a down payment and had extended the schedule for the remainder of the payments. They were no longer paying for the air fares and other expenses of our engineers going to Iraq to carry out the installation. They wanted the contract administered under Iraqi law, not British. The only thing they hadn't changed was the bottom-line price. But they had thrown a contract at us that would increase our costs and reduce our profitability.

'This is totally unacceptable,' I told them, trying to remain calm and find a way to work out the problems. 'We have a deal and I expect you to stick to it.'

The Iraqis remained calm. Ali Ali spoke first: 'This is the contract that we want you to sign. You must sign this document or there will be no deal at all.'

John Wareing is a fairly impatient sort of character and he made his feelings known in no uncertain manner.

'This is outrageous,' he shouted. 'This is no way to do business. It is ridiculous. You're holding a gun to our heads.'

The Iraqis did not react to our rejection of their contract. They simply folded up their papers and said that they would discuss the matter further with us at ten the next morning at the embassy. On the table when they left was a copy of the contract they were proposing we sign.

After they had gone Mark and I made it clear that we had no intention of accepting the Iraqis' new contract. We had made a deal. We had shaken hands. Then they had changed the ground rules.

'You don't do business in that manner,' I told John.

But he was reluctant to leave without a contract. He started to go through the Iraqi contract. He had a red marker pen and was putting lines across entire pages, scrawling 'rubbish' and 'Mickey Mouse' in the margins.

On the way to the embassy the next morning I told John that under no circumstances should he pull the Iraqi contract out of his bag. For one thing, I didn't want his copy with all his comments on the table. For another, I did not want to concede an inch to the Iraqis by suggesting that we would even consider their version.

'We've got to argue that we are sticking to our contract,' I said. 'It may take more time, but we must win the argument. We can't start the negotiations all over again by adopting any form of their contract.'

The Iraqis were trying to squeeze us, but we had our top man there, and he was not going to want to go home empty-handed or make a second trip to Bonn. My feeling was that they would back down in the end.

At the embassy we had been arguing for ten or fifteen minutes when John got impatient because he felt we were getting nowhere, and pulled out his copy of the contract. The moment he did so, I could see the Iraqis' eyes light up. Then, as he was flicking through the pages and complaining, they saw his comments. They started to get more and more difficult, and the meeting dragged on and on.

Towards the middle of the afternoon John said: 'I've got to get this signed today. Both Mr Henderson and I have to leave tonight. We must be in Coventry tomorrow morning.'

He asked the Iraqis to check for the last flight from Bonn to London. He said to book seats for me as well as him, since he was not prepared to leave me to talk further. It was a negotiating tactic to put pressure on the Iraqis and they suddenly realized that the contract might slip away. They believed John was prepared to walk away from the deal.

Ali Ali left the room and came back with the flight news. The last plane was due to leave at 8 p.m., but it was fully booked. The next flight was at five, but there was only one seat. He had taken the liberty of booking it for Mr Wareing.

'We know that you have to leave, Mr Wareing,' said Ali. 'But can't you leave Mr Henderson?'

John agreed, but he demanded time alone with Mark and me. He was quite angry, and made it clear that we could not deviate from certain points. Do a deal, he said, but the price remains the same. Because of his distrust of the Iraqis, he insisted that the down payment go up to 30 per cent instead of the twenty we had agreed on initially and the ten that the Iraqis were arguing for. Thirty seemed out of the question, but I didn't tell him.

I drove John to the airport and then went to the hotel, where the talks were to resume. Only Talat and Yass Abbas were there with Mark and Ron. They were sitting in the restaurant having a meal and laughing.

'What's so funny?' I asked, taking the place they had left for me.

'The Iraqis deliberately got rid of John Wareing,' said Mark, with a big grin. 'There were plenty of seats on the eight o'clock flight. You both could have gone then.'

I must have looked angry, because Mark reassured me: 'Don't worry. There's no problem. They're going to agree to our original contract.'

But there was still a problem. The Iraqis refused to meet John's demand for a 30 per cent down payment. On Monday, I flew back to Coventry to discuss it with him. I explained that 20 per cent was a fair down payment, and tried to tell him that the negotiating tactics of the Iraqis, while unpleasant and seemingly unethical to him, reflected deal-making in the Middle East and Eastern Europe, too. Finally, he agreed to accept 20 per cent.

I was not happy with the way the Iraqis had negotiated. But after more than twenty years in sales, working in difficult countries with tough negotiators, I didn't take it personally. It was business. And it was business that was going to keep TI Machine Tools operating at full capacity for the next year.

For most of my career, I had considered myself responsible for myself and the security of my family. But since returning to the company two years earlier, I'd seen that I had a bigger burden to carry. The orders that my sales people and I obtained kept the factory running, kept men and women employed.

Often, driving around Coventry, I would pass Alfred Herbert. The plant had been closed down a few years earlier and the receivers had sold off bits to other companies. TI had bought the lathe operation. But the company itself no longer existed; neither did hundreds of jobs that had once been filled by skilled, dedicated toolmakers. I was determined not to let that happen at Fletchamstead Highway. No matter what it took, it was my job to keep the order book full and the factory open. I was about to find out how far I would go to fulfil that commitment.

8

One warm evening in July 1987 Mark Gutteridge and I were having dinner with Anees Wadi and Safa al-Habobi at an expensive restaurant in Mayfair. Wadi always went to the best restaurants – not always the best in quality, but the most expensive all the same.

Not long after the negotiations had finished in Bonn, Wadi had mentioned to Mark that the Iraqis were considering buying a machine-tool company. They were having discussions with Wickman Bennett, our competitors in Coventry. I saw possibilities for TI Machine Tools.

'I understand you're interested in a machine-tool company,' I said to Safa in the restaurant that night. He nodded slightly, but there was no expression on his face. I plunged ahead.

'You should consider TI Machine Tools. TI Group have been trying to sell us for the past year. You could negotiate a pretty good deal as far as price is concerned. And our products would be a better range for you than Wickman Bennett.'

Safa had talked before about his hopes of turning Iraq's military factories into civilian facilities once the war with Iran ended. He had boasted about surpassing Egypt as the leading industrial country in the Arab world. With that in mind, the CNC lathes and other products manufactured by TI offered better flexibility for conversion to commercial uses than those of Wickman Bennett.

The idea of the Iraqis buying the company was not without risk. I'd been stung by their negotiating tactics in Bonn, and didn't fully trust them. Since Bonn, Wadi and I had had several long conversations about the Iraqis' methods. He convinced me I had not understood the way they do business.

'In their world,' he had explained, 'you don't have a contract until you've actually signed it. Until then they will use different people and different strategies to get the best possible deal.'

It was a hard lesson for me: that you have no agreement until you put your signature on a piece of paper. I'd always honoured agreements made on a handshake.

However, there appeared to be some truth to Wadi's words. Since signing the contracts the Iraqis had observed the letter of the agreements. The 20 per cent down payment had been wired to our bankers on time. Their engineers were already working with ours on technical matters so that we could start production on schedule.

There was another, more important reason for raising the issue of buying TI Machine Tools. The business did not figure in the strategy of TI Group. Because the earlier attempt to sell us had collapsed, I was concerned they would break up our division unless someone bought it soon, irrespective of the full order book. They could sell sections of the operation to other companies.

The break-up of the company was the worst thing that could happen. Selling it off section by section would mean a loss of jobs, particularly in the areas that weren't sold. Even those sections that were bought would be streamlined into someone else's operation, meaning more jobs lost. I saw a much brighter future for the business if it remained intact.

I also saw the possibility that the three recent contracts were only the beginning of business with Iraq. When the war ended the Iraqis would be buying large quantities of machine tools to gear up for civilian production. If they owned the company we would be in a prime position for providing the machines. Considering everything, this was a golden opportunity to ensure the long-term survival of TI Machine Tools. With those things in mind I told Wadi and Safa that Mark and I were willing to play an active role helping them buy the company. Safa indicated that he was interested, but he did not commit himself that night.

My contacts with the intelligence service had dropped off again. There had been a few meetings with an intelligence agent named Louisa Symondson, an expert on Russian affairs, but by my reckoning we'd only met six times in 1985 and 1986. My present job simply meant I wasn't travelling as extensively as I had in the past, so I wasn't as much use to them.

When TI Machine Tools started selling orders to the Iraqis, I wasn't worried about the government not knowing. I had known for years that the intelligence people had recruited another source within the company: Mark Gutteridge. I was the one who had given them his name. Eventually Mark and I had discussed our work for the intelligence services, although we weren't supposed to. We never actually told each other exactly what information we gave to the intelligence people, but we were certainly aware that we were both in touch with them. In a lot of ways it was a comfort to have somebody on your side when you were in the difficult countries.

In the autumn of 1987, when we first started working on orders with the Iraqis, Mark had told me he was passing the information on to his contact at MI5. He didn't go into how much detail he was sharing, but I gathered he was giving the intelligence people some good information: the types of machines we and other companies were selling to the Iraqis, where they were being installed in Iraq and what they were being used for.

This didn't bother me at all; the government ought to know what we were doing with Iraq or any other country. I had nothing to hide; neither did the company. For years, I had provided intelligence to my handlers. I was relieved Mark was doing the same. It also provided a comfort, for if the Iraqis bought the company it would give the government an even better view of what they were up to.

In the days immediately following the dinner with Safa and Wadi I travelled frequently to London for meetings with them, and often Mark went with me. Other days I was on the phone with Wadi five or ten times. They were clearly interested in the company, and with a man on the inside they sought as much information as possible before approaching TI Group. What were the values of the assets? How full was the order book? How pressed was TI to sell the operation? What sort of price should they offer?

Towards the end of the month they wanted Mark and me to go to Baghdad to talk to people there about the company. My sense was that this was a last step before they decided whether to make an offer, but I wasn't sure.

There was no way Mark and I could explain to John Wareing why we were going to Iraq. We could have lost our jobs; that was the risk we were taking in helping the Iraqis. So Safa asked John to send us out to talk to the factories that were buying the machines they had just ordered. John approved the visit, although he told us to make it short.

We flew to Bonn on the afternoon of Monday 20 July. The next day we went to the Iraqi embassy and formally signed the ABC contract, the last of the three negotiated the previous month. The embassy stamped Iraqi visas in our passports and on Tuesday night we boarded Lufthansa flight number 650 for Baghdad.

Mark had attended a trade exhibition in Iraq in the early eighties, but I had never been there before. The plane landed at the modern airport a minute before midnight, and we were met by a man who introduced himself as 'Mr Talib'. He was a security official at the Nassr factory, but they had sent him out to give us the red-carpet treatment.

Talib collected our passports and bags. We followed him to the front of the queue at customs control and went straight through. He then ushered us ceremoniously into a large Toyota waiting at the kerb and drove away as if making a getaway from a crime.

As Talib sped into central Baghdad, the first thing that struck me was the lights. The city was lit up like a Christmas tree. Street lights illuminated the wide roads, and windows in office blocks and homes were lit up. There was no blackout; nothing like my early memories of Coventry. In fact, there was no impression that the country was at war with Iran.

We checked into the Novotel, which was similar to others in the worldwide French chain. Talib said he would collect us at 8 a.m. for the trip to the Nassr factory.

It was hot by that time in the morning, but the Toyota was air-conditioned and the forty-five kilometre drive to the Nassr plant was comfortable. In the daylight, I saw the first signs of a country at war. Anti-aircraft guns were on top of the hotels and placed at other strategic points around the city. Along the main road out of Baghdad, north towards the factory, there were numerous anti-aircraft gun emplacements and we passed military vehicles.

The factory itself was unlike any I'd seen before. It was surrounded by gun emplacements and sand-bagged checkpoints; there were high walls and watch-towers at regular intervals along the walls; and the main entrance was guarded by a dozen men in uniform, all carrying rifles. Our car was waved through without slowing down and we pulled up in front of what appeared to be the main office building.

The Nassr complex covered three to four square kilometres. There were a lot of individual buildings spread around. By our standards, it was very big, and, Talib had explained, very diversified in its products.

At the main office we were introduced to Fadel Jawad Kadhum, who was identified only as someone 'from the ministry'. Because he wore an olive-green uniform, I assumed he was in the military. Only later did I learn it was the uniform of Saddam Hussein's ruling Ba'ath Party and that it signified Fadel's importance within Iraq. We also met Adel Alami, deputy director general at Nassr and Safa's second-in-command, and Mr Janan, an engineer who spoke very good English.

Mark and I gave a presentation on TI Machine Tools that took a couple of hours, showing slides with us and handing out company literature. We talked about its products, its structure, its turnover, its profitability. The point we tried to make was that we were offering them a going concern with a full order book. We didn't emphasize the military aspects of the products, but we described the flexibility of the machines.

At the end, they said nothing about whether they were interested or not. They were very courteous: they thanked us and gave us a tour of the Nassr plant. But not all of it. Some areas were clearly not for visitors. Even inside the heavily fortified complex, these locations were guarded by additional armed men.

One place they did show us was the central tool room. This was the first time we met Mr Jabbar, a senior Iraqi engineer. He and the other Iraqis who showed us the facility were proud of it, and they had every right to be. It was probably the largest and best-equipped such facility I had ever seen anywhere in the world. It was a very new building, like all the buildings at Nassr.

We saw machine tools from Britain, the USA, Switzerland, German, Italy, France. This wasn't low-technology equipment, but current, up-to-date, high-tech machinery. It was the best the West had to offer.

As we were walking around. I was surprised to see a Matrix thread-grinding machine. None of the machines ordered in the June deal had been delivered yet, of course. I stopped and asked Jabbar about the Matrix machine. He smiled and said it had been supplied by the Swiss company that had installed the tool room in the mid-eighties.

'We are very pleased with the machine,' said Jabbar with a grin. 'It is extremely accurate and dependable.'

We saw something else of interest on that first tour: a metal casing. What attracted Mark and me to it was the size. It was far too large for any of our machines to handle.

'What is that?' I asked Jabbar, pointing at the casing.

'It's for a bomb. A big one. A thousand pounds. It's from an American design.'

Of course. Once he said that, it was clear the shape could not belong to anything but a bomb – a big one indeed.

Later that afternoon, when we had got back to our hotel, Mark and I had a couple of beers in the bar and talked about what we had seen, the factory, the technology, the types of people we had met, the bomb casing. The technology was fantastic, as good as anything anywhere. Jabbar and the other engineers we met seemed intelligent. Fadel was a bit of a mystery, though. He had said very little but had been treated with great deference by the others.

We couldn't decide whether the Iraqis were really interested in buying the company. We thought they were, but we didn't know quite how they would proceed. Would they need our help or were they just going to do it on their own? We also discussed what was in it for us if they took over. By this stage we were planning our own roles.

'Paul, you could be managing director and I could be the sales director of the business,' preposed Mark.

'I think we might be able to get a small stake in the company, too,' I said, reflecting remarks made by Safa and Wadi in the earlier talks.

I'd remained interested in being an owner of the company since the first talk of a management buy-out in 1986, after the Wickman Bennett bid had collapsed. This seemed to be an idea that could work with the Iraqis. A machine-tool business relies heavily on its products, but management is important, too. It would be particularly so for the Iraqis, and they would probably want to retain as many of the British directors as possible. Safa had said as much earlier.

What we were hoping was that to keep us they would give Mark and me a share, rather than our having to buy it. But after our Bonn negotiations, we should have realized that the Iraqis were not ones for giving anything away.

The evening after the tour of Nassr I had my first authentic Iraqi meal. Talib, whom we nicknamed 'Mr Fix-It', had arrived with Jabbar and went to a traditional fish restaurant. At their insistence we ordered *masgouf*, a large fish of 10–12lb that appeared to be a relative of the carp. We got a close look because we were taken into the restaurant kitchen to select our fish live from a tank full of them.

As we watched, the fish was split, gutted and cleaned. Then they put it on two spikes and placed the spikes around a fire that burned a strongly scented wood. The cooking took an hour and a half or two hours. While we waited, we learned that our new friends liked to drink whisky.

The following morning there was a brief return to Nassr. The Iraqis wanted to ask us questions they'd obviously thought about after the previous day's discussion. We still received no indication of whether they were interested in buying the business. But Mark and I had concluded that, as they had gone to the trouble to ask us out to Baghdad, then they had to be interested.

I'd hoped to visit other factories and discuss other prospective contracts before returning to London that night. One of the places on my list was Al Hutteen, the plant south-west of Iraq where the TI machines for the 122mm and 155mm shell components would be installed. But since John Wareing had limited the length of our visit to two days, it was decided that we didn't have time. It struck me then that he might have suspected Mark and I were getting too close to the Iraqis, a dangerous possibility for our future employment.

It was a burning hot day, 120 degrees Fahrenheit or more by the time we left the factory. Although it was dry, it was burning. We were wearing lightweight business suits, but even so as soon as we stepped out of the car or left a building, our clothes were wet through and stuck to us. Talib kept saying that we needed something on our heads, because even though we weren't seeing any more factories, we were to have a sightseeing tour before our plane left after midnight.

From Nassr we drove back towards Baghdad and continued about sixty miles south-west to what had been the ancient city of Babylon on the plains between the Tigris and Euphrates rivers. Iraqi archaeologists had been working for years near the banks of the Euphrates to resurrect the glory that was Babylon. As we were driving there, he told us the legend of the Hanging Gardens of Babylon, which were considered by the Greeks as one of the Seven Wonders of the World.

King Nebuchadnezzar, who ruled Mesopotamia in the sixth century BC, built the hanging gardens to enchant his homesick queen, who came from a mountainous land. The city itself had a population of a million and covered nearly eight square miles. Its most glorious feature was the gardens, a series of terraces rising from the Euphrates toward the city and connected by marble stairways. The terraces were planted with full-grown trees, shrubs and flowers.

Talib angrily described how German archaeologists had first excavated Babylon in the early party of the century, carrying away the bright-coloured pottery and other works of art to a museum in Berlin. Now, he said, Iraqi archaeologists and workers were planning to restore the city to its ancient splendour.

When we arrived at the site, it was a ruin. A few small walls of rough-looking bricks had been rebuilt and workers were stirring up dust. Of course, I made no mention of my disappointment to Talib, who took a fierce pride in the project. Before we left, Talib had picked up one of the bricks being used to reconstruct the walls. Words in Arabic were inscribed on the brick. He read them to us: 'The Babylon of Nebuchadnezzar was reconstructed in the era of Saddam Hussein.'

In fact, Saddam Hussein had cast himself as a latter-day Nebuchadnezzar, who achieved a place in the Old Testament as the conqueror of Jerusalem. This legacy was part of Saddam's message of Arab supremacy over the Jews in Israel.

When I got back to Coventry I told John Wareing what I'd seen, and some of what had happened at Nassr. Since we came back with the last of the signed contracts from Bonn, it wasn't any problem.

Within a day of my return Wadi was in touch. The Iraqis wanted to buy the company. How do we go about it? he asked. They wanted us to go to London for meetings with Wadi, Safa and Roy Ricks. It was hard for Mark and me to get away from the office during the week. But we travelled down after work for meetings at MEED International's office in Duke Street that lasted until midnight or later.

Fadel came over from Baghdad a few days after we got back from there and we went down to meet him. 'What is the sort of price that we should be offering to purchase the business?' he asked in perfect English. This was a surprise. I didn't remember his speaking English when we were at Nassr. His style of dress had changed, too. Gone was the drab Ba'ath Party uniform and in its place was a tailored Western suit and silk tie.

'You could probably buy the business for £4 million,' I said, repeating the price that Mark and I had discussed over the last few days with Safa and Wadi.

'You ought to approach TI Group and find out if they are

interested. Once you've established that interest, you can take the next step down the road. You will have to get three years of financial and production records. Then I can go through them with you.'

Many times during those busy days and nights I stopped to think about what I was doing. The Iraqis were getting an inside look at the company from me. Wareing would certainly fire me if that fact was discovered. But as I wouldn't be participating in the negotiations with the TI Group, I didn't see it as a conflict of interest.

My overriding concern remained securing the future of the company where I'd started work thirty-three years before as an apprentice. I didn't want another empty factory in Coventry. And I didn't want to see my colleagues out of work.

Of course, there was something in it for me, for I stood a chance of becoming managing director. In fact, the more help I was to the Iraqis, the better my chances. But my interests were not selfish. I could find another job. I could go to another company, as I'd done with Lancer Boss. Or go back to Hi-Tek, which John Belgrove had turned around and which was in profit again. It would be easier for me than the men who had worked on the shop floor all their lives.

Things were moving fast. By the end of July, Wadi had written a letter to TI Group expressing an interest in buying the company and asking for financial and production records from recent years. TI was definitely interested, and responded with the documents and a letter offering open talks.

I did not participate in the negotiations, but I learned from Wadi that the Iraqis' first offer was some £2.5–3 million. TI had rejected it as too low, but showed an interest in continuing the talks.

My earlier concern over helping the Iraqis buy the business disappeared. TI Group was so keen to see the machine-tools division sold that it guaranteed a bonus to the directors, equivalent to one year's salary, to make sure the deal was successfully concluded. Moreover, John Wareing had indicated that he would not remain as managing director if the Iraqis bought the business, opening the way for me to take the position.

At that point the Iraqis were operating through Wadi's MEED International and they asked for a tour of the plant so that they could see what they were buying. This was when I suspected again that Wareing might know about my dealings with the Iraqis. In fact, he and I had a clash that pretty much convinced me he knew.

The Iraqis were to visit the plant on 18 August and Wareing issued an internal memo the previous day. This was copied to the board of directors and said: 'A number of visitors will be in the plant tomorrow representing MEED International and their end-user in Iraq. The attached itinerary is self-explanatory. I intend splitting the party into two groups for the works tour. One party will be accompanied by myself and Mark Gutteridge and the other by Lawrie Izzard and Ron Ash. I would be grateful if you would join our visitors for a buffet lunch at 12.15 in the sales conference room.'

I was enraged. The first thing was that, even though I was the sales and marketing director, I'd been cut out. It made sense for Mark to attend, since he had worked with the Iraqis. But it made no sense at all for me to be cut out and someone like Lawrie Izzard, the operations director and head of production, to go. So I confronted Wareing.

'This is completely unacceptable,' I told him in his office. 'These are people I've dealt with, people I've signed a £19-million contract with. It is discourteous not only to them, but to me if I am not part of this tour.'

'I'm the managing director and I'll decide how this company is run,' he fired back. 'I'll decide who the hell takes the visitors around. Your job is not to decide who takes care of that and it's not to decide anything else that has to do with the sale of this company.'

'For Christ's sake, John, I'm responsible for sales and you must include me in this. You are belittling me if you don't.'

'It's my decision. You can take it or leave it.'

Wareing issued no further memos on the subject, but later in the day his secretary phoned me. I had been delegated to take one of the groups around the factory.

Alarm bells were going off good and proper by then. The only reason John would have tried to cut me out was if he knew I was more involved with the Iraqis than I should have been. But there was no way he could have had any evidence.

Once they had come around and visited the factory, the Iraqis were quite satisfied. It was then just a question of how much they would pay. They appointed Bailey, Shaw & Gillett, a firm of solicitors in London, to advise them on the negotiations. A lawyer from the firm, Nick Mallett, became the chief negotiator for the Iraqi group. S. G. Warburg were appointed to represent TI Group.

The Iraqis also wanted some of the TI Machine Tools management to take a stake in the business. As I had expected, they wanted to lock in the management team and I helped them identify the five key players. In addition to Mark Gutteridge and myself, they were Lawrie Izzard, the operations director and head of production, Malcolm Thorneycroft, the engineering director, and Michael Downes, the personnel director. The intention was that those three would continue in their positions and I would become managing director. Mark was to be sales director.

I had been hoping that the Iraqis would give me 5 per cent of the business as a thank you for my efforts. By the end of August I had been spending every weekend in London, going over financial documents with the Iraqis and helping them out in other ways. But my future partners were not like that: they didn't think the same way and it didn't happen. They wanted the management team to invest our own money in the deal.

At that point I spoke to Izzard, Downes and Thorneycroft about their willingness to go in on the deal. All three agreed and came to London with Mark and me to talk it over with the Iraqis. However, the plans were still being kept secret from TI Group and John Wareing.

The corporate structure set up to acquire and control the company was rather complicated, but no more so than in any other business deal. Because I was a British citizen, I helped the Iraqis set up the companies that they needed to buy TI Machine Tools. As a result, my name appeared as an officer on them, but they were controlled by the Iraqis.

TMG – the initials didn't stand for anything – was set up as the entity to buy TI Machine Tools for the Iraqis and the management buy-out team. It was the overall holding company. A second company, Technology Development Group, or TDG, was set up to invest in the deal for the Iraqis. It would be owned and controlled by Safa al-Habobi on behalf of a supposedly private Iraqi company called Al-Arabi Trading Company, which, I was later to learn, was owned by the Iraqi Ministry of Industry and Military Procurement.

Anees Wadi and Roy Ricks had decided to invest in the deal, too. So another company, Technology Engineering Group, or TEG, was created to serve as their investment vehicle.

The five managers who were going to invest got together and formed a company called Echosabre, which was to be the holding company for our shares in TMG.

When all the companies were registered, TEG and Echosabre would each invest £100,000 in TMG. In exchange, each would receive 2½ per cent of TMG's stock. The Iraqis, through TDG, would invest the remainder of the purchase price for the business and control the remaining 95 per cent of the shares in TMG. Then TMG would acquire the machine-tool business and serve as the overall holding company for the shares.

I was concerned that the Iraqis, holding all but 5 per cent shares, could at any point suddenly sell the business out from under us. I didn't think they saw the company as a long-term investment, and I was worried that they would buy the company, transfer the technology to factories in Iraq and then walk away.

My ultimate aim was to buy the company back from the Iraqis. Three or four years down the road, with the company turning a good profit, I and the management team would buy the business. In the meantime I planned to smarten up the factory with better technology and develop new products. I knew the things we needed to do and they could be done, with the help of the Iraqi order book. Then the managers would become the owners.

With that need for protection in mind, a joint-venture agreement was drawn up between Echosabre and TDG, the Iraqi investment company. It granted the managers an option to increase our stake to 40 per cent and gave us the first option to buy the business if the Iraqis chose to sell. More important from my point of view, the agreement gave the management group the power of veto over the sale of the company to anyone else.

The Iraqis didn't like the joint-venture agreement. In fact, it had become a source of tension between Fadel and me. He was spending time in London working on the final negotiations, and I sensed that he was distancing himself from me. I thought he was quite happy with me in a sales and marketing role, but he had doubts about me as managing director. This would be confirmed very soon.

It was October 1987 when the Iraqis and TI Group sat down to finalize the price. TI wanted £6.5 million, based on their asset valuation of the business of £22 million. I knew the business pretty well by this time and I told the Iraqis that TI was overvaluing it. Based on the machine tools in the factory, the spares, the order book and other assets, I said the true value was no more than £17 million. A fair price for the company at that value was £4 million, I told them. Plus, TI should be required to assume the machine-tool division's £22-million debt to the parent company.

Using my information, the Iraqis struck a bargain with TI. They would pay £6.5 million for the business. But £2.5 million of the purchase price would go into an escrow account. Once the year-end accounts for 1987 were settled and the books completely audited for taxes, the true value of the division would be established. At stake would be the money in escrow. A formula was established whereby the closer the final valuation to £17 million, the more of the £2.5 million would be returned to the Iraqis. However, if the value really was £22 million, the money would go to TI.

TI would get £4 million on signing, with the remaining amount held in escrow. TI agreed to assume the existing debt for the company. On signing, they also agreed to return the £3.8 million that the Iraqis had deposited earlier as down payment on the three contracts Mark and I had brought back from Bonn. With that money coming back to them, the Iraqis would be paying only £200,000 for the company – if the valuation went in their favour. Ironically, £200,000 was the precise amount that TEG and Echosabre, the minority shareholders, were investing in the company.

So the Iraqis were about to buy one of the largest machine-tool manufacturers in Britain for nothing. Or, at most, for £2.5 million. It was a fantastic deal, and it confirmed to me that TI Group was desperate to get out of the machine-tool business. Had the Iraqis not appeared on the scene to buy it, I believed the company would have been broken up and sold off in pieces in a matter of months.

The final signing was scheduled for Friday 23 October. On Tuesday of that week, the Iraqis sent the management a final version of the joint-venture agreement. I couldn't believe it: they had altered all of the key terms of the agreement. Our option to acquire up to 40 per cent of the stock was restructured so that it would cost us a great deal more money. Far more seriously, they had eliminated the management's right to veto the sale of the company. This would strip us of our protection if we didn't like a prospective buyer.

I was bloody angry about it. After all the months of personal time I'd spent helping them, after the way I'd guided them in setting up this fantastic deal, they were screwing me. And they were screwing all the other managers too.

I demanded a meeting in London for the next day in Nick Mallett's offices. The other directors, who were as alarmed as I was, felt that I should take a solicitor. On reflection, I think it was a mistake, but I didn't fight it. Peter Beddows, a Leamington Spa solicitor, went down with me.

No sooner was I in the door at the solicitor's offices in London than I sensed Fadel was surprised and not happy to see me arrive with Beddows. I insisted that they honour the original agreement. They refused. Within minutes the whole meeting blew up.

'We'll buy this company without you,' Fadel shouted at me. 'You will not be party to any of it.'

'Well see about that,' I retorted as Beddows and I stormed out of the room.

As well as being extremely angry, I was very disappointed. I could see a lifelong ambition of mine, wanting to be managing director of Coventry Gauge and Tool and eventually owning the business, shot down in a matter of minutes.

Beddows was dumbstruck. 'I have never been treated like that in my life,' he said as we left the building. 'I'm flabbergasted.'

Wadi, who had been at the meeting, followed me out of the building and stopped me a few feet away.

'Paul, Paul, wait a minute,' he said soothingly. 'Don't leave London. I want you to meet Dr Safa at seven o'clock tonight. He's staying at the Hilton in Park Lane. We can work this out.'

'What's the point?' I asked, still steaming. 'It's all over.'

'No, it's not. This is just Fadel. It isn't what Dr Safa wants.'

'OK, I'll be there. But I don't see much point, Anees.'

Beddows agreed to stay with me, but the meeting in the bar at the Hilton that evening was not much better than the afternoon session. There was no shouting, but it was uncomfortable. Safa was loyal to Fadel and would not object outwardly to what had happened, yet I didn't think he agreed with what Fadel had done.

'Your mistake was bringing a solicitor,' said Safa, in front of Peter Beddows. 'We're in this together. We've been in it together until now. If there was something wrong, we are the kind of people you talk to and we try to accommodate you. We don't like outsiders.'

I explained my opposition to their draft of the joint-venture agreement. It had stripped the management of all protection.

'I felt that you had been underhand in the way you dealt with me,' I told him. 'I felt the only option was to bring a solicitor.'

The meeting ended with Safa assuring me that it would be sorted out. 'Don't worry, Paul. We'll be in touch tomorrow.'

It was midnight by the time I walked into our home in Westwood Heath. Esther was asleep. But in the middle of the floor inside the door was a note from her: 'Call John Wareing. It doesn't matter what time you come in.'

I called. Wareing said that Fadel had been in touch with him and advised him of the falling out.

'He approached me about becoming managing director of the company after the take-over,' said Wareing. 'I told him that I'd do it, at least on a temporary basis. Twelve months or so.'

By this time I was numb from the double-dealing. God knows business has its share of intrigue. But nothing like this had ever happened to me.

'Fine,' was all I could muster in response to Wareing's revelation.

'I should also tell you that I called all the other directors down to my house this evening and informed them of this. I've called a meeting of the board for seven tomorrow morning. You should be there, too,' he said before putting the phone down.

Earlier that evening I had spoken to Lawrie Izzard, Mike Downes and Malcolm Thorneycroft. They had not mentioned the meeting. I wondered why.

As I was ready to go out of the door early on Thursday morning, Esther came downstairs. She'd been fast asleep, so I hadn't told her what had happened. Now, as I described it to her, she became pretty upset. 'After the way you've helped these people,' she said, close to tears. 'You've gone through all of this. I have hardly seen you for four months. And this is the result. This is so unfair.'

I gave her a kiss on the cheek. 'It's business,' I said, and left for the factory. I'd made up my mind, standing there with my wife. I was going to fight it. No way was I going to lose to Fadel.

The showdown came immediately. We all gathered in the board-room. I was tense and trying to control my anger. The others seemed to prefer staring at the table to looking me in the eye.

Wareing's first move was to make it clear that there would be no place for me under the new ownership. I would lose my job and be out of the company. Then he made a mistake that gave me the opening to salvage the whole deal: he asked the directors sitting around the table to support him as managing director.

'I'm going to leave the room now,' he said. 'Those who support me can leave with me.'

John Stride, the financial director, and David Wilcock, the marketing director, got up and walked out. Lawrie Izzard, Mike Downes and Malcolm Thorneycroft stayed.

I explained to them what had happened at the two meetings in London. I told them that I was returning there immediately. I promised them that, by the end of the day, I would have the original joint-venture agreement signed.

'The choice is yours, fellas,' I told them as we sat around the conference table. 'I'm going to win. I'm going to be the managing director. If you are not on my side, I am still going to London. The difference is that I'll put up the whole £100,000 and I'll have all the shares.'

The three of them decided to stick with me, which left Wareing in a tough spot with Fadel. While Wareing didn't say as much, I later learned that the backing of the other directors was one of the conditions that Fadel had laid down for keeping Wareing on as managing director. He didn't get the support he had anticipated, which left me some room to manoeuvre. I told Wareing I was leaving for London and drove to the station in Coventry.

As I stood on the platform waiting for the train, the loudspeaker announced a telephone call for Mr Paul Henderson. There was a message to call John Wareing.

Lawrie Izzard, who was in Wareing's office, took my call. 'You're wasting your time, Paul. Don't bother going down to London. John has spoken to them and they said they are not prepared to change the agreement back.'

'That's my choice,' I told him. 'I'm going to London.'

I arrived at Nick Mallett's office calm and determined. Nick stood behind his executive swivel chair looking a bit grim. Fadel had given him instructions that morning, he said. He was not to change the agreement.

'I have the one drawn up by the Iraqis here,' he said, handing over the version that took away our rights. 'Sign this one. Then there is no problem.'

'Sorry. I'm not signing it.'

Nick was embarrassed. He had drawn up the original agreement. I used his phone to call Wadi and Safa at Wadi's office. Wadi took the call.

'Dr Safa's got steam coming out of his ears,' he said. 'He's furious at what Fadel did with Wareing. You stay there. Don't do anything.'

I went into the waiting room. Half an hour later, Nick came out. 'We're back to the original agreement,' he said, sounding worn out by another turnaround. 'Let's get it signed and out of the way.'

On Friday 27 October 1987 TI Group sold its machine-tool division to TMG as planned. The company was immediately renamed Matrix Churchill Limited. I had once again brought together two of the most respected names in the British machine-tool industry.

I didn't move out of my office in the sales department right away. It took me a little time to accept that I'd become managing director. So I was a bit slow to move into John Wareing's oak-panelled office, with its own bar and cocktail cabinet.

The sale was publicized in trade publications, the theme being the management buy-out of TI Machine Tools Division. Although the Iraqis didn't want to come out front, the fact wasn't hidden from the workforce, for I told them in a series of meetings the Monday after the sale that we had new majority shareholders and that they were Middle Eastern. I also told the workforce that the management had an option to buy 40 per cent of the company and that it was our intention to do so.

I had lived a year in the past seven days. But I was halfway to my dream of owning Matrix Churchill. I thought the way ahead was clear, and I expected to get there through hard work and determination. Of course, I couldn't know what lay ahead for the company and for me.

9

I missed the first sign of trouble. I was extremely busy putting the last touches on a new business plan for Matrix Churchill, one that included a difficult decision to cut back about 100 jobs, so I didn't recognize the significance of the three-sentence memo.

Export licences for the three Iraqi contracts signed in Bonn – the 122mm, the 155mm and the ABC – had been applied for in August. The applications were submitted to the Department of Trade and Industry, which had authority over exports. The licences themselves said the machine tools were destined for 'general engineering' uses in Iraq. They described the technical capabilities and accuracies of all the machines, but did not specify their exact end use.

In my experience the DTI was never concerned about the end use of a machine. The pattern had been the same all through my career, dealing with countries in Eastern Europe, China, India and Pakistan. In addition, while machines would be built to produce specific components, our lathes and grinders could be used for many purposes. So it was our custom and practice on all export applications to list 'general engineering' as the use of the machines, as we had on the Iraqi documents.

On 12 November 1987 Trevor Abraham, the commercial contracts manager at Matrix Churchill, sent me a memo about the export licences for Iraq. Despite numerous calls to the DTI, he said, the licences had not been granted. Trevor said he had been told that day that the applications had been passed to the Foreign Office and the Ministry of Defence, with a recommendation that they be approved.

However, in a small phrase at the end of a sentence, Trevor hit on the real issue. He wrote that the final approval 'is now a political decision'.

What had happened was that, because of the war between Iran and Iraq, the licence applications had been referred to a group called the Inter-Departmental Committee, or IDC. It was made up of the DTI, the Ministry of Defence and the Foreign Office. The representatives of those ministries on the IDC would review applications to Iraq, Iran and other sensitive countries, and could reject them.

I still didn't foresee a problem. The company had been selling this type of machine all over the world, and indeed the previous year we had sold some to Egypt for cartridge and shell manufacture. I just thought it was a question of time before the licences were issued.

I turned out to be right, at first anyway. On 2 December we were notified that the licences for all three orders had been approved. We had some machines in stock that could be used to fulfil part of the contract, so we sent them to our packers and had them shipped to Iraq. They went by truck, through Europe and Turkey into Iraq.

I thought that was the end of the problem, and the factory went on manufacturing machines for the Iraqi orders. After all, I knew that the government was fully aware of what the machines were to be used for in Iraq, despite the 'general engineering' description on the applications. Because he had told me, I knew that Mark Gutteridge had described them in great detail to his intelligence contact and the information had been circulated within government.

In fact, Mark had met quite regularly with his contact since the Iraqis began negotiating to buy the business. In June that year he had described Iraq's acquisition of British machines, including our own, to set up munitions production lines at Nassr and Al Hutteen. Then, in August, he briefed his contact, who used the name Michael Ford, about the role being played by Anees Wadi and MEED International in brokering the Iraqi deals with manufacturers from Britain and other countries.

At that meeting on 6 August, Mark had described our visit to Nassr, right down to the 1000lb bomb being built from American designs. He also provided a detailed list of the annual production targets for the munitions lines.

Then on Wednesday 28 October, less than a week after the sale of TI Machine Tools, Mark met Ford again at the DeVere Hotel in Coventry and gave him the details of the purchase by the Iraqis and the management group.

There was good reason to remember that session. Mark had brought along 100 sheets of drawings from the company files of all machines, layouts and components for all three Iraqi contracts. Some of the drawings had been done by company engineers; others had been provided by Wadi on behalf of the Iraqis. The Iraqi-supplied drawings were based on Soviet designs and still carried some Russian script.

Mark had removed the documents from the files at the office and Ford was to photograph them so they could be returned the next day. But Ford's camera wasn't capable of photographing the blueprints because they were too large. Mark had to repeat the exercise later that week so that Ford could have an MI5 photographer handle the task, which they did on 30 October.

From my own contacts with the intelligence service, I knew material gathered from one agency's source was regularly passed on to other departments, and that care was taken to protect the source. Ford had indicated to Mark that his information was being provided to other government agencies, so I knew the DTI, Foreign Office and Ministry of Defence were aware of the uses of Matrix Churchill machines when the export licences were approved on 2 December.

I hadn't really been bothered by the delay or the involvement of the IDC. This was business as usual. And my mind was occupied with the business of running Matrix Churchill. One of my hardest decisions in those first weeks once again involved Mark Gutteridge. I had to appoint a new person to fill my position as sales director for the company. From the first talk of selling the company, Mark had expected to get the job. But Fadel Jawad Kadhum, vice chairman of the holding company, TMG, had started to question me about whether Mark was the right man for the job, which would involve not only export sales but also domestic sales.

Mark had no experience in the UK market. Also, he had not managed a lot of people. I had another guy, John Harris, who was the UK sales manager, and had also had overseas experience and managed larger groups of people. I discussed the appointment with the Matrix directors and the consensus was that John Harris should have the appointment as sales director, not Mark Gutteridge.

At the end of the day, I thought it was the right decision to give the job to Harris. He was the key to the UK market and Mark was very export-oriented. Bearing in mind that we had fairly large orders from Iraq and expected more, we needed somebody who was going to push domestic sales. I did not want Matrix Churchill to be dependent on Iraq for orders.

Still, this was a difficult decision for me. I couldn't appoint a director without approval from Safa and Fadel, so I discussed the question with them. Fadel supported Harris and so did Safa. But Safa thought a lot of Mark, and was concerned about whether he would stay with the business if he didn't get the job.

'I don't think Mark will stay with the business,' I told him frankly. 'I'll do my best to persuade him, but he is going to be very unhappy.'

'I'll speak with Anees,' said Safa. 'He may be able to influence him to remain.'

The next day I brought Mark into my office. I let him know it wasn't totally my decision, but he would not be getting the sales director's job, and I explained the reasons.

'You will continue as export sales manager and obviously you'll be our key contact with the Iraqi market,' I told my friend, trying to find a way to make the news easier.

'You've let me down,' Mark replied, fighting to control his anger and disappointment. 'I've worked with you in setting up this deal. I've put a lot of time and effort in, like you. Only to find out now that I'm not getting the position and won't be a shareholder.'

'Mark, there's nothing to stop you being a shareholder of the business. There's nothing stopping that.'

'I've been stabbed in the back. I won't be staying here much longer.'

It was a particularly difficult thing for me to do because Mark was a friend. In his shoes, I could understand his point of view. It was the second time that I'd overlooked him and promoted someone else.

A few days later I met John Belgrove. He had been running Hi-Tek since I'd left and business was starting to pick up. John agreed that we should approach Mark and offer him shares in Hi-Tek. There was a strong chance that Hi-Tek would be handling some business with Iraq. Wadi was looking into all sorts of deals for the Iraqis, beyond machine tools. With Mark there, Hi-Tek could work with Wadi on some of those transactions.

John agreed, so I approached Mark. I was officially out of Hi-Tek. John Belgrove and Esther each owned the business, fifty-fifty. They would each sell 5 per cent to Mark and he would join the business later in 1988. I would be sorry to lose Mark, but at least we would have maintained the friendship and he would have a good job.

Mark was reluctant to take the job. He had already talked with

Wadi, who was trying to persuade him to go to work with him and Ricks. Mark was sitting on the fence. But he assured me he was not angry, and either way he reckoned he would get a good position when he finally left Matrix Churchill. Whether Mark went to Wadi or Hi-Tek, it solved a difficult personal problem for me, which was just as well, because a much tougher one was around the corner.

Matrix Churchill Limited was progressing well as a business. We'd trimmed the workforce to about 700 and the development staff were working on a new range of advanced-technology CNC thread-grinding machines. It would be at least a year before they were ready to market, but it marked the first time in many years that the company was devoting a significant amount of work to research and development.

Largely on the strength of the Iraqi orders, the business had ended 1987 by breaking even. It was the first year in ten that the company hadn't lost money. And I'd started the new year off with a bit of a bonus myself.

The final valuation of the company's assets had been completed. Rather than the figure of £22 million given by TI, the net asset value was barely over £16 million. It meant that the £2.5 million in the escrow account was returned to the Iraqis. They had indeed bought the company without spending any of their own money.

One day in January of 1988, after the escrow money had been released, Safa and Fadel drove up to Coventry to see me. It was Fadel who did the talking. 'Because you did such a good job and saved us £2.5 million, we are paying you the interest that the money earned in escrow as a bonus,' he said, handing me a check for £9072.

It was a nice gesture, and helped ease some of the sting in the way they had treated me over the joint-venture agreement. However, Fadel and I were still not on good terms. He still seemed to have doubts about my ability as managing director.

The problem came early that same month. Trevor Abraham got a phone call from Anthony Steadman, director of export licensing at the Department of Trade and Industry. Steadman was the person who, the previous November, had told Trevor the licences were being referred to the IDC.

Trevor rushed into my office and described Steadman's call. This time, Steadman had said, the Iraqi export licences were to be revoked. There were suspicions that the machines were going to be used in the munitions industry, said Steadman. That, he added, could violate the policy set out in 1985 by Sir Geoffrey Howe of Britain's not aiding either side in the Iran–Iraq war.

'I admitted to him that some of the machines were going to be used for munitions manufacture,' Trevor told me. 'They seemed to already know. I'd no reason to hide it anyway.'

'Of course there was no reason to hide it,' I said. 'But this is a major problem. We'll have to deal with it right away.'

Trevor was accurate in saying some of the machines were going for munitions. At that point we knew the contracts for the 122mm and 155mm shells were military. But the ABC contract was a bit of an enigma to us; we didn't really know what those components were for. It was the last of the contracts signed and, in early 1988, the Iraqis were still sending us drawings.

The DTI had never been told explicitly that the Iraqi contracts were for military uses. We had identified them as general engineering, as we did all other contracts. But the government had known, through Mark Gutteridge, that the machines were for military applications and had approved the licences just a month earlier.

Later that day I told Mark there was a possibility that the licences would be revoked. He was shocked and angry on realizing that his information had probably called attention to the exports.

'I told my intelligence contact I'd give him information about the Iraqis on one condition: it would have no effect on Matrix Churchill business,' he said. 'What we are doing is not illegal. I gave him the information in good faith and told him I didn't want it used against Matrix Churchill. I told him it would cause the loss of jobs if we lost the business.'

Angered by the government's action, Mark dropped a bombshell in the conversation. For the first time, he told me that Safa and Fadel were high-ranking Iraqi intelligence officers. He had been told so by Michael Ford back in October when he described the sale of TI Machine Tools to TMG.

'British intelligence were aware of this before they bought the business,' Mark said. 'They knew all along that it was the Iraqi government buying the company.'

I don't think Mark would have shared this incredible information with me unless he had felt betrayed by Ford and the intelligence service over the use of his information in a way that threatened Matrix Churchill.

Obviously I was concerned that the chairman and vice chairman of the company were agents of Iraqi intelligence. I wasn't shocked. How could I be? I'd spent years working as an informant for British intelligence. So had Mark. But Safa and Fadel appeared to be more than mere informants.

Certain things fell into place after Mark's revelation. For example, I had wanted to do a publicity blurb when the new owners took over the company. I wasn't ashamed that we had Iraqi owners. I suggested to Safa and Fadel that we feature them, with pictures, in a publicity leaflet for the company. But they refused outright, and wouldn't even talk to me about their backgrounds.

The fact that they were working for intelligence made me suspicious of their ultimate objective. Did they intend to extract as much technology as possible from Matrix Churchill and then walk away, not caring what financial shape the company was left in? Was it their intention to use Matrix Churchill technology to develop their own machine-tool industry and then force us to import and sell their machines?

I realized I would have to be careful of what I said to the Iraqis, although I didn't see that I was personally at risk. I was not involved with the British intelligence service at that time. But I would have to be careful about the technology we provided to Iraq.

The immediate problem was the possibility of having the export licences revoked. Loss of the Iraqi contracts would not only cause redundancies at Matrix Churchill; it could close the company. For me the bottom line was that the Iraqis would have withdrawn from ownership immediately. They obviously bought the business because they wanted the machines and the technology. They would have lost interest very easily and Matrix Churchill could end up in receivership. The best it could do without the Iraqi orders was to survive as a company with 100 or 150 jobs, not the present 700.

There would also have been an immediate loss of £1 million. Nassr and Al Hutteen had already given us £3.8 million in down payments on the contracts. We had outstanding bank guarantees and the Iraqis would have called in the guarantees if the machines were not delivered. We would have had to honour them, but £1 million of the money had already been taken out of the business by Safa and company.

When TMG bought the business, TI had refunded the £3.8 million pounds to TMG. The money had then been given as a parent-company loan to the new Matrix Churchill. But then Safa and Fadel, who controlled the board of TMG, had ordered £1 million of to be taken out of the company accounts. They had £100,000 of it paid to Wadi as a commission for his role in the sale of the business. This meant Wadi's original investment of £100,000 in the acquisition of Matrix Churchill had been returned.

Safa had taken out a sizeable chunk of money as well. On his instructions, the remaining £900,000 had been wired to account number 706655 at the United Arab Bank in Paris. The account belonged to the Al-Arabi Trading Company, the registered owners of Safa's TDG. There would be no way of getting it back.

With the million gone, its biggest orders blocked and the possibility of its owners returning to Iraq, there didn't seem to be much future for Matrix Churchill if the licences were revoked.

It wasn't only Matrix Churchill that faced potential disaster. Steadman had told Trevor that the review of licences involved other British machine-tool companies, too. Altogether, the four major British machine-tool manufacturers had £50 million in orders pending from Iraq. Most, if not all, of them were related to munitions projects. At a time when other business was difficult to find, losing those orders would be a severe blow. Others with big Iraqi orders were Ben Simon's Wickman Bennett, Keith Bailey and BSA and Colchester Lathes, which was part of the 600 Group.

The government's action angered me for two main reasons. First, they had known all along what our machines and those of the other companies were being used for in Iraq. Second, and even worse in my mind, British industry was being subjected to restraints while our German and Swiss competitors were selling far more advanced technology not only to Iraq but to Iran as well. Why was our government singling us out and threatening redundancies?

The day of Steadman's call I contacted John Nosworthy, the director general of the Machine Tool Technologies Association, the industry trade group. Nosworthy was a good man, and I reckoned he would coordinate an industry response. He promised to set up a meeting as soon as possible at the MTTA offices in London and try to arrange a meeting with Alan Clark, the Minister for Trade and Industry.

I also wrote a letter to John Butcher. He was a minister in the Department of Trade and Industry and the local Member of Parliament for Coventry. Matrix Churchill and Wickman Bennett were both in his constituency, so I knew the MP would be concerned by the potential loss of jobs. I asked him to set up a meeting with Clark.

Nosworthy soon phoned back and said that, with the help of John Butcher, we'd probably get a meeting with Clark. He said Wickman Bennett wasn't going to be involved. The company had not applied for export licences for most of the machines it had sold to Iraq because it believed that licences were not necessary. Ben Simon apparently felt he could handle the situation himself. But Keith Bailey of BSA and Brian Carter, the managing director of Colchester Lathes, were eager to attend a meeting with Clark.

The meeting was arranged for late morning on Friday 20 January 1988. I took an early train to London and went to the TMG offices in Duke Street to brief Safa. Of course, I had informed him immediately about the potential problem, but that day I wanted to reassure him that I thought the issue would be resolved.

It was a clear, cold day as Bailey, Carter, Nosworthy and I entered the DTI, a modern building within a short walk of the Houses of Parliament. After a security check and a brief wait in the lobby, we were escorted to Clark's personal office on the fifth floor.

Alan Clark was in his fifties, tallish, thin and smartly dressed. He was one of the most colourful Thatcherites, and I'd read stories about him in the press. He was the son of Lord Clark, who had become famous as host of the BBC television series *Civilisation*. The family money came from a threadmaking business and Alan Clark owned Saltwood Castle in Kent as well as residences in Scotland and Switzerland. One story that I remembered had been about his smart wardrobe. A journalist asked him about the $2000 suits worn by the American mobster John Gotti. Clark had replied that you were lucky if you could get a decent suit for $2000.

Clark greeted us warmly, introducing us to Tony Steadman, a technical man named Bill Morgan, and Clark's personal assistant. After exchanging pleasantries, Clark sat down at the head of a large conference table in the room. We sat on one side of the table, the DTI people on the other.

The Minister opened by congratulating us on getting the export business for Britain and creating jobs. He went on to say that he did not need convincing because he fully supported continuing the current export licences for shipping machine tools to Iraq. He said he was optimistic the licences would not be revoked.

'I know that at least £37 million worth of orders are at stake for this year alone, with a strong possibility of follow-on orders in the future,' he said.

Clark's number was low. He hadn't included the machines for which Wickman Bennett had decided export licences were not required. But his sentiments were on target – it was just what we had hoped to hear.

'I know Iraq is awash with machinery from Germany, Switzerland, France and Italy,' he said. 'You should be able to obtain business there as well. I'll support your case, even if it goes up to the Cabinet committee level. The UK must be able to complete these existing contracts without interruption.'

Clark implied that we should ship our machines as fast as possible under the current licences in case some bureaucratic interference occurred. As for future business, he stressed the need for careful wording on the applications. 'I know what the machines are being used for. You know what the machines are being used for. So let's get down to talking about the licence situation and future business,' he said.

In future applications, Clark advised us to couch the use of the machines in a manner that stressed the civilian aspects for which they could be used. He said the applications should stress the civilian use and should be supported by as much technical detail as possible.

The Minister warned us that his advice was based on the current state of play. 'If the political overtones of the Iraq–Iran conflict change and if the United States becomes more supportive of one side than at present, then the current order may change,' he said.

Toward the end of the half-hour meeting, Brian Carter of Colchester Lathes raised a question about a phone call he had received from a reporter on the *Daily Telegraph*.

The journalist had told Carter that he was aware of our meeting with the Minister and knew that it concerned export licences for the shipment of £50 million worth of machine tools to Iraq. He also seemed to know that the Ministry of Defence and Foreign Office were opposing the sales.

'The reporter,' said Carter, 'seemed remarkably well informed.'

Clark urged us not to use the press to bring pressure on the government to ensure that the licences were not revoked. That, he said, would only focus unwanted attention on the issue and might draw in the Labour Party.

He said he knew the editor of the *Daily Telegraph* and would speak to him about it. He sent his assistant out of the room to get the editor on the telephone and, as we were saying our farewells and departing, the assistant returned and said he'd got the editor on the line.

We walked into the street thinking, what's the problem? Clark was going to clear the licences. We should stress the peaceful aspects of our business on future applications and we could go on selling to Iraq. Not only would the current orders be filled, but we would also be able to supply orders for the future.

I went over to TMG to relate the welcome news to Safa. As far I was concerned, the Minister had acknowledged that he knew the machines were being exported for military purposes. We weren't asked what the machines were doing. If there was concern that they were going to munitions plants, Clark would certainly have asked each one of us what components could be produced on our machines. By not asking, it was implicit that he knew. Besides, he'd said as much with his comment about 'you know' and 'I know'.

The only troubling point had been Clark's reference to a possible change in American policy. As far as I knew, US policy was the same as the British: quiet support for Iraq and the regime of Saddam Hussein. That much I had learned from Gordon Cooper, who had been running Matrix Churchill Corporation, our sales and service subsidiary in Cleveland, Ohio.

As sales director of TI Machine Tools, I had been the president of the American operation, although I'd had little to do with it and Gordon actually ran things. Around the start of 1988, Safa al-Habobi said he wanted to replace me as president. Cooper would report to him from then on. I didn't think about it much. Safa certainly had the right, as chairman of TMG, to run the US business, too.

Since then, however, I had learned bits and pieces from Gordon, a friend and former Coventry Gauge and Tool apprentice. Safa had sent over Sam Namen, one of his associates from Iraq, to set up a purchasing business through Matrix Churchill Corporation. It was to buy American technology for Iraq. Gordon said it was all rather secretive. He said Namen and Safa would often begin to speak in Arabic when he came into the room. There seemed to be a lot they were hiding from him.

The American export policy was quite similar to that of Britain. Companies in the USA were receiving export licences to sell Iraq sophisticated technology with both commercial and military uses. Whereas we were shipping machine tools, the Americans appeared to

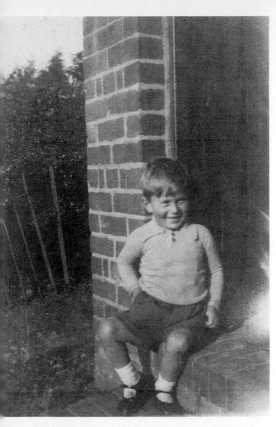

Sitting on my grandmother's doorstep in Malvern, to where I was evacuated in 1942 at the age of three.

Me aged six and my brother aged ten at our home in Coventry.

Esther and me on our wedding day, 16 July 1960.

eceiving the Gauge and Toolmakers' Prize in 1958 from Sir Stanley Harvey, who wned Coventry Gauge and Tool Co. Ltd.

etirement party at Matrix Churchill International for projects engineer Charlie Harris the mid-1970s. Left to right: Charlie Harris, me and Charlie Tearne, who were both les directors, and Joe Walker, a commercial assistant.

Diary entry for my appointment with an intelligence officer described as Mr Kilby of the MoD.

Further meeting with Mr Kilby on 5 July and appointment with intelligence service in London on 31 July.

The diary entry by my secretary, Anne Smith, for my meeting on 31 July with Miss Eyles of the MoD ties in with the meeting of that date referred to above.

Anne Smith's diary entry for my meeting with Miss Thompson of the MoD on 13 July.

Diary entry for my meeting on 4 November with Miss Lambett of MI5.

Signing the manufacturing agreement for the Wrocław CNC lathe with Andrzej Dyszy, export director of Poland's Metalexport.

An Exhibition of Sculptures, Banners, and Assemblages by

WLADYSLAW HASIOR

Royal Festival Hall
28 July–20 August 1977

The Polish Ambassador

has pleasure in inviting you to the

Special Preview of an Exhibition of

Sculptures, Banners and Assemblages

by

WLADYSLAW HASIOR

Thursday, 28th July 1977
at 12.00 noon

ADMIT TWO

Royal Festival Hall, South Bank, SE1

Waterloo Entrance

Refreshment s

Invitation to exhibition of work by the Poli
artist Wladyslaw Hasior, which Esther and I attended and whi
was organized by the Polish Cultural Institute in Londo

My daughter, Sue, outside Canterbury Cathedral on the day of her graduation in European Studies from the University of Kent in 1989.

My son, David, on duty at Stanley airfield with the 1st Battalion of the Coldstream Guards soon after the 1982 Falklands conflict.

David, second from right, in dress uniform, being presented to the Queen at a cocktail party given by Her Majesty for the 1st Battalion of the Coldstream Guards.

be providing more along the lines of advanced computers for testing and design operations.

A company called Gerber Systems had provided computers to run machine tools. Unisys Corporation was selling advanced computers used in production control in several factories. Hewlett Packard computers were used in numerous plants for testing and calibrating equipment.

The American government had also permitted Iraq to buy helicopters, radio equipment and imaging devices for reading satellite photos. Some of the largest companies in the USA were doing business with Iraq, such as General Motors, Honeywell Incorporated, Hughes Aircraft Company and the Bell Aerospace division of Textron Incorporated.

It was also well known among those of us doing business with Iraq that the government there was receiving huge loan credits from the USA. The Americans were supposed to be providing Iraq with guarantees so that they could buy US commodities such as rice and wheat. But I'd been told by several Iraqi associates that some of those funds were being used to pay for machine tools and other material from Europe. If I knew, it seemed unlikely that the American government did not know. So I assumed it was simply another aspect of the policy of favouring Iraq against Iran being pursued in London and Washington.

It was early February when Mark Gutteridge came into my office with a knowing smile on his face. Before the meeting with Clark, he had told me there was nothing to worry about over the licences. Now, he wanted to add an 'I told you so'; which I certainly didn't mind hearing.

'The licences won't be revoked,' he said. 'There's no problem with these and there'll be no problem in the future.'

There actually was no official word from the DTI that the licences would not be revoked. After Mark's comments, I heard from John Nosworthy of the MTTA that Steadman from the DTI had called to say the licences would not be revoked. Steadman had again emphasized that the industry should take a low profile with the press.

On the basis of these reports, Matrix Churchill filed an application to export to Iraq thirteen large CNC lathes. These were twin-spindle lathes, mounted on a vertical bed of steel. This contract had been inherited from TI Machine Tools, but there had been delays because the Iraqis could not decide on the quantity of the machines.

These machines, too, had to do with artillery shells. I'm not a munitions expert, but as it had been explained to me, shells have tiny nubs which spiral around the rear of the shell. These nubs spin the shell as it is fired out of the barrel, similar to the way grooves in a rifle barrel impart spin to a bullet. The result is an artillery shell that travels farther and is more accurate.

Normally, these small nubs are welded onto the shells after they are machined, which is not very elegant from an engineering point of view. A Belgian company had developed a technique to generate the nubs on a copy lathe as part of the machining process. The Iraqis had asked us to come up with a similar process for our big 750 Series CNC lathes. In developing the design, our engineers had discovered multiple civilian applications for the technology and we ultimately incorporated it into our standard product range.

Originally we had proposed selling the Iraqis twenty-six of the 750 Series lathes, which are expensive machines costing about £300,000 each. In the end the Iraqis had placed an order for thirteen machines worth almost £4 million. They were destined for the Al Hutteen factory.

Once the earlier licences were cleared and we had worked out the details for the nub-turning contract, it was mid-February 1988 when we applied for the export licence. Within a month we received a letter from the DTI saying that this type of machine did not require an export licence. We could go ahead and ship the machines to Iraq.

In addition, the governments had issued a residency permit to Dr Safa and provided Dr Fadel with a multi-entry visa. I took this as another signal that we had no problems; we could get on with selling and exporting to Iraq.

10

Dick Burnley stood in the doorway of my office, gripping a piece of paper.

'Would you be so good,' he said calmly, 'as to explain this bill to me? I think our chairman has gone over the top here.'

I took the sheet of paper. It was an invoice from Harrods. Someone in our finance department had passed it on to Burnley, the financial director of Matrix Churchill. As I examined it I didn't know whether to laugh or cry. The bill was for £6000 worth of garden furniture – four chairs, a couple of loungers, a table and an umbrella.

'Bloody hell,' I mumbled.

I had thought carefully about the problem of Safa al-Habobi's spending in recent months. But what could I do? He was, after all, the chairman of TMG, the parent holding company. But £6000 on garden furniture was not the first outrageous purchase to go through our finance department, and Burnley would not be the only director to raise questions.

By the spring of 1988 Matrix Churchill had bought Safa a £1 million house and a Mercedes-Benz. The company was also paying for a nanny for his two children and a driver for the Mercedes. Safa's wife had run up bills of £100,000 for decorating the house. But £6000 worth of garden furniture was too much.

'Don't pay it just yet, Dick. I'll see if I can sort it out,' I said.

It was Anees Wadi who had overseen the transformation of Safa al-Habobi from a scruffy Iraqi engineer into the thoroughly westernized chairman of a large British company. But it was the business that had financed it, right down to a small fortune for straightening his teeth. I remembered well the start of the process, though at the time I had no idea how expensive it would prove.

'You know,' Wadi confided to me one evening at dinner, not long

121

after the Iraqis had acquired the business, 'we've got to transform Dr Safa. He must have the right image. He's the chairman of a large British machine-tool company. We have to get him to dress properly. He's got to have a chauffeur and a nice place to live and everything that goes with it.'

'We' meant Wadi would choose what Safa needed and Matrix Churchill would foot the bill.

First Wadi took Safa to the finest tailors in London and had him measured for a dozen business suits, plus shirts and silk ties. It was not long before Wadi had transmuted Safa into a very well dressed executive, with shiny shoes and nice teeth. And the company rented a large, sunny flat for the family near Regent's Park.

Since Wadi had a Mercedes, Safa needed one too. Matrix Churchill bought him the biggest model, a 500 Series in royal blue at a cost of over £40,000. The company advertised for a driver and the first of many was hired. Safa, we would learn soon enough, had trouble keeping domestic staff. Drivers would come and go every couple of months, unable to stand the abusive treatment and demands from Mrs Safa. The same was true with the string of nannies we hired for the two children.

One day when I was in London Wadi had taken me aside. 'You know, Paul,' he said, 'Dr Safa is not happy in the flat. He is concerned about security for himself and his family. The flat isn't secure enough. He's always worried.'

Knowing by that time that Safa was in Iraqi intelligence, I could understand the reasons for his concern. But I saw nothing wrong with the flat.

'What does Dr Safa suggest?' I asked, fearing the worst.

'We should buy him a house.'

'A house? The company should buy him a house?'

'Yes. It's a good idea. But we mustn't tell Dr Fadel about it. He wouldn't understand.'

Fadel was on the TMG board along with Safa and me, and had access to all Matrix Churchill's accounts. If the company bought a house for Safa, eventually he would find out. But in the end it was me who slipped up. I was at the TMG offices in Duke Street. Wadi had discovered what he deemed to be a suitable house and estate agent had arranged for us to see it that afternoon. I was in Safa's office talking to him and Wadi. 'Are we going to go and see that house for you?' I asked.

Both men looked at me blankly. Then they looked over my shoulder. I turned round to face Fadel, who had entered the room as I was speaking. I didn't know how much he had heard, but I was quick to leave the room. I heard the argument begin before I was far from the door. From the little I overheard and from what Wadi told me later, Fadel had accused me of trying to buy the house behind his back to curry favour with Safa. Wadi and Safa had defended the purchase, but it was left unclear whether they had defended me.

My relations with Fadel had not improved much since the Iraqis' acquisition of the company, and this was sure to make things worse. When we were alone later that day, he made it quite clear that he was angry.

'I'm a board director,' he told me sternly. 'You should tell me what is going on. You have no right to act behind my back.'

'It's not my responsibility,' I countered. 'I am not the chairman of the board. If I were, I'd inform the board of what actions were taken. But it's Dr Safa's responsibility. Not mine.'

Fadel had lost the argument with Safa and Wadi. That afternoon the two of them and I visited the house. The address was 71 West Heath Road, on the edge of Hampstead Heath, an attractive and very expensive part of London. Newly constructed and decorated throughout, it was a spacious, two-storey house, built of red brick and with white, Georgian-style windows. There were five bedrooms, a good-sized lounge, a reception hall and two large kitchens. Outside was a garden with a swimming pool.

Safa must have returned later that evening with his wife, because the next day Wadi phoned me. It was just right; they would take it. Matrix Churchill, of course, would pick up the bill of £1.1 million. The company obtained a loan of £750,000 and the rest was paid in cash from company funds.

Companies often owned properties where employees or visitors could stay temporarily. TI Group had kept a flat in London that I had used occasionally when they owned the business. But it was very unusual for a company to buy a house solely for the use of one of its directors; particularly at such a price. And that wasn't the end of it.

The first thing Safa did was spend a great deal of money on a security system. Not only were surveillance cameras put on the outside of the house and an elaborate alarm system fitted. He also had a metal security door installed that shut off the family bedrooms from the rest of the house.

Then there was the decoration. On my visit I had seen that the house was agreeably decorated and all new, no one having lived in it. But Mrs Safa found nothing about it to her liking. Wadi had rung me one day not long after the purchase to explain that Matrix Churchill would have to open an account at Harrods since Mrs Safa needed to buy some things for the house. In a matter of weeks she had hired a decorator and run up a bill of £100,000 at the Knightsbridge store. Then came the garden furniture.

When Dick Burnley left my office I called Wadi and told him about this latest Harrods bill. I hoped he would raise the matter with Safa for me.

'This is totally the wrong image for the company and Dr Safa,' I told him. 'Ordinary employees in the finance department are seeing these bills. You've got to have a word with Dr Safa.'

A couple of days later I had a meeting with Safa, who brought up the subject himself.

'I understand you've got some problems with the amount of money my wife is spending at Harrods,' he said.

'Just a few,' I replied. 'For example, this sort of money on garden furniture. Mrs Safa could have spent £1000 and got some very good furniture.'

'OK, OK,' he said, raising his hand to let me know he had heard enough on the subject.

The next day he called to tell me that the garden furniture was being exchanged for something more suitable. The next bill was for £750, and that one we paid.

I had no idea what sort of income Safa was drawing from TDG. But he was taking director's fees from Matrix Churchill of only £1000 a month. But in terms of benefits in kind, such as the house, the car, domestic help and the dental and medical bills for the whole family, his actual remuneration from the company was the equivalent of £300,000 a year. That was way over the top for a machine-tool company. My salary as managing director had started at £45,000. I had a company car, a Jaguar Sovereign, but I drove it myself, and my other costs were nothing compared with Safa's.

The Iraqis had always spent a lot of money. They stayed at the best hotels: the Inn on the Park in London, the George V in Paris. They ate in the best restaurants. My feeling was that they came to the West with an inferiority complex, and this was their way of saying: 'We are not inferior. We can afford the best, just the same as anyone else.'

By the spring of 1988 I had known Safa for nearly a year, during which time his outlook, as well as his lifestyle, had undergone a quite dramatic transformation. I had recognized at the start that he was an intelligent man and a very good engineer. But living in London and acquiring the things that come with wealth had changed his attitude. He was now more comfortable and outgoing, and more confident, particularly as his English improved.

To a large extent Wadi had led the way for Safa. Wadi knew how to live well. He had his big Mercedes and a flat in Swiss Cottage, and he often kept a suite of rooms at the Inn on the Park. He ate in the most expensive restaurants and loved to gamble. Whether he introduced Safa to the gaming tables I don't know, but the pair of them would often gamble in London's casinos until the early hours. I was not sure what the stakes were, although a story Wadi once told me indicated that they were very high.

He had been staying at the Inn on the Park for a week, eating there often and entertaining guests. Although he had his own flat, I always thought he used the hotel to ensure his privacy. In the years that I knew him Wadi never invited me or anyone else that I knew of to his home. I was at the hotel when he was checking out at the end of one week. The bill must have been £10,000. 'I won enough last night at the casino to cover this,' he said with a laugh.

I had my doubts that Safa would ever risk so much. But even before Mark Gutteridge told me that Safa and Fadel were high-ranking intelligence officers, I had begun to change my opinion of him. When I first met Safa, in Bonn in 1987, I made the mistake of judging him by his appearance. When Fadel had come to London for the first time, I had assumed he was Safa's superior. Fadel had left his green Ba'ath Party uniform in Baghdad. In the West he favoured Christian Dior suits.

I had begun to guess that I was wrong about their relationship after Safa overruled Fadel on the joint-venture agreement with management at the time of the company's acquisition. Then when Safa and Wadi won the argument over the house, it reinforced my suspicion that Safa was the man in charge.

Because I had come to respect Safa al-Habobi as a shrewd and intelligent man, it also meant that I had to be extremely careful with him. So it was that in the first half of 1988 I negotiated an agreement with officials at the Nassr establishment to transfer Matrix Churchill technology to the Iraqi factory.

Selling machine tools is one thing. It involves manufacturing a machine and selling it complete to the customer, who then plugs it in at his factory and, once it is set up, can produce a component. By contrast, the transfer of technology, which is rather a fancy name, is in fact a licensing agreement. So for £2 million we would be selling the Iraqis the right and the technology to manufacture our CNC lathes at the Nassr plant. They would get the complete technology to design the 2 Series and 3 Series CNC lathes.

In addition Iraqi engineers would come to Coventry and be trained at our factory. Rather like apprentices, they would work in all the departments and learn the trade of toolmaker. On their return to Iraq they would be able to produce the CNC lathes using our technology.

Despite my concerns about the Iraqis manufacturing our machine tools in Baghdad, there was nothing I could do to block this transfer of technology. Even the Department of Trade and Industry was not helpful. It was provided with full details of the contract, and was aware that eventually the Iraqis would be self-sufficient in the manufacture of CNC lathes. DTI officials were also informed of the in-depth training of Iraqi engineers at our Coventry factory. Yet the department had quickly approved the transaction, telling us it did not need an export licence. No more problems with sales to Iraq. But I was already planning for the future.

By mid-1988 Matrix Churchill was in the process of designing a complete new range of CNC lathes, more sophisticated than the 2 and 3 Series, with far more advanced technology. So I already had in mind that what we were selling the Iraqis was old technology. By the end of 1989 the 2 and 3 Series lathes would be replaced.

To my mind we had to keep ahead of the game with the Iraqis. For them to continue to be interested in us and not make Matrix Churchill dispensable, my plan was that we always had to have something new in the pipeline. The other side of the strategy was that, by developing a new range of products, the company would be well placed for the time when the management was able to buy it from the Iraqis.

The technology transfer was Matrix Churchill's fifth contract with the Iraqis. It followed the three negotiated in Bonn and the one approved earlier in 1988 for the sale of the big 750 Series lathes.

Safa was continuing to direct enquiries our way and kept the business with Iraq going strong. So it was no surprise when he called me from London in early April 1988 to tell me that he had people with him and wanted them to come up to Coventry to take a look at the factory that afternoon. He said the two men were named Christopher Drogoul and Paul Von Wedel. They were from the Atlanta, Georgia, branch of Banca Nazionale del Lavoro, a large bank owned by the Italian government and more often referred to simply as Banca Lavoro.

'I'm not sending them in my car because I need it here,' said Safa. 'We've hired a vehicle to take them up to Coventry.'

It was a dreadful day, chucking it down with rain. Shortly before lunch I watched from my office window as a long, grey Daimler Princess pulled up outside the front door of the factory. It was the sort of car that royalty uses. Inside were Adnan al-Almiri and Hana P. Jon, who worked for Safa at TDG, and one American.

'Sorry, Drogoul couldn't make it. I'm Paul Von Wedel,' said the American after they had scrambled out of the limousine and into reception. He was a short, balding fellow who looked more like a car salesman than a banker.

I gave Von Wedel a tour of the factory and then we sat down to talk with Trevor Abraham. The American said that Banca Lavoro could finance out of Atlanta any and all contracts we signed with Iraq at rates that were substantially lower than anything we could obtain elsewhere. The figures he proposed were a fraction of what we were paying our bankers, Lloyds Bank, and other institutions.

For example, Von Wedel told us his rate on a confirmed, irrevocable letter of credit: a financial document that guarantees payment for the supplier from the bank. In order for the bank to confirm the letter of credit, the customer must deposit the funds with the bank. It was a necessary security when dealing with countries such as Iraq. Lloyds charged us 1 per cent per year on a confirmed, irrevocable letter of credit. Von Wedel said Banca Lavoro could do it for a quarter of 1 per cent per year. The other fees he listed were equally attractive. Indeed they were so good that we could not see how the bank could offer them. Trevor and I were both suspicious.

'Does this have the backing of your headquarters in Italy?' Trevor asked.

'Yes, it does,' said Von Wedel. 'That's not a problem.'

'Well,' Trevor persisted, remaining sceptical, 'where do you get such cheap funds that you can commit them at these rates?'

'Through the Export-Import Bank of the United States,' answered

Von Wedel. 'These are government guarantees – a sure thing that lets us offer these very favourable rates.'

Trevor and I took Von Wedel to lunch at the Malt Shovel. We were still so surprised by the rates that we asked the American more questions over our meal. But each time he had a ready and reassuring answer.

'Bring us your business with Iraq and we'll show you what we can do,' the banker said as he left.

After Von Wedel and the Iraqis had gone I asked Trevor: 'How the hell can they do it? These rates are unbelievable. They are great for us, but how can they do it?'

'I'm not sure,' replied Trevor. 'It doesn't make sense.'

We decided to find out if Banca Nazionale del Lavoro was a credible institution. I wrote to our bank manager at Lloyds and asked him about the foreign bank. I also indicated the rates we had been offered. He rang me a few days later with his assessment. 'There's nothing wrong with Banca Lavoro,' he said. 'It's one of the biggest banks in Italy, owned by the government. As for the rates, we can't match them. Can't even come close. You should take them while they are available.'

At the time the only pending Iraqi contract in need of financing was the transfer of technology. It was a £2-million order – not a huge one. It seemed a good way to test Von Wedel and his bank. I was still suspicious that the rates were too good to be true, and I believed that there would be a delay of at least six months in receiving the money. But this was not the case at all. When we submitted our documents for payment to Banca Lavoro in Atlanta later in 1988, we were paid right on the nail. It turned out to be an excellent arrangement.

As for the Iraqis, there was no need to steer them towards the bank, as Von Wedel had suggested we do. They were fully aware of the money available through the bank they referred to as BNL. In fact, I learned from Gordon Cooper in Cleveland that Matrix Churchill Corporation was using the Atlanta bank to finance a number of large transactions with Iraq. Cooper's impression was that Safa had a close personal relationship with Christopher Drogoul and possibly with a woman who worked at the bank.

On the morning of 6 June, a couple of months after Von Wedel's visit, I got a similar telephone call at the office from Safa. He had some more people he wanted to send up to the factory. This time they were from a company in Chile called

Industrias Cardoen. Safa mentioned it had something to do with arms manufacturing.

'These are important people,' he told me. 'You show them around personally. Look after them.'

The company's name did not ring a bell with me, so I walked over to Ron Ash's office and asked him. Ron, our defence projects engineer, had previously worked for the Royal Ordnance.

'Sure, I know about Cardoen,' Ron said. 'They're a very big arms manufacturer in Chile. Santiago is the headquarters.'

A bit of quick research and a few phone calls before the party arrived confirmed what Ron had said. Industrias Cardoen and associated companies formed one of the world's biggest private defence manufacturers. A press article from 1983 said that the company sold a full line of weapons, from aerial bombs, grenades and machine-guns to artillery, rockets and armoured vehicles, which they marketed all over the world. But in recent years one of their biggest customers had been Iraq.

The founder and chairman was Dr Carlos Cardoen, who was from Chile but had been educated as a metallurgist in the USA and reportedly spoke several languages. Press clippings portrayed Cardoen as something of an adventurer. He had mortgaged his home in the seventies to finance the expansion of the family mining business into defence products. Rewarded with an increased turnover and rising profits, he now lived in a mansion, flew his own helicopter and made his own rules.

Carlos Cardoen arrived at the Coventry plant shortly after lunch in Safa's chauffeur-driven Mercedes. With him was a man he introduced as Augusto Giangrandini, his principal assistant. Cardoen was slim, with black hair swept back over his head. I judged him to be in his early forties, a few years younger than me. Extremely courteous and immaculately dressed, he was obviously a mature businessman. He was also reserved and quietly spoken. I took a liking to him almost immediately.

Giangrandini was the opposite physically and in personality. He was a big man, overweight, a larger than life character who was shaking hands happily with everyone he met as we toured the shop floor.

While we sat in the boardroom with Ron Ash and Trevor Abraham after the tour, the Chileans said openly that they were involved in a munitions project with Iraq. Both men were knowledgeable about machine tools and said that the project was very big and would require a lot of machine tools.

Cardoen said that he had done business with Iraq in the past, but this sounded like a bigger project than the previous ones. In addition he revealed that he was being paid in oil. I knew from Wadi that the Iraqis were pressed for hard currency and they had plenty of oil, so it made sense that they should barter oil for arms.

Later Cardoen told me that Iraq's State Oil Marketing Organization had allocated his company a million barrels of oil a month to pay for its business. Cardoen then sold the crude to oil traders and the proceeds were deposited in his bank accounts. It meant that he would be paid even when the Iraqis were short of hard currency. 'I am guaranteed payment in oil,' he said.

Cardoen had been using Japanese machines at his plants in Chile. On that first visit to Matrix Churchill he was straightforward in saying that he did not expect our company to be able to compete with the Japanese, whose prices were much lower.

'We were asked by Dr Safa to come up here and have a look at your operation,' explained Cardoen. 'It looks very good, very modern. I like what I see. You are much too expensive, but you do have a special relationship with Iraq. We will send you an enquiry.'

We parted on friendly terms. I expected to get a request for quotations on the Iraqi project that Cardoen was working on, but I had no idea then what the machine tools were, except that they were something to do with munitions.

Within days the enquiry arrived. In fact it came so fast that it must have been left by Cardoen at the TMG offices in London. They had sent the drawings from which we were to prepare our quotes. The project was a 'turn-key' operation to manufacture artillery fuses in Iraq. It required a large number of our smaller CNC lathes to produce the components for the fuses. The machines would not make the fuses themselves, but rather some of the mechanical parts that would then be assembled as fuses.

In a turn-key project the contract requires the supplier to set up an entire factory and hand it over to the customer ready for use. All the latter has to do is turn the key, so to speak. It can be good business, even if the supplier does not manufacture all of the equipment himself. He can simply buy from other companies and mark the goods up to ensure a tidy profit before selling them on to the customer.

Cardoen was assembling the machines and other material for the fuse factory, which would be built somewhere in Iraq. The quotation that we put together was for twenty-four 2 Series CNC lathes and the same number of 3 Series machines. Since Cardoen's visit to Coventry we had had discussions about the technical requirements with his engineers and were preparing the quotation. Cardoen's initial response was that our bottom-line price of over £6 million was too high. The Chileans could buy Japanese machines for 30 per cent less. We couldn't take 30 per cent off our prices – the profit margin was not that big – so our first reaction was that we stood little chance of winning the business.

Later in June Safa called and asked about progress on the contract. When I told him it looked like we were too expensive, he said he would get back to me. A few days later we were invited to Miami to meet Cardoen and his people to discuss a contract for the fuse factory. Obviously the Iraqis, since they were the buyers, had some influence with Cardoen when it came to choosing the machine tools.

On a Sunday in July I flew to Miami with Ron and Trevor. It was unusual for the managing director to attend a negotiating session, but Safa had insisted that I go. It was raining heavily when we arrived that afternoon at Miami's palm-lined airport. The rain had stopped by the time we got to the hotel that Cardoen's people had booked for us, and now that the sun was out it was beginning to grow humid.

The next morning we took a taxi to a four-storey office block in Miami Lakes, which lies outside the city. There we went to the suite of a company called Swissco Management Group, one of several businesses that Cardoen owned in America. In fact Giangrandini told us that Cardoen owned the building containing Swissco's offices, as well as a considerable amount of other office buildings and property in Florida.

Cardoen's office had a tiger skin on the floor. From what I had heard, I assumed he had shot the beast himself, but I didn't ask. In addition to Cardoen and Giangrandini we met Carlos Schurmann, the fuse project manager and Ron's counterpart as the technical expert, and Juan Valdivieso, the financial manager and equivalent to Trevor.

At the time Cardoen was living in Miami, or was at least on an extended visit. The first day he took us to lunch at an Italian restaurant not far from the office, and his wife and one of his daughters joined us. That night Giangrandini took the three of us to dinner at a Cuban restaurant in the part of Miami they call Little

Havana. He was a well-known and clearly popular customer there, and for us, the chance to try various unfamiliar dishes made it into an entertaining evening.

The contract negotiations took three days. The discussions were complicated because Industrias Cardoen was being paid in oil by the Iraqis. Trevor and Valdivieso worked out a financing arrangement whereby a British bank would extend credit to Cardoen. The credit would be backed by the British government's Export Credit Guarantee Department, which provides loan guarantees to assist in overseas sales by British businesses.

Before going to the USA Trevor and I had decided that we could lower our prices by about 7 per cent and still make the project attractive from a financial standpoint. When Cardoen and I sat down on Thursday to negotiate the final terms and price of the contract, the agreement we reached was roughly 5 per cent lower than our original quotation, so I was pleased with the outcome.

Around the time that we signed the Cardoen contract we were close to finalizing another, larger contract with the Iraqis. This was what we called the 'ABA contract' and it was to provide machinery to manufacture components for production of the Ababel rocket at the Nassr factory. As I understood it, the Ababel rocket was about a metre and a half long and was used in a mobile multi-rocket launcher. As the contract progressed I learned that the technology for the launcher was from Yugoslavia and that the launchers were mounted on special vehicles so that they could be moved around the battlefield.

I was familiar enough with export regulations to recognize that we had no business selling Iraq anything to do with missiles. A set of laws called the Missile Technology Control Regime had been adopted by most Western countries and it strictly banned the sale of anything related to ballistic missile production. But the Ababel was a rocket – not any kind of a missile as I understood the term.

ABA started off as a big contract, and the Iraqis wanted it urgently. In addition to sixteen CNC lathes and a large drilling machine from Matrix Churchill, the manufacturing process required twenty-two machines known as vertical machining centres.

Developed in the sixties, machining centres are different from lathes in one basic way: a lathe produces circular parts and a machining centre prismatic parts. Lathes rotate components and machine them against tools that are fixed in place. A machining centre keeps the component fixed in place and moves the tools around it, rapidly and automatically selecting different tools from a carousel that may hold up to 240 cutting tools.

Matrix Churchill did not manufacture the size of machining centre required for ABA. But we were working on a major installation in Alcester with a company that did, called Flexible Manufacturing Technology. The joint project was a highly automated plant to manufacture front axles for Ford cars. The plant was owned by Rockwell Maudslay, a British subsidiary of the big American company Rockwell Corporation. We had good relations with the company and I liked its managing director, Michael Bright.

I had therefore gone to Bright and he had agreed to work with us on the ABA contract. The quotation we prepared for the Iraqis totalled £18 million, with £12 million of it going to Flexible Manufacturing Technology for twenty-two of its machining centres and the rest to us for the lathes and drill. We had added 15 per cent to the price of the machining centres as our profit on that part of the order.

The fast-moving deal ran into a problem in July. Trevor flew to Iraq to work out the financial details with officials at Nassr, but he found the Iraqis uncertain about whether to proceed with the ABA contract. Events in the region seemed to be moving away from military production. There were press reports that Ayatollah Khomeini was on the verge of giving up in the eight-year war with Iraq.

Trevor returned with a signed but undated contract for a smaller version of the project. It called for twelve machining centres, eight CNC lathes and the drilling machine, at a reduced price of £12 million in all. The contract was not dated because the Iraqis were still not sure they wanted to go ahead. Naturally it would not come into force until it was dated as well.

The UN negotiated an end to the long and bloody Iran – Iraq war with a ceasefire agreement between the two countries in August 1988. Remembering Safa's boast that Iraq would transform itself when the conflict ended into the region's leading industrial nation, I assumed the ceasefire meant new business from the Iraqis. The ABA contract might be cancelled, but machines we had supplied for the munitions components could easily be adjusted to manufacture a wide range of commercial products. And there would be new commercial business.

This did not happen, however. Saddam Hussein had decided privately that his country would become a different kind of power in the Middle East. The first signal I received of this came a few weeks after the ceasefire. Adel al-Alami, who had succeeded Safa as director general of Nassr, came to Coventry. There he and I signed the scaled-down £12 million version of the ABA contract. This transaction, like the transfer of technology, was financed by Banca Lavoro's Atlanta branch.

Around this time we got a second enquiry from Cardoen in Santiago. The Iraqis had decided to expand the fuse plant the Chilean company was building for them, so more machines were needed. However, these would be performing different functions. This time Cardoen wanted machining centres and some smaller lathes.

Trevor and Ron flew to Santiago and thrashed out the financial and technical aspects of the contract. Only three Matrix Churchill lathes were to be quoted; the remainder of the order was for Japanese-designed and manufactured equipment. Eleven CNC lathes would be made by the Japanese company Star and twenty-four machining centres by Takisawa, also Japanese. It was another £6 million order.

Since the early eighties we had had a business relationship with Takisawa: under a joint-venture agreement we assembled a range of their vertical machining centres in Coventry and sold them in Scandinavia and other parts of Europe, and the Middle East. Thus we had the rights to sell the machines as part of the second Cardoen contract. For the Star lathes we approached Star's UK distributor, Brown and Sharpe.

Industrias Cardoen accepted our quotations in November and the contract was signed during a visit to Santiago and Miami by Trevor and Ron. As with the other Cardoen order, the Iraqis were paying the Chilean company in oil.

Towards the end of 1988 Matrix Churchill had all its Iraqi contracts in place. The company had a substantial order book, not only with the Iraqis but with British customers too. Along with the Rockwell Maudslay plant, we were selling a large number of machines to the Rover Group for their new small car, the Metro. In addition I was trying to re-establish my relationship with Eastern Europe and the Soviet Union. We had even started negotiating to acquire a small British company that imported and distributed

Russian machine tools, and this would give us an advantage in selling our machines to the USSR. All the forecasts indicated that we were set to make a profit in our first full year. But this money was not going to be distributed to shareholders, for it was my opinion that it was more important to put it back into the business, and Safa and Fadel agreed with me.

Throughout 1988 we did a lot of work smartening up the factory, installing more computers and automatic machines, and reorganizing some of the departments. The apprentice programme from which I had graduated nearly thirty years earlier had been discontinued under TI Group. It was now started again, with the first intake coming to work in 1988. We also began forging contacts with local schools, showing students that engineering was not a 'dirty' job but a technologically advanced one.

The company had invested £600,000 in a new IBM computer for production and financial control. It enabled us to control the entire production process, from ordering the raw material at the right time to establishing the dates for testing the finished machines so that they could be shipped on schedule.

Matrix Churchill had lost ground in the technology of thread-grinding machines, where Coventry Gauge and Tool had once been the world leader. Now, a lot of effort and money was being invested by the design and engineering department in developing new thread-grinders. They were also putting together a new line of more technologically sophisticated CNC lathes.

I had always been impressed by the cleanliness of Japanese machine-tool factories. All the lines were painted that marked out the gangways and production areas, and the floors were clean. Although the factory at Fletchamstead Highway was old, I wanted it to look as good as any Japanese factory. In fact when the Rockwell Corporation officials from the USA visited the factory before signing the Rockwell Maudslay contract, one of them told me: 'This is as good as any Japanese plant.'

The dream was coming true. After losing an average of £2 million a year for the past ten years, Matrix Churchill was going to make a profit. New products were in the pipeline. The workforce had stabilized, and there appeared to be no danger of redundancies. In truth we were so busy that some work had been sub-contracted to two other machine-tool companies.

Apart from the arguments about Safa's expensive lifestyle, which in any case had moderated somewhat by the end of the year, the first full year of Matrix Churchill Limited's operation had been impressive. I was only sorry that Mark Gutteridge was no longer part of the company. In fact the appointment of John Harris as sales director had not worked out and Mark had still been with the company I would have offered him the job. As it was, we appointed an outsider in November 1988. The new sales director was Peter Allen.

Understandably angry when he did not get the sales director's position, Mark had kept his promise to leave Matrix Churchill, and on 1 August 1988 had started work as a partner in my former consultancy firm, Hi-Tek.

By the time Mark left, he was not involved in many of the high-level meetings with Safa, Fadel and their countrymen in Iraq. Nor had he been involved in the Cardoen contracts. But I was aware of his relationship with the intelligence service, and I kept him informed of what was happening. I was not unduly concerned about the information getting back to British intelligence. At the time Mark left the company all our export licence applications had been cleared, and since his departure we had not experienced any further problems.

Shortly before he left, Mark told me that his intelligence contact had asked him if he could put somebody's name forward to take over from him at Matrix Churchill.

'I gave them your name, Paul,' he told me with a smile. 'My contact even said he knew of you. Said they'd been in touch with you before. You might be receiving a call one of these days.'

11

Roz Webb, my secretary, buzzed me. A man was on the line for me, saying he was a friend of Richard Stanbury. Did I want to talk to him?

Stanbury was the name used by one of my former contacts in intelligence. He was with MI6, the collectors of overseas intelligence. No one would know his name unless they were part of the intelligence service. It was the end of August 1988, with Mark Gutteridge gone less than a month, and here was the call already. I told Roz to put him through to me.

'Mr Henderson,' said the caller, 'my name is John Balsom. I'm a colleague of Richard Stanbury.'

'Yes, what can I do for you, Mr Balsom?'

'We'd like to know if you'd be willing to have a word with us. A short meeting. At your convenience, of course. I work in London, but I get up north quite often.'

I had been expecting the call, so it aroused no anxiety. 'I'd be happy to meet you. Matter of fact, I have to be in London next week.'

'Great. Do you know which day?'

'Tuesday. I have an early afternoon meeting just off Oxford Street.'

'Well then, how about if we meet at, say, four-thirty in the lobby at the Inn on the Park. You know the hotel, Mr Henderson?'

'Yes, I know it well. Four-thirty on Tuesday is fine.'

I was not worried about recognizing the intelligence man. From experience, I knew he would know what I looked like. John Balsom: I wondered if it was his real name. Probably not, I thought, since none of them used their own names. Even the secretaries probably had false names.

The Inn on the Park, just off Hyde Park, is very swish. It was a favourite of Anees Wadi's, who from time to time availed himself of a suite of rooms there and often dropped into the bar for drinks. The Sunday after the Iraqis bought TI Machine Tools Division in 1987, Safa had taken Esther and me there to a celebration luncheon.

That Tuesday in early September 1988 I was sitting in the reception area on the ground floor, just to the left of the entrance when a man walked up and asked if I was Mr Henderson. I nodded.

'John Balsom,' he said, extending his right hand as I stood up. 'Pleasure to meet you.'

He showed me a small black wallet that contained an identification card saying Ministry of Defence. I did not think for a minute that that was where he really worked. It was part of the charade.

Balsom was slim, with a lot of black hair parted at the side and swept back over his head. I guessed he was in his middle thirties, but he could have been older. At five feet eleven, he was about an inch taller than me. Right away he struck me as intelligent and well educated.

We sat in two comfortable chairs, close together and at right angles to each other. My large brown briefcase, packed with material from my meeting with Safa al-Habobi and Wadi, was at my feet. Balsom carried nothing. We could have been two businessmen having an informal, late afternoon meeting.

'You know,' he said, in a normal, conversational voice, 'we've been in touch with a colleague of yours.'

'Yes, Mark told me.'

My mention of the name seemed to surprise Balsom, for he frowned.

'Ah, well, yes, Mark,' he said. 'Ah, I've had a look at your file. Had a chat with some of your old friends as well. We thought you might be willing to help us again.'

'Of course, Mr Balsom. That's why I agreed to this meeting with you. By the way, are you aware that Anees Wadi is staying here tonight?'

'I had no idea.'

Obviously he recognized the name. He seemed genuinely surprised and a bit agitated at the prospect of Wadi seeing us together. It would have been easy enough to explain: a business meeting – nothing complicated. But I was surprised myself. I would have thought that the intelligence service would have known where Wadi stayed so often.

Regaining his composure, Balsom started to discuss how keen the government were to keep an eye on the Iraqis. With the Iran–Iraq war just ended, Whitehall was worried that Saddam Hussein might turn his resources to more destructive weapons: nuclear warheads, missiles, and chemical and biological devices.

'From your unique position, you could be an enormous help to us,' said Balsom.

'I suppose I could.'

He did not press me for details about Matrix Churchill or the Iraqis. I sensed that he was sizing me up, deciding how useful I might be, how much I would be willing to tell them. I do not believe that MI6, or MI5 for that matter, had recruited a managing director before. Furthermore, since I was employed by the Iraqis, I might not have been so willing to provide information.

We chatted a little longer before Balsom stood and thanked me. We had talked for about an hour, or perhaps slightly less.

'We'll be in touch,' he said, offering me his hand.

Balsom kept his word, and our second meeting took place in October. I was surprised when he suggested the same hotel, but I didn't mind. He asked general questions about the financial structure of the business and dealing with the Iraqis. He appeared to be an expert on the Middle East, or even on Iraq, for he knew a great deal about the region's politics and history.

'What about Carlos Cardoen? Any dealings with him?' the intelligence man asked.

'I've met Dr Cardoen on two occasions. We have a rather sizeable contract with him. He's building a fuse factory for the Iraqis. He visited Coventry and I went to Miami to sign the contract with him in July. The Iraqis are paying him in oil. It's a barter.'

'What else is Cardoen selling the Iraqis?'

'I'm not sure. I've heard aerial bombs discussed. All I really know about is the fuse factory. That's all we're involved with.'

'How about Space Research Corporation? Or Gerald Bull?'

'Only vaguely. Dr Safa mentioned SRC not long ago. I can't recall what he was talking about, though.'

'OK. Let me know if you hear anything about SRC, please.'

This second meeting also lasted about an hour. At the end Balsom gave me a telephone number where I could reach him, and said:

'Give me a call if you get any interesting information. We'll arrange a meeting.'

Again he had not asked the sort of detailed questions that Miss Eyles had about machine capabilities and components being manufactured; not even on the Cardoen fuse contract. I sensed that he was still unsure. Would I cooperate? Had I switched sides when the Iraqis bought the company? The answer would come if I rang him.

It was January 1989 when I called the number Balsom had given me. When I mentioned Space Research Corporation, Balsom said he would be on an early train to Coventry the next day.

SRC, I had learned since the October meeting, was based in Belgium and run by Dr Gerald Bull. He was Canadian and had a reputation as a brilliant artillery designer. He had done work for both the Canadian and US governments, but now carried out mostly private defence contracts in other countries.

I was not certain how much Bull was doing with Iraq, but earlier in January I had had a call from Safa about a contract that SRC had signed to supply the technology for fuses to Iraq. Apparently even the expanded fuse factory that Industrias Cardoen was assembling was not enough to satisfy the Iraqis.

SRC had signed a £21-million contract to build and equip a fuse factory for Iraq. The contract required that the company set up the plant on a turn-key basis, similar to Cardoen's but using Swiss, German and Italian machine tools. SRC had an interesting partner in the deal. TDG, the company I had helped Safa set up in 1987 and the major shareholder in TMG, was supposed to be coordinating some of the purchases.

But when these partners tried to order the machine tools for the plant, the manufacturers had refused to help. It seemed that Bull's small company and Safa's TDG could not secure the bank guarantees required by the tool manufacturers before they would start work on the orders. Indeed no company would manufacture such expensive machines without a guarantee of payment.

'See if you can help them out,' Safa instructed me. 'It could be good business for Matrix Churchill as well. I will send you up a copy of the contract.'

I had phoned SRC and spoken to Michael Bull, the founder's son, who had repeated what Safa had told me about the problem, but in more detail. I had agreed to consider supplying all of the machine tools for the factory. Bank guarantees would be no problem for us.

Since Balsom had asked about SRC, I had telephoned him after my conversation with Michael Bull. The day after I called I collected Balsom at Coventry station and we drove to the Malt Shovel, where we had lunch and talked at some length about Bull's fuse contract. I also handed him a copy of the SRC–TDG contract with the Iraqis, which he took away for evaluation by MI6's specialists.

'We're not really interested in conventional armaments,' Balsom told me. 'Find out all you can about Bull and SRC and any other projects they might be working on. They are a very important link.'

I gathered from our conversation that Bull's company was providing Iraq with more than a fuse factory. At our first meeting Balsom had mentioned that his chief concern was Iraq's potential development of missiles and nuclear weapons.

At the Malt Shovel, too, the MI6 man remained pretty tight-lipped about what he knew. But he was comfortable enough to ask detailed questions about other projects and about the way the Iraqis had set up the infrastructure of their factories. It appeared that I had passed his test, and he had amassed a large number of queries.

'What about Project 117? Do you know anything about that?' he asked.

'Yes, I do. The Iraqis also call it the "Lion of Babylon".'

I had visited Baghdad several times in 1988, and each time been treated as an honoured guest. On my first trip the year before, the Iraqis had moved me from the Novotel to the Al Rasheed, the best hotel in Baghdad, where guests of the government stayed. Almost the entire ground floor of the hotel was occupied by the lobby, and there were several good restaurants, a large swimming pool, a gymnasium and a ten-pin bowling alley. By contrast with some Arab countries, whisky and beer were plentiful in Iraq, and the atmosphere was quite friendly. I often ran into other businessmen I knew from Britain or Europe, and there seemed to be plenty of Americans too.

One day I was walking across the lobby when someone called my name. I turned to see the managing director of Bipromasz, a Polish state company. I had known him from my earlier days in Eastern Europe, and now joined him for a drink and a chat. Bipromasz was negotiating a deal to refurbish ageing Soviet tanks and other tracked military vehicles that had been used in the war against Iran, and planned to set up a complete factory outside Baghdad to handle this work.

I had sold machines to this man in the past, and told him I would be interested in providing quotations for the project. Fine, he had said, and later I received a list of the company's requirements, which were marked 'Lion of Babylon' and 'Project 117'.

I also told Balsom what I knew about Project 144. This was headed by a Brigadier Rahim, who was educated at Liverpool University, and reporting to him was Brigadier Marouf, a graduate of Stanford University in the USA. I had met both men while attending a fifteen-day international trade fair in Baghdad in November 1988, where Matrix Churchill had had a small stand in the British pavilion. The DTI had sponsored the pavilion, and I had taken this as another sign that selling to Iraq was acceptable.

In connection with the fair, British government officials had visited Baghdad for trade talks. Among the trade ministers who had gone to Iraq was Tony Newton, who had recently joined the Department of Trade and Industry. At the close of the talks Newton confirmed that £340 million in government-backed loans would be available in 1989 for British companies doing business with Iraq. This was double the amount on offer in 1988, and 20 per cent of it was made available for the sale of military-related products to Iraq.

'This substantial increase reflects the confidence of Her Majesty's Government in the long-term strength of the Iraqi economy and the opportunities for an increased level of bilateral trade following the ceasefire,' Newton had said in a press release distributed to British companies exhibiting at the fair.

A similar type of loan guarantee had been used by Matrix Churchill to finance the export of machines to Iraq under the two Cardoen contracts. Expanding the programme was another clear signal to go on selling to Iraq.

It is worth pointing out that the Chief Secretary to the Treasury at the time was John Major. In this capacity he oversaw the sharp expansion in British financial assistance to the Iraqis for purchases from British companies, including purchases of defence goods. After all, Matrix Churchill was far from the only British firm using export credits to finance sales to Baghdad.

There was certainly no denying that civil servants in the Export Credit Guarantee Department at the Treasury were aware that at least some of Matrix Churchill's loans were being used for military purposes. When we applied for credits on the first Cardoen contract, officials in the department had quickly discovered and reported in memos that Cardoen was a manufacturer of explosives and military goods. Yet the loan was approved.

The generous export guarantees provide another parallel with the USA's policy towards Iraq. Since 1983 the US government had given the Iraqis more than $4 billion worth of similar credits to buy American agricultural produce and timber. But in my dealings with the Iraqis I had also learned that some of those credits were buying more than grain. Millions of dollars worth of the American credit guarantees were being used by Banca Lavoro to finance other Iraqi purchases. Several times Safa had mentioned that some of the technology and machinery he was buying in Europe was being paid for indirectly through the USA's loan programme. As with most matters, however, Safa was not forthcoming with the details.

The end of the Iran–Iraq war in August 1988 had attracted companies from around the world to the November trade fair in the Iraqi capital. Western companies were eager to increase their business with Baghdad, and present at the fair were manufacturers from Japan, West Germany, Switzerland, the USA, France and Scandinavia.

None of the stands, however, was as large and attention-grabbing as that of 600 Services, which represented Colchester Lathes. They had erected a first floor over their machines that contained a restaurant offering free food and a band playing Dixieland jazz. During the Iran–Iraq war 600 Services had maintained an office in Baghdad with a staff of about twenty, and Iraq was a big market for its parent firm, the 600 Group.

'We should put up a stand like that at the military fair in the spring,' Safa had said to me one day as we walked around the 600 Services display.

'I think it's a bit over the top. What we really need is an office in Baghdad,' I replied.

At the Malt Shovel I told Balsom that I had discussed Project 144 in some detail with Rahim and Marouf because Matrix Churchill's ABA contract was part of the overall project. The ABA contract dealt with the Ababel rocket, which was part of a multiple-rocket launcher that would be mounted on a truck, but Project 144 was much larger.

Rahim and Marouf described to me how there were plans in hand to manufacture a large, long-range missile. They had asked Matrix Churchill to provide a machine to produce a ring one and a half metres in diameter as one of the missile's components. We refused because we could not manufacture a machine that large. However, I also had no intention of participating in a missile project.

In addition to the actual missile, the Iraqis were working with a British company which was supplying a plant to treat components with a coating that would withstand temperatures of up to 3000 degrees Celsius. Such temperatures, I gathered, were generated by the missile propellant.

Part of the assembly of the missile was apparently to be done by robots, while another aspect of the project involved the manufacture of industrial robots by the Iraqis under a licensing agreement with Beroe, a Bulgarian company. The actual technology was from a Japanese firm.

By the time I had finished, Balsom was well pleased. He was convinced that I was supportive of MI6, despite the fact that my company was owned by Iraqis. One of the other things I had mentioned was my plan to go to the military trade fair in Baghdad in late April 1989.

'We must talk before you attend the military fair,' he said. 'It could be very interesting.'

I did not raise it with Balsom, but something interesting had also happened at the November fair which would turn out to be important at the military fair.

I had been transferred to the Hotel Melia, a very good hotel, smaller, more intimate and less frequented by other Westerners than the Al Rasheed. All the same, since the Iraqi government put up its guests at the latter, I asked Safa why I had been moved.

'We didn't want to make it obvious that you are a guest of the government,' he explained. 'We want you to have a lower profile.'

This lower profile extended to the airport, for Talib did not meet me before I cleared customs and passport control, as he had done previously. As a result, I had to go through a customs check for the first time in Iraq.

We had been cautioned in 1987 that Iraq insisted that visitors have an AIDS test if they were staying in the country for more than seven days. In the past, bypassing customs had meant no test for me, but this time I would be tested on the spot. Fortunately Matrix Churchill employees carried their own needles when travelling to Iraq in case such tests were required. The result was negative.

The customs inspection was very thorough, both entering and leaving. For the first time in my travels to Iraq I felt like I used to when going in and out of the Soviet Union or Bulgaria. You are locked in, at the mercy of the government, and it would prove a very difficult place to leave if you were in trouble.

The military trade fair was scheduled to take place from 28 April to 2 May 1989, at the international fair grounds in the Mansour district of Baghdad. Because Matrix Churchill was Iraqi-owned, Safa felt it was important to put on a show of strength, and insisted that I attend.

A British company called Promotor International Limited was the organizer for the UK companies. It had sent out a promotional leaflet describing the theme of the fair as 'Defence Equipment For Peace and Prosperity'. The leaflet encouraged British manufacturers to attend by stating: 'A high level of interest is being shown in the postwar Iraqi market, both here and in continental Europe, and now is the time to ensure a strong British presence in Baghdad as a national group.'

On Friday 21 April I was preparing to leave for Iraq when Roz told me that Balsom was on the line.

'I'd like to talk to you before you go off to Baghdad,' he said.

'I'm really busy at the moment,' I told him.

'I'll come to Coventry. It's important.'

'All right then. Come on Monday. Will it be all right to meet at my office?'

'Yes. I'll be there,' said the MI6 man.

On the Monday Balsom signed in at the gate, and after his name it said 'DTI'. I had warned him not to identify himself even as Ministry of Defence in case the Iraqis ever checked the gate records. A visitor from the Department of Trade and Industry would be easier to explain.

The meeting lasted three hours. I gave Balsom a tour of the shop floor and explained a bit about the machine-tool business. Then we drove to the Malt Shovel, where my sister-in-law, Mavis, arranged for us to have a private room in which to talk over lunch.

Balsom was insistent, though in a nice way, that I should obtain as much information as possible while at the Baghdad military fair. Because of my relationship with the Iraqis, he presumed, I would enjoy access to information from behind the scenes. Remember the people you meet, he told me, especially anyone in a uniform.

'Paul, you realize you are taking a serious risk, don't you?' he then asked.

145

'Yes, but I'm a careful man. I learned that in Eastern Europe and Russia.'

'The Iraqis are a different kind of people from the Russians or the Poles. These are dangerous characters. Ruthless. You would be in serious trouble if they discovered you were a spy.'

Balsom paused for a few seconds, apparently thinking hard, before asking me: 'Are you happy taking such risks?'

What an odd question, I thought. Happy? At the start there had been a bit of glamour, but that had worn off long ago. It had never occurred to me that I might have missed the thrill of being an agent. I had never thought it made me *happy* in any fashion. It was something I did to help my government – as simple as that. I wasn't sure how to answer Balsom's question.

'I don't really see it as risky,' I said to him finally, avoiding the 'happy' bit. 'I am cautious. I know when to stop pushing for an answer. Don't worry.'

'Well,' he replied, 'I've brought you something as a reminder. I want you to know exactly the sort of people you are dealing with. Especially Saddam Hussein.'

He reached into his briefcase and handed me a copy of a book with a black cover, entitled *Republic of Fear*. 'It's just been published. Read it. Under no circumstances take it into Iraq with you.'

I had been cautioned before by intelligence contacts. There had been brushes with foreign authorities, and you never forget detention by the KGB. But never before had I been warned so forcefully of the danger.

Balsom's keen interest in my information and his quick trip to Coventry led me to believe that the material I was providing was more important than ever. I felt I could control the situation and the dangers. I was not brave, but I was not stupid either.

To underline his warning Balsom insisted on talking with me again the next morning, before my British Airways flight to Baghdad. We agreed to meet at the Post House Hotel at Heathrow.

At home that night I dipped into the black book. Written by an Iraqi dissident under the name Samir al-Khalil, it was a chilling account of Saddam Hussein and his Ba'athist regime. There were stories of children's eyes being gouged out and people being dumped into vats of acid. As I sat next to Esther, who was doing the *Daily Telegraph* crossword, such brutality seemed a world away. And yet at the same time it sounded only too real.

Particularly harrowing was an account of the execution of opponents of the regime in Baghdad's Liberation Square. A Ba'athist Minister had told the crowds: 'The great and immortal squares of Iraq shall be filled up with the corpses of traitors and spies! Just wait!'

I hid the book before I left for Heathrow. I knew I could not take it to Iraq, and I certainly did not want Esther reading it. But I now knew a great deal more about the man to whom I would be carrying a gold-plated birthday gift. For, shortly before the fair, Safa had told me that the opening day, 28 April, was Saddam's birthday. He had suggested that a gift was in order for the Iraqi leader.

'You mean money or something,' I asked, incredulous.

'No, nothing like that. A token of esteem for Saddam. It should be related to the company. Nothing cheap. You don't want to insult him.'

I did not propose to give Saddam Hussein a two-ton lathe for his birthday. But some of the other directors and I finally came up with an idea. We had a model made of one of the 2 Series lathes, complete with CNC controls, about four inches high and a foot long, and very detailed. We had it gold-plated and mounted on a fine piece of oak. The total cost was about £3000.

I was carrying the model with me when I arrived in Baghdad. Safa was pleased when he saw it, and took it from me, saying that he would take care of delivering it. I never saw the model again, and I never met Saddam myself, so I assume that he received it.

By this time Matrix Churchill had opened an office in Baghdad. I had offered the manager's job to Mark Gutteridge, but he wanted to stay with Hi-Tek, so we hired Jim Bartholomew, whom I had known since my selling days in Eastern Europe. It was Jim we worked with when Hi-Tek and Jim's company, Renata, were in financial trouble in the early eighties.

Jim had opened a small office in Baghdad's Mansour district. Yass Abbas, the project manager at Nassr whom I had met in Bonn in 1987, came to work for us, along with several other Iraqi engineers. Safa had his own office for when he was in Baghdad, and several cars were bought for him and the staff.

A Toyota saloon was assigned to me when I was in town. I had a good laugh the first time I saw it, because the registration number was 556, but since the figures were in Arabic script they looked like 007.

At the military fair our stand was larger than the one we had had at the commercial exhibition the previous November, as we were showing a wider range of products. The first machines for the ABA contract were near completion and we obtained permission from the Iraqis to exhibit one of the big machining centres from the British company Flexible Manufacturing Technology. We had also reached an agreement to distribute some of BSA's machines in Iraq, so we demonstrated one of the firm's multi-spindle chucking automatic machines on our stand, set up to produce munitions components. In addition Matrix Churchill lathes were on show.

Matrix Churchill was one of the few exhibitors showing technology with civilian and military applications. One of the few machine-tool displays was from the Nassr factory, which was exhibiting one of the first CNC lathes assembled under the transfer of technology agreement with Matrix Churchill. 'Nassr', read the label on the machine.

There was no mistaking the military nature of the fair. Almost every other stand displayed strictly military hardware: artillery, machine-guns, rifles, radar, field radios, and models of tanks and fighter aircraft. British Aerospace had a model of a Hawk trainer at its stand; the real plane was sitting at Baghdad's airport. Dozens of other British companies displayed military goods of all types, and a list of defence products requiring export licences for display at the exhibition was four pages long.

The British were not the only ones marketing arms material at what was jokingly called 'Saddam's birthday bazaar'. The French also had military aircraft on display at the airport, and other goods at their stand. So did the Italians, the Chileans, the Swiss and many other countries. The Iraqis themselves had a display of full-size models of several missiles and artillery pieces.

Just before the fair opened there was a rumour that an Egyptian plane on its way to the event had mistakenly flown over the presidential palace. The plane had apparently been shot down by Iraqi anti-aircraft guns, and the unfortunate pilot had died. The story was never confirmed, but it seemed to indicate that the Iraqis were still jittery about Iran.

I walked over to the large stand where Carlos Cardoen's company was displaying its products. Cardoen greeted me as a friend and showed me round his exhibit, which was filled with models and photographs of defence products, ranging from artillery pieces and armoured vehicles to cluster bombs. The latter were intriguing devices, for, as he explained it, a 1000lb bomb casing would be filled with up to 400 smaller bomblets. The large casing was programmed to open at a certain altitude, dispersing the smaller bombs over a wide area. The bomblets would then explode, saturating up to 90,000 square metres.

'The area covered by mine is more random than those produced by the Americans,' Cardoen explained. 'But mine is much cheaper to produce, and much more profitable for me.'

I did a lot of intelligence gathering, collecting material from the various exhibits: leaflets on new weapons, brochures on the line of tanks for sale and descriptions of advanced military technology. As an exhibitor, it was easy enough for me to obtain such printed material.

The Iraqis, however, were very secretive. There were no leaflets at their stand – only models and mock-ups of the missiles, rockets and other hardware. Nevertheless, I was able to gather a fair amount of information about the Iraqi projects through the country's English-language newspaper, the *Baghdad Observer*. The Iraqis could not resist boasting about their achievements, so I simply collected copies of the paper.

Balsom's intense need to know about Iraq's missile project had given me an idea. One afternoon I asked some officials at the Iraqi stand if I could tour Project 1728. I had passed the building that housed the project on the way back from Nassr many times and there were hints that it was part of the long-range-missile development programme.

The Iraqis knew that I was the managing director of a company owned by their government, which made me something of a favoured guest. They were polite but steadfast in their refusal: there would be no visit to that installation.

Ten years earlier I used to spend days at such fairs in Eastern Europe and the Soviet Union – all pretty boring for the most part. Since Matrix Churchill had so many contracts in Iraq, I was kept busy outside the exhibition, but the diversion was not always pleasant. On Monday 1 May, the day before the fair was due to end, I was sitting in the Matrix Churchill offices in Baghdad with Safa, Carlos Cardoen, Augusto Giangrandini and Jim Bartholomew. The subject was the delay in shipping the machine tools for the two Cardoen fuse projects, and the mood was tense.

The Matrix Churchill lathes, Takisawa vertical machining centres and the Star CNC lathes for the contracts were all waiting for British export licences before they could be shipped to Iraq. We had delivery schedules to meet, Cardoen and the Iraqis were both anxious to get the project under way and £12 million was at stake for our company. Trevor Abraham and I had both been pushing the DTI for approval, but so far we had not been granted the licences. They told us that the matter had been referred to the Inter-Departmental Committee.

Then Giangrandini raised the possibility of shipping the machines to Iraq by a different route. 'You could send them out through a customer in Turkey or Eastern Europe,' he suggested. 'Or, better still, you could assign them to Industrias Cardoen in Chile.'

I could see Safa liked the idea. All he cared about was getting the machines to Iraq. He did not care what the export application listed as the destination. When he began to speak in support of the idea, I cut him off. 'There is absolutely no way that we could change the ground rules on these applications,' I said firmly. 'Any attempt to divert this equipment to another country would be discovered easily. I cannot withdraw the application that says "final destination Iraq" and then submit another one for the same machines that says "Chile". It would be stupid. And it's against the law.'

Safa refused to back down. The debate was heated and lasted thirty or forty minutes. Finally Safa slammed both hands down on his desk and stared at me.

'You will instruct Matrix Churchill to find an alternative country as a destination for these machines,' he ordered. 'You will send the telex immediately. And I want to see a copy of it after it is sent.'

Safa's demeanour always changed when he returned to Iraq, just as his wardrobe did. Gone were the Western suits and silk ties. Back were the open-necked shirts and khaki trousers. Gone too was most of his civility in dealing with me. He often lost his temper, apparently needing to show that he was my boss.

Refusing to send the telex would have cost me my job for certain. Safa would then have the chance to install his own managing director: most likely an Iraqi engineer who would follow every order. They could have drained the business and left it for dead. Yet lying to the government about the destination of the machines could land me in jail. That also was certain.

With only seconds to come up with a solution, I told Safa that I would send the telex and left the room. What I did not tell him was what else I intended to do. The telex should have gone to Peter Allen, the sales and marketing director, who dealt with licences. Instead I addressed it to Stephen Brittan. It was a name Safa would recognize, for Brittan was the project manager on the two Cardoen contracts. But Steve would have no idea what to do with the telex, and would wait for my call.

I sent the message and delivered a copy to Safa's office. Later that evening, in my room at the Hotel Melia, I phoned Coventry.

'You have the telex?' I asked Steve.

'Yes. What do I do about it?' he replied.

'Nothing. Just ignore it.'

'Fine. That's just what I was going to do anyway.'

No action was taken in response to Safa's demand. But if the licences did not come soon he would start issuing orders again. I was under no illusions: he would fire me for not taking the action he had decided was required to ship the machines.

At the end of the fair executives from the exhibiting companies were invited to a cocktail party in a large auditorium at the Al Rasheed. It was hosted by the Iraqi Minister of Industry and Military Industrialization, the principal procurement agency. The head of MIMI, as it was called, was Hussein Kamil, the son-in-law of Saddam Hussein. One of the Iraqis had told me that Hussein had saved Saddam from an assassination attempt in the early eighties and had been rewarded with marriage to Saddam's eldest daughter, Ragha. Hussein attended the cocktail party and I shook hands with him when I arrived.

Senior officials thanked the companies for attending. The last of the Iraqi speakers made a reference to Carlos Cardoen, calling him 'a very good friend of Iraq'. Then Cardoen delivered a speech on behalf of the exhibitors, promising even more trade and cooperation with Iraq.

The telex had just been a test; the truly nerve-racking dilemma came two days later. I was packing my bags to leave the country. I had more than a hundred pieces of literature and newspaper articles, including some thick catalogues, all about military products. As I had discovered in November, when the red-carpet treatment ended, the Iraqis were very thorough about examining baggage. There was no question of hiding the material. What will they think when they see all this military literature? I wondered. How will I explain it to them? What happens if they confiscate it?

I decided the truth, or at least a version of it, was the best response. Still, I was nervous as I filled my suitcase with the material for Balsom.

In the customs area my bags and briefcase were opened, and the contents spilled out onto a table. Holding up leaflets showing Cardoen's cluster bombs, an inspector seemed to have discovered a live bomb.

'What is this? Why do you want this? Where did it come from?' he demanded, loud enough to attract the attention of everyone in the vicinity.

'I've been to the military fair,' I explained, holding out my exhibitor's pass, which I had kept handy for this moment. 'I collected the literature for my business. My business, understand?'

The inspector did not answer. A supervisor heard the commotion and came over. He was an angry-looking fellow with a short, dark beard. I repeated my explanation. The supervisor flicked through the material and grabbed my exhibitor's pass. Turning it over, he compared my photograph with the one in my passport. Then he picked up the literature and began to sift through it more carefully. I could hear the watch ticking on my wrist. He seemed to take for ever. I glanced at my watch. Two minutes had passed since he had become involved. It seemed an eternity.

Finally the supervisor handed me back my exhibitor's pass and my passport. With a shrug he then dropped the literature on the table and ordered the inspector to repack my bags. He watched this procedure and then, with a nod, motioned me through customs and towards the waiting plane.

It was 19 May before Balsom and I found time to meet again. At a meeting lasting only twenty or thirty minutes I handed over the literature. He was very appreciative, thanking me several times. As he looked through it, I mentioned that we were having difficulty with the DTI. The licences for the Cardoen machines were being held up. While I was in Baghdad, I told him, there had been a rather heated discussion with Safa about the delays.

Balsom listened but made little comment. He was far more interested in the literature from Industrias Cardoen's stand and from the French companies. And, as in our earlier sessions, the material he liked most was the press cuttings about Iraq's plans for a long-range missile and other weapons systems.

From those earlier meetings I had gathered that Gerald Bull and his Space Research Corporation had some role in the missile project. Balsom looked up sharply when I mentioned that I had heard Safa and his company, TDG, were teaming up with SRC to acquire a company in Northern Ireland. The company, I had heard at the military fair, had something to do with missile technology. The name sounded like Lear Fan.

Gathering up the material to leave, Balsom asked if I had seen an actual missile. I told him I had been refused a tour of the installation where I thought the work was being done on the top-secret Project 1728.

'There were some models on display at the fair,' I explained. 'There was no way of telling how far along they are in building them.'

'A model is easier to construct than a real missile,' Balsom said. 'But they are well advanced in developing missiles. I'm certain of it.'

12

The British Airways 767 had just lifted off and was heading out over the Tyrrhenian Sea. Safa and I settled into our seats in Club Class and got our first drinks. It was Friday 14 July 1989, and we were on the way back to London after a trip that had taken us to Switzerland and Livorno in Italy.

As I watched Italy disappear below the clouds, I thought again about the Banca Nazionale del Lavoro. It was only natural. I had noticed one of the bank's offices on the drive from Livorno to the airport in Pisa that afternoon. Before that, we had been in Geneva and Lugano, signing contracts with suppliers for our contract with Nassr to build a £26-million hot-die forging plant in Iraq. It was being financed by Banca Lavoro. Once again, I had been surprised by the excellent rates the bank was giving us. I decided to have a word with Safa about the bank.

'How is it that Banca Lavoro can give us such good rates?' I asked, putting down my magazine and turning to him. 'Does their parent bank know?'

'The parent bank knows all about this,' said Safa. 'It is an arrangement between the governments. Between my country and the Italians.'

Safa was unusually talkative. Our relationship had been strained since the argument in Baghdad. Perhaps he was glad to be on the way home. Or pleased with the new contracts. Whatever it was, he told me a long and detailed story about the way Banca Lavoro had come to finance so many Iraqi projects.

In 1980 Iraq contracted for the construction of ten military ships with Fincantieri, a shipbuilder owned by the Italian government. The ships were four frigates, with short-range missiles, and six corvettes. Corvette-class ships are larger vessels and they were to be armed with rocket launchers, anti-submarine torpedos and helicopters from other Italian firms.

'The price was $2.6 billion. We made a large down payment,' explained Safa. 'But there were problems.'

Soon after the contract was signed, President Carter's administration told General Electric, the American firm supplying engines for the ships, that they could not be exported. Carter's people opposed providing any goods that would help either Iraq or Iran, although the countries were not yet at war.

When Ronald Reagan succeeded Carter as president, the war had started and American policy towards Iraq began to change. In 1982 the Americans resumed unofficial diplomatic relations with Baghdad. As part of this new policy, exports were again licensed for Iraq. The engines were shipped. The destination read 'the Italian navy'.

In 1984 the Italians sent the first of the ten ships. It reached Alexandria, Egypt, and was preparing for the last leg of the trip to the Iraqi port of Basra. But the US Congress applied pressure and blocked its departure.

'This, I think, was the work of the Israelis,' Safa told me with a glare. 'They have great influence with the Americans, especially in Congress.'

These ships were clearly aimed at the war effort, and would have made Iraq a major naval power in the Persian Gulf region. While Western nations were quietly selling dual-use technology and less conspicuous military goods to Iraq, there would be nothing quiet about ten warships steaming into Iraqi ports.

The Italians finished building the remaining ships, but could not deliver them. They also refused to return the Iraqi deposit or the other money paid at various stages of the work.

'As far as the Italians were concerned,' explained Safa, who grew quite angry as he related the story, 'they had completed the work and been paid for what they'd done. The failure to deliver was not their fault. They were not responsible. My government made it quite clear to the Italians. If they wanted any more business with us, they had better do something about the frigates. That was when the arrangement involving Banca Lavoro was established.'

The Italian government owned the bank and there was a long history of political manipulation. As Safa explained the 'arrangement', Rome agreed the bank would provide loans and other credits to Iraq at extremely low rates to make up for the financial loss of the ships.

These transactions were to be routed through the bank's Atlanta branch because it would not attract attention.

Safa finished his story and turned away. I thought about what he had said. The story made sense. If Saddam Hussein couldn't get the Italian ships, he could use low-cost Italian loans to pay for other military goods. It would explain the low rates the bank was giving us and other Western suppliers. For British and American companies were not the only ones benefiting from the Banca Lavoro rates. Germans, Swiss, Italians, Belgians, Yugoslavians, even the Russians – all were receiving advantageous rates from the bank for their deals with Iraq.

I never knew how much of what Safa told me was true. I soon discovered, however, that he was wrong about something important. The Atlanta branch had attracted attention, with unfortunate consequences for Matrix Churchill. In a bit of a turnabout, this time it was the intelligence service giving me information.

Shortly before noon on 18 August, John Balsom signed in at the gate of the Matrix Churchill plant and was brought into my office. I stood and shook hands, motioning him into a chair on the other side of my half-moon-shaped desk.

'How was the journey?' I asked as my secretary made coffee.

'Fine, no problem,' he said.

Once the coffee had arrived, Balsom opened his briefcase and withdrew a copy of the *Financial Times*. Handing it to me, he said: 'Seen this yet? I thought you might be interested.'

I glanced at the headline and, alarmed by it, quickly read the article beneath. US federal agents had raided the Atlanta offices of Banca Lavoro two weeks earlier, on 4 August. They'd shut down the office, questioned employees and confiscated thousands of pages of documents. The records supposedly described the bank's loans to Iraq and companies doing business with Iraq. They came to billions of dollars and the paper said it had been done without authorization from bank headquarters in Rome. Authorities were examining the records to discover the names of companies that received the loans. The story suggested the firms might be part of an Iraqi military purchasing network.

I laid the paper on the desk. I was surprised by the raid. Then again, the whole arrangement with the bank had seemed strange. Not even Safa's explanation had quite satisfied me.

'This is a shock,' I said to Balsom. 'I had no idea it had happened.'

'Yes, quite a surprise all round. What's the effect on your business?' he asked.

I thought for a minute, reviewing in my mind the Matrix Churchill contracts financed by Banca Lavoro.

'There's very little exposure with regard to products manufactured by Matrix Churchill, except for the transfer of technology and ABA contracts,' I said. 'But I'll alert the financial director so he can work out the implications of this.'

I faxed a copy of the article to Safa in London. I assumed he was unaware of the raid; otherwise I was certain he would have let me know.

Our largest contract involving Banca Lavoro, I explained to Balsom, was the new hot-die forge project for which I had been signing contracts with suppliers in Switzerland. But the contract was still in the early stages. If the deal fell through, it would not be a significant loss to the company.

I was uncomfortable with the transaction anyway. It was outside our field of experience, but Safa had insisted that we provide quotations. I'd come to believe that his reasons had more to do with TDG's bank account than with the Matrix Churchill order book.

The issue had first come up on a trip to Baghdad earlier in the year. Safa had called me into his office and handed me a copy of an unsigned contract between Nassr and Thyssen Industries, a large German company. It was to set up an advanced hot-die forging plant in Iraq. It was a turn-key contract, which meant Thyssen would put up the building, supply and install the machines and get the plant up and running. It was a sizeable venture, with a bottom-line price of £26 million.

Forging is the step before a component is worked by machine tools. With a hot-die forge, hot metal is compressed into a preformed mould. The moulding is removed when the metal cools and the forging is removed. Then it is turned, ground, milled or otherwise machined into a final component.

Matrix Churchill's only experience with hot-die forging had been selling machine tools to forging companies. But Safa had something else on his mind. 'Take the contract and come up with a competitive proposal,' he told me. 'But that is the price. It cannot be any more than £26 million.'

A couple of days later I was at Nassr chatting with two Iraqi engineers who had heard we were putting together a quotation for the plant. Neither man said as much, but I sensed they were uncomfortable with the prospect of Matrix Churchill winning the contract. We were novices compared with Thyssen.

But, soon after I returned to Coventry, the technical staff had put together a bid, and not long afterwards Safa signed the contract. It was clear that he had tremendous influence at Nassr – or somewhere within the Iraqi government.

When I saw the contract itself I had a bit of a shock. The deal was between Nassr and Technology Development Group, Safa's London company. Matrix Churchill would do the work, but TDG would collect at least 10 per cent commission on the £26-million order.

This was not the first time Safa and TDG had taken a commission from a Matrix Churchill deal, and the practice was not unusual. For example, on both Cardoen contracts, TDG had received substantial commissions. Some of the payments went out of Matrix Churchill accounts to TDG accounts in Zurich and Paris. But 10 per cent on a £26-million order was an unusually large commission.

It was negotiating with suppliers for the forging contract, I explained to Balsom, that had taken Safa and me to Geneva and Lugano. We had signed agreements with several companies to supply equipment for the project.

The technical know-how would be coming from a Swiss company in Lugano. It was called Schmiedemeccanica, known as SMB, and it had been Safa's choice. I had wanted to select a German company, but Safa insisted on SMB. It was obvious that he was very friendly with the company's president, Gianni Martinelli. Later, I was told that Safa had a 17 per cent shareholding in SMB.

What interested Balsom most, however, was the Livorno end of our journey. Safa and I had missed the last plane out of Lugano and Martinelli had lent us a car and driver for the five-hour drive to Livorno. When we arrived at our hotel in the Italian port city at 10.30 that night, there was a note. We should meet Fadel Jawad Kadhum and the others at a nearby restaurant. I hadn't known Fadel was going to be in Livorno. Safa hadn't even told me why we were going there.

Italians eat late and the restaurant was still crowded and noisy when Safa and I walked in. Seated at a large table in one corner, we found not only Fadel but Carlos Cardoen and his top man, Augusto Giangrandini. The Chileans greeted me warmly.

'What were they doing there?' asked Balsom, interrupting the story.

'I wondered the same thing,' I told him. 'I was still in the dark.'

Safa and I ate our meals and the others drank and talked. I was sitting next to Giangrandini and it was loud enough for me to be able to ask him what was going on in Livorno. He was never one to keep a secret and seemed to enjoy talking about all sorts of deals.

'We have a factory here,' he said with a broad smile. 'You must have driven past it on the way in. High walls. Gargoyles on the top of the fence. Cosmos Cardoen.'

'It was dark. I don't think I saw it. What do you manufacture?'

'Underwater vessels.'

'You mean submarines?'

'Small ones.'

He also told me that evening that the Iraqis were having discussions with Marconi Underwater Systems, a British company, but he did not go into detail.

It turned out that Safa and Fadel were negotiating with Cardoen to acquire underwater technology, presumably to build submarines. The following morning, Safa and Fadel accompanied Cardoen and Giangrandini to the factory. I was not invited. Safa had kept a secret of whatever was going on with Cardoen and his submarines. Two weeks later I made a five-day trip to Baghdad to discuss details of the forging contract, but the submarine business was never mentioned again.

As we sat in my office Balsom and I talked a bit more about relations between Banca Lavoro, Matrix Churchill and Safa. Beyond a hope that it made things tougher for Safa to operate, he didn't seem particularly interested in the raid on the bank. After one o'clock, we drove to the Portofino, one of my favourite Italian restaurants, in nearby Kenilworth.

Over lunch and a bottle of Chianti, Balsom and I chatted about our families. I'd always found him quite likeable, and he seemed to return the feeling. He said he was going to America in a month to get married. I talked a bit about my son, David, who was in the Coldstream Guards doing a stint in Northern Ireland, and my daughter, Sue, who had graduated from Kent University.

Driving back to Coventry to drop Balsom at the station, I raised the export licence issue. I told him that I couldn't understand why the licences were not forthcoming for the two Cardoen contracts.

'From what I hear, it's the Foreign Office creating the problems,' he said. 'Let me find the name of someone for you to talk to there.'

Since Balsom was about to do me a favour, he asked for one himself. He said he'd like me to come down to London and spend a day with his boss and some technical experts from his office.

'They have a lot of questions they'd like to put to you about what you've seen in Iraq,' he explained. 'I said I thought you'd be willing.'

'Well, you know, I will do it if it's necessary,' I told him. 'But we have to do it such a way that I can explain where I am to Safa. It's a problem if I'm gone all day.'

'We'll think of something.'

After dropping Balsom I arrived back in the office about three o'clock and telephoned Gordon Cooper in Cleveland. Balsom's news about the raid concerned me. However, I was more worried about the continuing delay in the release of the export licences. But I imagined Gordon might be a bit more alarmed.

There was a long pause after I told him the news. Clearly he was as surprised as I had been. The raid had apparently received very little press coverage in the USA.

'Bloody hell,' he said finally.

Most of the projects arranged by Safa through Matrix Churchill Corporation in Cleveland were financed by the Atlanta branch. All of them, Gordon thought, included a hefty commission for Safa. Even money that Gordon thought should have gone into the Matrix Churchill account was transferred instead into accounts that Safa had in the Bahamas and the Isle of Man.

Gordon made a few telephone calls and called me at home that night. He said Paul Von Wedel, who had visited the Coventry plant in 1988, had been questioned by the federal authorities. But Christopher Drogoul, the manager of the Atlanta branch, was in Paris on holiday when the raid occurred. Cooper didn't know if Drogoul was back in America yet.

I later learned what had happened to Drogoul. He had not gone directly back to Atlanta, but instead had flown to London for an emergency meeting with Safa and an Iraqi banking official, Sadik Taha. Only after conferring with them had he returned to America. Yet Safa had kept the whole thing secret from me.

On 4 September I was in London on business with Safa. Balsom had asked for a brief meeting, so we got together at Ye Olde Cheshire Cheese, a pub just off Fleet Street. He said he had thought of a way for me to manage a day with his technical people.

'I've got the name of the fellow at the Foreign Office you should see about your export licences,' he said. 'It's Rob Young. He's head of the Middle Eastern Affairs division.'

I jotted down the name and listened to Balsom's solution.

'You call Young and get an appointment to see him,' said the intelligence officer. 'Best would be early in the day or late in the afternoon. Then we'll work our session around that. Should provide you with a perfect excuse.'

'Sounds good, John,' I said. 'I'll ring Young and try to get an appointment as soon as possible.'

Balsom then handed me a copy of the *Observer* of 3 September. There was an article by Alan George about the Iraqi arms-buying network. He said the Foreign Office had blocked the attempt of TDG and Space Research Corporation to buy Lear Fan, the former aircraft plant in Northern Ireland. He said the government wouldn't allow the purchase because Lear Fan's carbon-fibre technology could be used in missiles. And he had also identified TDG as one of the shareholders of Matrix Churchill. I'd mentioned Lear Fan to Balsom before. He asked if I could add anything that wasn't in the press cutting.

Lear Fan's carbon-fibre material was originally used in aircraft. It was extremely strong and lightweight, which also made it useful for missiles. The company had gone into receivership in 1985 and the factory had been closed up. Early in 1989, I told Balsom, Safa, Fadel and TDG had joined with Gerald Bull and SRC to form a company called Canira, for Canada and Iraq. The company was set up to buy Lear Fan.

'Dr Fadel told me they had wanted the plant for the carbon-fibre technology, but he didn't say exactly what they intended to do with it,' I explained. 'They planned to train Iraqi engineers at the plant. He was very angry when our government refused to allow the purchase.'

What tripped them up, I believed, was applying for a development grant with the Northern Ireland Development Board. The board needed approval from the government in London. Because of the sensitive nature of the plant's technology, the purchase had caught the attention of the Foreign Office and been stopped.

'My opinion is that, if they'd not got so greedy and gone for the development grant, they would have succeeded,' I told the intelligence man.

A week later we met again. I told Balsom I had called Rob Young at the Foreign Office and had an appointment for the end of the day on Friday 22 September. Balsom seemed quite pleased, and said he would arrange the session with his people.

'Where shall I meet you?' I asked him.

'Why don't you take the train down to London,' he said. 'I'll pick you up at Euston. Plan on an early train.'

This was the first time we hadn't set a meeting place. It seemed odd. But I told him the arrangement was fine, although I really couldn't afford to spend a whole day talking with intelligence officials right then.

At the time I was under considerable pressure from the press. Since the first articles in the *Financial Times* and the *Observer*, the press had latched on to Matrix Churchill and its role selling machine tools to the Iraqis in a big way. Articles had tied us into the Banca Lavoro scandal simply because the Italian bank had financed some of our contracts with Iraq. I discussed the press comments with the other directors and we considered not responding to the dozens of telephone calls. But I decided to give a couple of interviews. We had nothing to hide.

The newspaper that seemed to know the most was the *Financial Times*, so I returned a call from one of their reporters, Richard Donkin. In an interview with Donkin I told him some of our machines had been sold to Baghdad to make parts for artillery shells. All of them, I emphasized, had had proper export licences.

'Even if some of the machines had gone into defence areas, I don't see anything wrong with that,' the article quoted me saying. 'They cannot produce anything but that which will contribute to the making of conventional type weapons. We have hidden nothing.'

The quotation was accurate enough and the other directors and I thought we'd weather the storm. But I was about to learn that the controversy in the press was making it more difficult to get our export licences approved at Whitehall.

In fact, I later came to believe that the stories were planted by officials in the Foreign Office to generate pressure to stop exports to Iraq by Matrix Churchill and other companies. There would be no way to prove it, but the stories were obviously coming from government officials. I knew from Balsom and others that the Foreign Office were the ones opposing us. It didn't make sense that anyone at the Department of Trade and Industry or the Ministry of Defence would be trying to sabotage us.

Later in September another press story appeared that deepened the anti-Iraqi sentiment in some quarters of the government. It also chilled me.

A journalist working for the *Observer* had been arrested trying to leave Baghdad. He was accused of spying, and the Iraqis were threatening to execute him. From the press, I learned that Farzad Bazoft, the son of a wealthy Iranian oil executive, had lived in England since 1975. He had gone to Iraq earlier in September to investigate a mysterious explosion at a secret missile plant at Al Iskandriyah, near Baghdad. The press claimed that the blast killed dozens of people, but the Iraqis acknowledged only nineteen deaths.

According to the newspapers, Bazoft and an Englishwoman who was working as a nurse in Baghdad had posed as a doctor and his nurse and driven to the plant one day. Allowed into the plant in their white medical smocks, Bazoft had taken photographs and soil samples. Bazoft had returned alone the following day. I was told that when he tried to get the British embassy to send the photos and soil back to London for him, they refused. So he had them with him when he tried to leave the country on 15 September. The Iraqi secret police stopped Bazoft at passport control and dragged him away to solitary confinement.

It was a frightening episode for me. How many times had I broken into a cold sweat as I moved through passport control leaving Iraq? The fear also struck hard because I knew about the secret plant. Matrix Churchill had been asked to supply a specialized lathe to turn solid-fuel charges into shapes for missile propellants. The lathe was to go to the plant, which was called Al Qaqaa.

A Matrix Churchill engineer had visited Al Qaqaa to examine the set-up for the lathe. He found that the Iraqis wanted to install it in a blast-proof room, where it would be operated by remote control. The lathe they sought was far more precise than those manufactured by Matrix Churchill and needed to be specially configured. With that as an excuse, I had turned down the request for a quotation. I wanted nothing to do with providing machines to manufacture missile fuel.

Bazoft's arrest forced me to reconsider my work for the intelligence service. I was meeting two or three times a month with Balsom and providing him with information that he clearly believed was very important. I had smuggled papers out of Iraq. I had asked questions about projects in which I should have had no interest. I had tried repeatedly to visit some of Iraq's most secret military installations.

I had always assumed that I was in control, that the risks could be managed. Many times, however, Balsom had reminded me of the dangers I faced in Iraq. Bazoft's arrest reinforced those risks. I vowed to be more cautious than ever, making this promise to myself even as I was being drawn deeper into the espionage world with my planned debriefing down in London.

Balsom met me as planned at Euston on the morning of 22 September. A chauffeur-driven black Ford Granada took us to Carlton Gardens, a small close off Pall Mall, near Buckingham Palace, where we entered one of the houses.

Inside I was introduced to three men, all of whom used only their first names. 'Peter' was obviously in charge, the man Balsom had said was his superior. The other two introduced themselves as 'Mark' and 'David'.

We exchanged greetings and took seats at the dining table. Balsom opened with a brief summary of my assistance to the intelligence service. Then he retreated to the rear of the room, turning the debriefing over to Peter and the other two.

'Now then Mr Henderson, what do you know about Project 1728?' asked Peter, apparently intent on wasting no time.

Project 1728 was rumoured to be Iraq's ambitious program to develop a ballistic missile capable of delivering a nuclear or chemical warhead. Its range was supposed to be anywhere from 600 to 1200 kilometres. But the information I had obtained pointed in another direction.

'There are a lot of rumours about that project. I can't give you any first-hand knowledge of what it's like inside the project building. The Iraqis have kept that one very secret. I haven't been allowed in, although I've asked about it several times. From snippets I've picked up, I'd say Project 1728 involves modifying Scud missiles from the Russians to give them a longer range.'

'Why do you think that?' said one of the junior men.

'It's connected to work done at the Nassr factory, but it's not on the same site,' I replied. 'I have lots of dealings with Nassr. They bought two standard machines from us for Project 1728. We don't know what they intend to manufacture with them. I have no real evidence that it's Scuds. This is just the information that is being fed back to me by our service engineers who installed the machines. And I've talked about it with Jim Bartholomew, our office manager in Baghdad, as well as a senior engineer at Nassr named Jabbar.'

'Please show us where Project 1728 is located,' said Peter, handing me a pointer.

I walked over to the wall-sized aerial photograph of Baghdad and its surrounding area and indicated a rectangular factory building thirty-seven kilometres north of the city, on the road to the far larger Nassr establishment.

'Is it heavily guarded?' asked one of the men.

'All the plants have military guards and are surrounded by high walls and towers. This one looks the same as the others.'

I moved the pointer a few inches on the map. 'Over here is a large military barracks. I've passed it many times on the way out to Nassr.'

'Tell us about Nassr, please,' instructed Peter.

The vast factory complex north of Baghdad was where Matrix Churchill had done most of its business with Iraq. Since then, I had been to Nassr many times. Each time I had seen more of the latest technology. I described the machines from Germany, Switzerland, the USA, Japan, France and Britain. Some production lines were turning out commercial goods: parts for cars and lorries and so on. Others, I explained, were dedicated to components for artillery shells and half-ton bombs.

We also discussed the Cardoen contracts and implications of the unsuccessful attempt by Safa and Gerald Bull to purchase Lear Fan in Northern Ireland.

'What else do you know about Bull and his company, Space Research Corporation?' asked Mark. 'Have you done business with them?'

'We are right now,' I said. 'SRC was trying to assemble a fuse-manufacturing facility for Iraq. They couldn't do it. Didn't have the commercial expertise. The Iraqis asked me to see if we could help them out.'

The intelligence men were extremely interested in our contract to provide machine tools to manufacture components for a rocket three metres long. We called it the 'ABA contract'. They referred to it as Project 144.

I explained that ABA was one of five sections of Project 144. The overall project involved the manufacture of industrial robots and development of a long-range missile. The two Iraqis heading the project were Brigadier General Rahim and Brigadier General Marouf.

165

I had brought a set of blueprints for the design of the small rocket. Steve Brittan, the ABA project manager in Coventry, had had them prepared for me, although he had no idea what I intended to do with them. Now I pulled them from my briefcase and placed them on the table. The drawings showed such elements as the design for the warhead booster and a carrier for the retractable fins at the rear of the rocket. The fins were designed to flip out once the rocket emerged from the firing tube. I slid the drawings across to Peter.

'May we have these?' he asked.

There was a look on his face that I had seen there all day: the look of an expert attending to a business he understood perfectly.

'By all means. They're copies I had prepared.'

'What is this rocket for?' he asked.

'I've been told that it's for a mobile rocket launcher. It's a Yugoslavian design known as Ababel.'

He seemed surprised. 'Do you know anything about Project Babylon?'

'Do you mean the "Lion of Babylon?" I've heard about that. We were asked to do some quotes. It involves refurbishing Iraqi tanks by a Polish firm and the manufacture of tracked vehicles.'

'No. Project Babylon is something different. A long-range gun being developed by Bull. A "supergun".'

Peter seemed to believe the rocket was a projectile for this so-called supergun. He suggested we adjourn for lunch.

The five of us walked to Pall Mall and stopped at a small, older building. There was no name on the outside, but there were security cameras. Just inside the door was an attendant in livery who opened the inner door so that we could pass into a bar. We had a drink and went upstairs to the dining-room.

The tables were well spaced, ensuring confidentiality. Ours was in a corner and the tables on either side of us were empty. Gradually I steered the conversation round to a matter of concern to me and Matrix Churchill: the delay in granting the export licence for the Cardoen machines. This was the issue that I intended to raise later at the Foreign Office.

Three ministries shared jurisdiction over export licences for machines such as ours. The DTI was the lead agency. But the Foreign Office and the MoD were consulted on applications with potential military uses. Balsom had explained to me earlier that the Foreign Office was the obstacle to approving the licences.

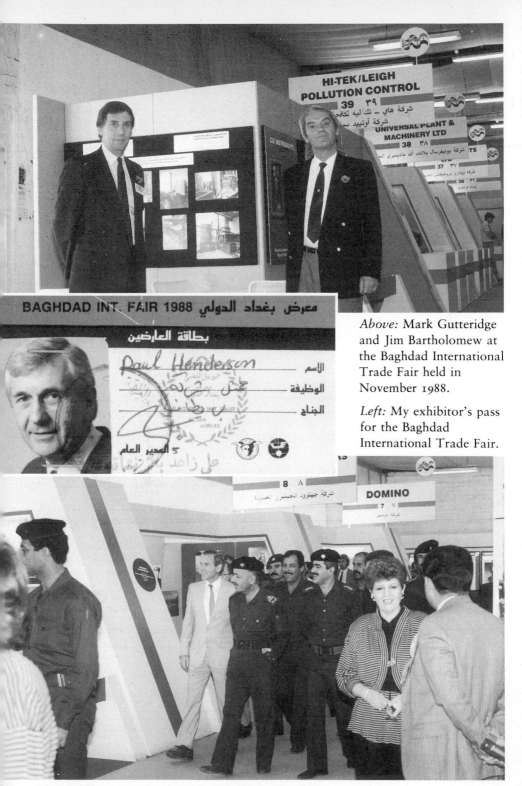

HI-TEK/LEIGH
POLLUTION CONTROL
39 ٣٩
شركة هاي ـ تك/ليه لمكافحة
شركة أوتييد سد

UNIVERSAL PLANT &
MACHINERY LTD
38 ٣٨
شركة يونيفرسال بلانت أند ماشينري المح

37 ٣٧
شركة ويلارى بروهيئمبر المحد
36 ٣٦
شركة قرامير

BAGHDAD INT. FAIR 1988 معرض بغداد الدولي

Above: Mark Gutteridge
and Jim Bartholomew at
the Baghdad International
Trade Fair held in
November 1988.

Left: My exhibitor's pass
for the Baghdad
International Trade Fair.

بطاقة العارضين

Paul Henderson

الاسم
الوظيفة
الجناح

المدير العام

8 ٨
شركة جمهوره انجينير المحدودة

DOMINO
7 ٧
شركة دومينو

The British Ambassador showing Iraqi military personnel around the UK pavilion at
the Baghdad Military Fair held in the spring of 1989.

VISITORS 24-1-89

NAME - COMPANY	VISITING	IN	OUT	DATE/REMARKS
MR BERNER				
MR JOHNSON				
M. WOOD				
KONO	B DOUGLASS	11.15	1.20	
MR DIXON				
BTI	MR HENDERSON	1.15	3.00	
MR PERRY				
MULTIPAS	J. CARTER	11.20	11.34	
M CUTTERIDGE				
HI TEK	R ALLEN	11.20	1.00	
B MORTIMER				
KENNAMETAL	A WRIGHT	11.50	2.35	
G. HODGE				
POWER PLANT	P. JAMES	11.55	1.20	
MR ANDRESS				
RANK XEROX	H. MAYNE	11.50	1.01	
D. ELLIS				
POTHROCE	C GOFF	12.10	12.54	
MR. PEARCE				SPECS
MR ICOE				
MR JONES				
MR FAULKNER				
ARC	G COATES	1.0	3.55	
MR GUSTAFSON				SPECS
MR ERIKSON				
MR HEDMAN				
VOLVO (SWEDEN)				
MR LEACH				
KENNAMETAL	A RICHARDS	1.15	2.45	
MR RUSSELL				
FSR	A MAYNE	1.44	3.20	
MR ALLEN				
ARC	K SHELDON	1.57	2.35	

VISITORS 18-8-89

NAME - COMPANY	VISITING	IN	OUT	DATE
LONG				
ROHM	WRIGHT	9.35	11.47	
STEPHENS				
XEROX	N. COOK	8.40	11.42	
WOOD				
SANDVIK	AVCOTT	9.45	9.58	
DUTTON				
HERTEL	BURNLEY	9.55	11.44	
MR BROWN				
JUNGHEINRICH	R HAYMAN	10.18		
MR STEAD				
WHITFORD CONTROL	J. DAVIES	10.85	11.55	
MR IRELAND				
PFANDER	A WRIGHT	10.27	11.03	
MR WHITE				
C CROWTHER	MR HOBDAY	11.05	11.56	FLOOR THD
C DENBIGH				
MTA	N RENSHAW	11.06	12.10	
MR McNALLY				
LNS UK	(?) COPE	11.15	12.21	
MR FROC				
MTA	K DAVIDSON	11.2	12.58	
MR BOLTER				
BTI	MR HENDERSON	11.30	3.10	
DOWNING				
SES	GANLEY	12.03	12.13	
MORTIMER				
KENNAMETAL	WRIGHT	12.16	12.39	
KELLY				
JOHNSON				
ETCHRINE	BONEHAM	12.25	2.14	

VISITORS 11-9-89

NAME - COMPANY	VISITING	IN	OUT	DATE/REMARKS
ROBBINS				
WHITEGATES	T. ANDERSON	2.45	3.35	
B. COX				
THAME ENG	K BARRETT	2.50		
G. SAUNDERS				
SIGMA	J. GANLEY	2.52	3.16	
I ENG				
BT.CON	REC	2.55	3.06	
BHUDRA INDIA				
PRINE CORPS	S. REID	3.20	4.30	
BALSON	HENDERSON	3.51		
DTI				
MILES				
XEROX	MAYNE	3.58	4.50	
M. CORNFOLD				
R THOMPSON				
ROCKWELL	J. ADAMS	5.25	6.44	
	TUES 12.9.89			
BARKER				
CZ INS	HORLOR	8.10	4.40	
BIRCH				
CONCEPT				
BERTSKY	G COATS	8.19	4.47	
GREENHILL				
SKETCHLEY	VENDING	8.20	4.30	
B ROURKE				
BEECHWOOD	JAMES	8.21	8.45	
BREE				
A DISPLAY	ALLEN	8.23	3.52	
HALL				
JOHNS				
COURTAULDS	CHRISTOPHER	8.39	9.57	

VISITORS 27.10.89

NAME - COMPANY	VISITING	IN	OUT	DATE/REMARKS
THORPE				
ROBBINS				
CCV POLY	MCLENNAN	12.17	5.42	
MR HAWKES				
SQUARE D	G MONCUR	1.47	5.39	
WHITMORE				
KONICA	PARKER	2.25	2.51	
JS TRANS				
CORPHA LTD	IAN PENTITH	2.48	3.42	
MR DONKOR				
MR THOMPSON				
ROCKWELL	J ADAMS	3.0	4.04	
MR BALSON				
DTI	G HENDERSON	3.10	5.09	
	SATURDAY 28.10.89			
F WEBB				
WEBB	D NICHOLS	8.10	11.50	
AUDY				
B & S	CONTRACTOR	8.18	1.20	
DAVIS				
AHS	CAR VALET	9.35	10	
J MAY				
B & S	CONTRACTOR	10.30	12.0	
	MONDAY 30.10.89			
B TURNER				
SKETCHLEY	VENDING	6.23	8.00	
MR DONKOR				
CONCEPT	A AVCOTT	8.00	4.00	
MR BIRCH				
CONCEPT	A AVCOTT	8.01	4.00	
MR BARTITUS				
CONCEPT	A AVCOTT	8.03	4.00	
ANDY + 1				
B & S	CONTRACTORS	8.16	5.55	

VISITORS — 1-12-89

NAME - COMPANY	VISITING	IN	OUT	DATE/REMARKS
MR ALLEN				
H + B	K BENBOW	9-20	10-25	
MR BAGLEY				
ALPINE ABRASIVES	A WRIGHT	9-22	10-30	
MR SKEATING				
DONALD COLLINS	B O'DEA	9-24	10-30	E.BRIDOUX
MR DUNHILL				
CEJ TOM	T/CONLAN	9-26	1-05	OUTSBOX
TICKLE				
SPROUL				
WRAGG	V ALLEN	9-34	11-05	
BALSON				
DTI	HENDERSON	9-35	10-55	
MR EDWARDS				
MR USHERWOOD				
R XEROX	A MAYNE	10-0	11-0	
S. FREE				
UNIVERSAL	I KEY	10-03	10-20	
MR HARGAN				
KENNAMETAL	M HAHN	10-06	2-58	
MR BROOK				
TAYLOR ALDER	P. ALLEN	10-10	12-30	
MR McMELLAN				
HOT MARKETS	R McCALL	10-21	10-21	
MR CURTIS				
ECKARDT	B BURT	10-21	3-30	E754UHY
MR HAWKINS				
R PRIME COUR	P AHLUWALIA	10-28	12-11	
SWAIN				
SALTER				
EURO	C RICK	10-28	11-13	
JAMES				
SANDVIK	S DEWIS	10-33	11-14	

VISITORS — 23-3-90

NAME - COMPANY	VISITING	IN	OUT	DATE/REMARKS
MR THOMAS				
MR HUDSON				
SANDVIK MCTOOLS	R KENNING	1-15	1-45	
MR GRASLING				
NEW BROS	SHARING	1-35	1-58	
HOTWIRE CON POLY				
METCALLAN	O TEACHING CO	1-00		
MISS ROSE O'KELL				
PENROSE	G. BLOOMER	1-00	12-15	
MR. PARISH				
KENNAMETAL	S DAWS	1-28		
K BACON				
MR GARDNER	G BLOOMER	1-45	2-07	
O I				
MR FRANKLIN				
DESOTO	D SUTTON	1-50	2-15	
MR HAILBROOKES				
WITHAMS	W BANKS	2-06	2-22	
MR PICHECKE				
BIRCKS LITHO	R McCALL	2-50	3-00	
S. KOTSIOPOLO				
COV POLY	DR THORNEYCROFT	3-00	3-38	
	MONDAY 26-3-1990			
B TURNER				
SKETCHLEYS	VERDINC	6-15	7-52	
MR PALNEIL				
HERTEL	S DEWIS	8-17	9-07	
I MAN				
B-S	GREEN	8-35		
WHENHAM				
TRIDENT	RANDALL	9-05	16-04	
BALSON				
DTI	HENDERSON	9-35	11-21	

VISITORS — FRIDAY 20-4-1990

NAME - COMPANY	VISITING	IN	OUT	DATE/REMARKS
SUE	SKETCHLEY	8-50	11-0	
REVIE				
AUTOCIM	BAIRD	8-56	10-47	
STREET				
FORSLUND				
HERTEL	THORNEYCROFT	8-54	12-09	
BANDY				
S - P	CLAYTON	9-22	10-55	
MR LISSAMAN				
QUALITY STANDARDS	C HORLOR	9-23	11-17	
BALSON				
DTI	HENDERSON	9-35	10-57	
CHILDENER				
VERNON	BROWN	9-40	12-04	
BRIGGS				
IMPACT	WRIGHT	9-55	16-18	
MS FREE				
UNIVERSAL	C BLOOMER	10-22	10-30	
LUSTY				
OLD ENG	PAYNE	10-45	11-54	
PARNELL				
HERTEX	WRIGHT	11-33	12-51	
STIRLING				
C.S.J	AUCOTT	1-34	1-45	
HARVEY				
E + Y	MAWBY	12-07	1-29	
MR BALFES				
MR BLAKES				
ALBA	MR DOWNES	12-43	3-09	
MR BANFIELD				
ISCAR	B FRANKLIN	1-15	2-8	

VISITORS — 26-4-90

NAME - COMPANY	VISITING	IN	OUT	DATE/REMARKS
MS MARKHAM				
HARRISON SUPPLE	R McCALL	1-10	1-30	
MR BALSE				
DTI	MR HENDRESSY	1-17	2-58	
MR TAUSETT				
MR SEATON				
STARTRITE	P ALLEN	1-56	2-23	
MR COCHRANE				
P E FANUL	P JAMES	2-00	3-29	
CHARLTON				
CUSTOMS	MERRYMAN	2-05		
DUNPHY				
M T A	RICH	2-29	2-45	
EVANS				
INFAST	BLOOMER	3-13	3-47	
	FRIDAY 27-4-1990			
B. TURNER				
SKETCHLEYS	VERDIN	5-20	6-20	
2 MEN				
NEWAGE	AUCOTT	8-39	1-20	
MCNALLY				
WB MAC	PAYNE	8-40	9-19	
DIXON				
	CRICKS	8-53	9-16	
ASH				
G G M AVT	EVANS	9-00	9-48	
MR THOMPSON				
OSAL - AB	P JAMES	9-16	9-56	
MR FISHER				
ENDIA	A WRIGHT	9-18	9-47	
MR JARIN				
TECHNOLOGY	MR HARRIMAN	9-22	11-40	

Record of visits to Matrix Churchill in 1989 and 1990 by my controller, John Balsom, whose surname was spelled in several ways by the gate attendant.

Me, right, with Brigadier Nazar, centre, of the Ministry of Military and Industrial Procurement at the Matrix Churchill stand during the Baghdad Military Fair in 1989.

Number plate of the three-litre Toyota saloon that was provided for my use in Baghdad. I was amused by the fact that the figures – 556 in our numbering system – in their Arabic form spelled the code-name of spy fiction's legendary James Bond.

Reprint ■ 20 October 1989

Machinery

and production engineering

INTERFACE

cial ssue

...NAGEMENT LED ...Y-OUT AT ...ACHINE TOOLS

...e Tools Ltd., the Coventry based machine tool
...der, has been acquired by its Board of Directors in
...on with the British investment consortium, TMG
...ng.

...st in a number of
...nt led buy-outs within the
...ol industry, has occurred at
...very successful three year
...tructuring and growth
...Company
...rchill Ltd., the banner under
...company will now trade, has
...order book which currently
...xcess of £40 million and a
...ange that has achieved global
...on as one of the most
...rs in the world.
...lders of London based TMG
...ering include a British
...ent bank plus a number of
...s investors
...0% of equity will be taken up by
...Directors of Matrix Churchill

...Henderson, previously Sales
...or, has succeeded John Wareing
...Managing Director and is joined on
...w Board by Malcolm
...neycroft, Lawrie Izzard, Michael
...nes, Dick Burnley (formerly
...opean Finance Director with
...cinnati Milacron) and John Harris,
...has been appointed Sales Director.

Products and services offered by Matrix
Churchill Ltd. will continue to include
the full range of Churchill CNC lathes,
and Matrix thread and cylindrical grinders,
and Matrix machining centres.
Additionally, new product launches are
already planned for 1988 including a
major new range
Manufacturing strategy has already
been revised to accommodate the
company's success. Volume production
techniques utilizing standard "building
block" modules and latest CIM
technology will be employed
In commenting on the acquisition Paul
Henderson stated "the change of
ownership will significantly strengthen
our foundations. The Board of TMG
Engineering obviously view us as a
growth business and our progress will
expand at a greater rate than would
have occurred had we remained with
TI. TMG plans continued investment in
both the Coventry machine tool plant
and the Foundry at Newcastle Under
Lyme."
The planned future program of
investment will ensure that Matrix
Churchill Ltd., a company with a proven

and respected pedigree extending over
more than 100 years, maintains its
position as UK market leader by
meeting manufacturing industry's
requirements for quality, reliability,
advanced technology and first class
after-sales support.

*Paul Henderson
– the new Managing Director*

...ENDERSON
...into a world force

MATRIX CHURCHILL

...the company's new logo incorporating the established Matrix and Churchill names.

Above: Lead feature on me and my
role in Matrix Churchill in the
trade journal *Machinery and
Production Engineering*.

Left: Front-page article on the
Iraqis' acquisition of Matrix
Churchill and the new
management structure, in a
special issue of the company
magazine, *Interface*, published
in November 1987.

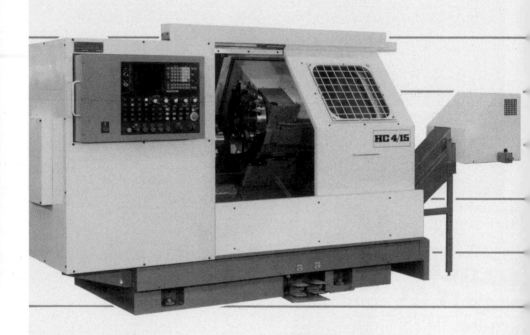

Matrix Churchill's HC4/15 CNC lathe, which can be used for munitions production. Eight were supplied to Iraq's Nassr establishment under the ABA contract.

P N 1124 The Governor, H.M. Prison, Wormwood Scrubs,
P.O. Box 757, Du Cane Road, LONDON W12 0AE

My prison number at London's Wormwood Scrubs.

champagne toast with Trevor Abraham and Peter Allen after the collapse of the
Matrix Churchill trial at the Old Bailey on Monday 9 November 1991.

Recent photograph of me with Sue, Esther and David and his wife Karen.

'You know I'm having difficulty with licences for the Cardoen project,' I said to Peter. 'The delay by the DTI is causing us real problems. We might lose the contract if we can't ship the goods soon.'

I explained that the government had known all along that our machine tools could be used for military purposes, but that they also had commercial applications. Cutting off our licences at this point could have a devastating effect on our business.

'The issue of machine-tool licences is difficult, particularly for machines that have dual-use technology,' said Peter. 'I have some sympathy for your position.'

He seemed to understand my dilemma and I interpreted his remarks as support from a high-ranking intelligence official.

Following lunch, we returned to Carlton Gardens. After a review of the morning session and a few more questions, Louisa Symondson arrived.

She had been my controller for a brief period and I spent another two hours or so answering her questions about my recent trip to the Soviet Union and the visits to factories there with the delegation from the Machine Tool Technologies Association. These were the early days of *glasnost* and she was interested in the impact of this new freedom on the manufacturing sector.

By the end of the afternoon I was tired. The intelligence agents seemed to have exhausted their questions, if not their voices, and we exchanged handshakes. Peter seemed especially grateful as he escorted me to the door of the safe house and thanked me.

Balsom and I walked along the Mall, down to Horse Guards Parade. The sun was still shining, but an autumn chill was in the late afternoon air. As we walked. Balsom thanked me as well and said it might be some time before we spoke again.

We stopped across the road from one of those typical government buildings. Balsom told me it was the Foreign Office. 'Rob Young is the man to see,' he remained me.

Before leaving, he also repeated that he was off to America to get married. If I needed to speak to someone in his absence, I was to call the number he had given me and ask for Peter.

I crossed the street and went to the desk in the lobby of the Foreign Office building. A security officer directed me down a long corridor, lined with stacks of documents.

In preparation for the meeting. I had written a four-page, single-spaced brief outlining our case. This had given me an opportunity not only to argue for releasing the licences, but it had been a chance to examine the progress at Matrix Churchill as it approached the end of its second full year under the new management.

Employment had climbed back to 800. The £2.4-million profit of 1988 was expected to nearly double by the end of 1989. The domestic market was good, and exports were going to more than forty countries. CNC lathes were accounting for 70 per cent of our turnover, and the new range of advanced lathes was expected to be ready for the market next year. If the projections were on the mark, Matrix Churchill would be Britain's largest machine-tool company by the end of 1990.

The brief said CNC machine tools could be used for civil and military applications. It also pointed out that, if British machine-tool companies did not sell to Iraq, there were plenty of competitors from other nations queuing up to do so.

I was candid about the impact of a refusal to grant the licences. Iraq was a high-volume, short-term market. There were a number of major commercial projects being planned there, such as plants to produce cars by General Motors and trucks by Daimler-Benz, the parent company of Mercedes-Benz. In addition, we had major orders already under way. It wasn't an exaggeration but the unfortunate reality – jobs would be lost if we could no longer sell to Iraq.

'At least 300 jobs would be declared redundant and the impact on local sub-contractors would be equally devastating,' I warned in the brief.

As I was ushered into his small office, Rob Young was pleasant enough, but stiff and official. He listened in silence as I went over the points on the brief. He didn't give any indication about whether he would support approval or not.

I left the meeting less optimistic than I had gone in. Still, I believed Balsom wouldn't have sent me to Young if the Foreign Office official hadn't been somewhat sympathetic to my case. In a later report on the meeting, Young said that I had not guaranteed that the machines would not be used in munitions production.

With the help of John Nosworthy of the MTTA, I had also set up a meeting with Lord Trefgarne. He had replaced Alan Clark as Minister of Trade at the DTI after Clark moved to the Ministry of Defence.

The meeting was set for five o'clock on Tuesday 26 September at the DTI offices at 1 Victoria Street. In advance, I had sent a copy of the brief prepared for Young to Eric Beston, the head of export control at DTI. When Nosworthy and I were ushered into Trefgarne's office on the eighth floor of the building, Beston was there along with the Minister and another export official.

Trefgarne greeted us pleasantly. He said he was pleased to see us. He had read my brief and wanted to hear the case in person. 'We're anxious not to prevent exports needlessly,' he said. 'It will help if you can take me through a few points.'

There were nine outstanding licences, one of which was for the four Japanese Star lathes for the Cardoen contract. The Japanese government had by this time issued the export licences to Takisawa for the twenty-four machining centres, and I told Trefgarne as much.

'I understand that the UK government must move with caution on these licences,' I said. 'But the delays are running into months now. Our competitors in Germany and Switzerland have no difficulty obtaining licences.'

'I'm sympathetic,' said Trefgarne. 'We'll try to have it resolved as soon as possible, Mr Henderson.'

There had been much press coverage about TDG and our business. An article in the *Financial Times* had been illustrated by a diagram of the Iraqi military buying network, with a branch labelled 'Matrix Churchill'. Trefgarne's only concern seemed to be who was actually running Matrix Churchill. I assured him that, although we had Iraqi directors, the day-to-day operations were in the hands of its managers, all of whom were British.

I acknowledged that the machines had commercial and military uses. I also knew the intelligence services had informed all of the Ministers about the real use of the machines. So I stressed the Iraqi plans for automotive projects such as the Daimler-Benz and General Motors plants. And the loss of jobs if the licences were refused.

Trefgarne appeared sympathetic. I left with his promise to act as quickly as possible. I expected him to push hard for them.

What I had no way of knowing then was that a tremendous row was going on behind the closed doors of Whitehall. William Waldegrave, a minister in the Foreign and Commonwealth Office, was adamantly blocking the Matrix Churchill exports to Iraq. His concern was not the use of machine tools for conventional weapons, such as artillery shells. He was arguing that any type of machine tool could be used to help Saddam Hussein develop a nuclear bomb.

'Screwdrivers are also required to make H-bombs,' he had scrawled across one memo concerning Matrix Churchill licence applications.

Waldegrave's attitude was unrealistic. Not only would his position have cost hundreds of jobs in the machine-tool industry; it would have halted almost all machine-tool exports to Iraq.

Officials at the DTI and the MoD had a more accurate view of the matter. They were arguing in briefing papers and meetings that there was no good reason to stop the sale of Matrix Churchill machines to Iraq since there was no evidence that they were being used to produce nuclear weapons or missiles. The DTI also made the point that the Iran–Iraq war, the reason for restrictions on exports to both countries, had been over more than a year now. But Waldegrave refused to change his position, setting the stage for a critical showdown between ministers from all three departments.

At four o'clock on the afternoon of 1 November the three ministers who were to decide the fate of our export licences met in a room at the House of Lords. They were Lord Trefgarne from the DTI, William Waldegrave from the Foreign Office and Alan Clark from the MoD. Each was accompanied by assistants who would take notes of the discussions. By later accounts, the session became heated.

Trefgarne told the others that Matrix Churchill had made a strong case for approving the licences and he favoured doing so. The machines, he explained, are dual-use technology which may not have any military application. He also repeated my assurance that the Iraqis had no say in the day-to-day operation of the company.

Waldegrave objected. Because intelligence information showed Iraq was trying to develop nuclear weapons and missiles, any effort that could help Iraq rebuild its military capability was a mistake. 'The Defence Intelligence Staff at the MoD are right now conducting a survey of Iraqi procurement activities in the UK,' he said.

Clark expressed surprise at news of the survey. He said he would see that it was stopped immediately.

'It is outrageous that the DIS should spend its time seeking ways to damage our trade surplus in this way,' he said.

Clark, who had been friendly to me nearly two years earlier, said restrictions on trade with Iraq and Iran should be dismantled.

'These guidelines were political in origin,' said Clark. 'There is no link to the security of the United Kingdom. Further, the political situation has changed. The ceasefire in the Gulf has been in effect for so long that there is little likelihood of it being broken.'

Trefgarne agreed, saying: 'The Matrix Churchill lathes are not state-of-the-art and, in any event, they would not affect a renewed conflict between Iran and Iraq.'

Waldegrave responded that the guidelines were still essential to protecting British interests by keeping arms suppliers from believing they had a green light to ship to Iraq. Anyway, he said sternly, any change in the overall guidelines would have to be debated at a higher level of the government.

Under pressure from the other two ministers, Waldegrave softened on the Matrix Churchill licences. They could be approved, he said, as long as the DIS continued monitoring shipments to Iraq by Matrix Churchill and other British companies. Trefgarne and Clark accepted the demand. The decision was taken to approve the export licences.

Later in the month the DTI notified the company that its licences had been approved. The machines, which had been waiting at our shippers, packed and ready, were shipped to Iraq. It had been a long and unnecessary battle with officialdom. The government knew all along what the machines were used for. They hadn't blocked similar sales before, and there was no reason why they should have done so this time.

It had taken a lot of time and effort, but at least the government was allowing us to legally sell machine tools to Iraq again. I was hoping I'd seen the end of my troubles with the government.

A similar debate was going on behind closed doors in the USA. The raid on Banca Lavoro in August 1989 had caused anxiety over some officials in the administration of President Bush. About $2 billion of the loans that the Atlanta branch had supposedly made without authorization from headquarters in Rome were guaranteed by the US government. Now, the Americans were planning to guarantee another $1 billion in loans to Iraq, but evidence of Iraqi wrongdoing in the bank scandal led to warnings about the granting of further credit.

The Americans also had strong evidence that Iraq was engaged in a worldwide effort to buy technology for its arms industry, including the manufacture of nuclear weapons. As early as December 1987 information on the Iraqi arms network provided to MI5 by Mark Gutteridge had been passed on to the CIA. Since then there had been a steady sharing of intelligence between the two countries.

For example, in November 1989 the CIA issued a secret report on the repercussions of the Banca Lavoro scandal. The six-page document included a boxed section about the Iraqi weapons procurement network that was drawn directly from the information provided to British intelligence by Mark and me. The report identified the companies that we had passed on to our handlers, such as TDG and TMG, and it described how TMG had gained control of Matrix Churchill in 1987.

The outcome of the debate in America was much the same as it had been in Britain. The Americans approved the additional $1 billion in credits for Iraq and even stepped up the issuance of export licences for sensitive dual-use technology.

Not long after Matrix Churchill received the news on its licences in late November 1989, Balsom called and asked if he could come up to Coventry. He had an idea he wanted to put to me.

On 1 December, a Friday, I picked him up at the station and we drove to the Malt Shovel for lunch.

'Paul,' Balsom said after we had sat down, 'we're interested in turning one of the Iraqis working in the procurement network. Which one would you suggest?'

I wasn't surprised. I'd been told much earlier in my espionage career that my information was useful in helping the intelligence services identify candidates for turning. But the matter hadn't been raised before by Balsom and, to be honest, I didn't think he had much chance.

Over the months, I had told Balsom about Safa al-Habobi and Anees Wadi. They both liked to live well. They drank and enjoyed expensive restaurants. They gambled not only at casinos in London, but, when we travelled to Germany and Switzerland, they would go off together gambling until the early hours of the morning.

By this time I wasn't sure what Wadi's role was in the Iraqi operation. I was beginning to think he was senior to Safa, that he was the number one. He clearly had great influence with Safa, and he was smooth enough to conceal it if he were the senior person. But Wadi didn't seem a likely candidate for a double agent. He seemed too confident and had too much wealth of his own. He wouldn't need the money MI6 could offer in exchange for his help.

I told all of this to Balsom and added another reason. 'Anees is spending more time in America,' I explained. 'He has set up another company in California. It's called Bay Industries and I think he is using it to buy American equipment for the Iraqis. I hear he even bought a $2-million house in Beverly Hills. He spends most of his time in America these days, as does Safa.'

With the press attention on the network and the outcry over Farzad Bazoft's arrest, Safa and Fadel had even talked recently about moving the whole TDG operation to another European country. They didn't find Britain as friendly as Germany, France or Switzerland.

As for Adnan and Hana, the two Iraqi engineers who worked with Safa at TDG, they didn't seem to offer much scope for Balsom. I explained that they were fairly low in seniority and probably wouldn't have access to the information that people such as Wadi, Safa and Fadel possessed.

'They toe the party line,' I said. 'They don't live it up and I don't think they go out much. I think they're both pretty wary of the regime in Baghdad and they want to stay in line so they can remain here. I don't think they'd be worthwhile even if you could turn them.'

'What about Fadel Kadhum?' I asked Balsom.

'Dr Fadel is too straight,' I replied. 'He's a member of Saddam's Ba'ath Party and the general director for the legal department of the Ministry of Industry. He's much too privileged to be approachable. And he's not in the UK much. He is not a resident and spends most of his time in Iraq.'

'Then I believe we have narrowed it to Dr Safa,' said Balsom.

I saw Safa as the most vulnerable of the group. He had grown accustomed to the Western lifestyle that Matrix Churchill's money was buying for him. While he also seemed to be accumulating money of his own in Switzerland, France and the Bahamas through commissions, he did not have Wadi's wealth. I was suspicious that he was a womanizer, although I never had any proof. But there were a lot of little things, from the night at Club 56 in Bonn to his staying late in London long after we'd done with business.

'There may be a small chance that Dr Safa would be willing to cooperate if he was promised asylum if anything happened,' I said. 'That, and you would have to pay him a substantial amount of money to do it. But I doubt it will work.'

We talked a good while longer. Balsom finally decided to turn up on Safa's doorstep at his home on a Saturday morning, tell him who he was and ask to talk to him.

Safa was security-conscious already, with the surveillance cameras at the house and the security door to the bedrooms. I'm sure he knew he was being watched, so an approach from the intelligence men wouldn't startle him.

I was concerned, however, that the plan would put me at risk. Safa was a high-ranking Iraqi intelligence officer, as was Fadel. If MI6 failed to turn him, it might not take him long to work out that the intelligence service had someone inside Matrix Churchill. Someone who had access to him as well as sensitive Iraqi projects. It could only be me.

A few days later Balsom telephoned. They had changed the strategy a bit. Balsom's colleagues had decided to telephone Safa first, identify themselves as MoD officials and ask to meet him at his home. Safa had refused, saying it was unacceptable. But he did agree to see them at the TDG offices, which by then had moved to Chiswick, in West London, closer to Heathrow than the previous offices in Mayfair.

'They went to see him at the TDG offices,' Balsom told me. 'But he wouldn't meet them alone. He had Mr Hana with him all the time.'

They'd seen there was no chance of turning Safa. He probably knew they were intelligence agents from the start, not MoD people. They pumped him with a lot of questions about his activities in Britain and left.

'He was very clever,' said Balsom. 'We got nowhere with him.'

Safa never mentioned the incident to me. However, he began spending less time in Britain. America seemed to command a lot of his time, and I knew from Gordon Cooper that the Iraqis had some big deals in progress there even after the collapse of the Banca Lavoro arrangement.

Matrix Churchill itself had weathered the Banca Lavoro scandal without a catastrophe. Peter Allen, our sales director, had gone out to Baghdad after the Atlanta raid to meet Iraqi banking officials, who had promised to find alternative means of financing the contracts guaranteed by Banca Lavoro. By the end of 1989 funds were provided through the West Deutsche Landesbank in Düsseldorf. The contracts were moving again, albeit behind schedule.

As the company's business with Iraq continued, so did the information that I was providing to the intelligence service. As Matrix Churchill was owned by the Iraqis, I was on preferential treatment when I visited Iraq and was allowed to see and discuss many things which were normally barred to foreigners. I was also able to learn about the projects of other companies through contacts with Matrix

Churchill's office in Baghdad. The result of this unique access was that British intelligence had a clear window on companies from all over the world that were building the Iraqi armaments industry.

For example, I had told Balsom what I had seen when I visited the Al Hutteen establishment. There was a completely automated production line for 122mm shell casings supplied by a Swiss company, Georg Fischer. As with most of the Iraqi facilities, this was a very sophisticated operation, with CNC lathes, overhead gantries, conveyors, measuring devices and so on. Also at Al Hutteen, I saw 155mm shells being produced on our CNC lathes, including nubs being turned on the twin-spindle lathes that we had supplied.

At the Nassr establishment, I had described to me the busy operations in Shed C. There, the Iraqis were producing 122mm shells, 80mm mortars and components of the Ababel rocket on machines supplied by Matrix Churchill and Wickman Machine Tools. Nearby, in Shed D, I saw a shell-forging line supplied by SPS of West Germany plus equipment for missile production, such as a process for coating the inner tubes of missiles to withstand extreme heat.

In early 1990, I had been invited by Adel al-Alami, the director general of Nassr, to witness the final take-over of an automated forging shop, which I was told had been supplied by a West German company. The component I watched being produced was a tank turret, but I was suspicious of the ultimate uses for this forging operation.

I had already been asked by the intelligence people about Project Babylon, which was the giant Iraqi supergun designed by Dr Gerald Bull. Among the material I had given them was a copy of the Matrix Churchill contract with Bull's Space Research Corporation to develop artillery fuses and drawings for a 210mm shell that the intelligence service concluded was related to the supergun.

But when I examined the forging shop, I found more signs of what would become the infamous gun. There were very big computer-controlled internal and external turning machines manufactured by Ravensburg of West Germany. There also was a special honing machine designed to finish large internal bores to a very high accuracy. This, too, was manufactured in West Germany, but the name of the supplier was not visible. Altogether, it appeared to me that this shop was capable of producing supergun barrels.

On a visit to another facility, the Nissan 7 Factory, I saw 155mm artillery shells being produced on what I believe was an automated

CNC turning line supplied by BSA Machine Tools, and 122mm shells being turned out on CNC lathes from Colchester Lathes, another of the British suppliers to Iraq.

I provided the intelligence service with the names of all these companies and the production occurring at the facilities I visited. Sometimes the details were sparse. But of Project 144 at Nassr, for example, I learned enough to provide MI6 with a virtually complete description of the Iraqis' efforts. The project comprised five sections:

1. The manufacture of industrial robots at the state electrical plant at al Quadissiya under a licensing agreement with a Bulgarian company, Beroe. The robots were in fact designed by a Japanese firm, Fanuc, and Beroe had obtained a manufacturing licence from them.

2. A 600km-range missile for which a facility was created to manufacture an inner coating that would allow the missiles to withstand temperatures of up to 3000 degrees Celsius and a burn time of 10 minutes.

3. A 900km-range missile for which Matrix Churchill had received drawings of some components. This missile had a diameter of approximately 1.5 metres.

4. An air-to-surface missile in the early stages of design.

5. The ABA project, which was the design and manufacture of the rocket to be fired from a mobile launcher with a range of 50km. Matrix Churchill had a contract to supply CNC lathes, together with CNC machining centres manufactured by Flexible Manufacturing Technology of Brighton. This was a Yugoslavian design and also known as Ababel.

A related project on which I provided intelligence information was the manufacturing of solid-fuel missile propellant at the Al Qaqaa establishment. Matrix Churchill had been asked to provide prices for special machines to turn the solid fuel, but we had declined the deal because of the danger involved. Nonetheless I had told MI6 all that I knew about it. I also shared information that I picked up about TDG's attempt to buy the Lear Fan plant in Northern Ireland to provide carbon-fibre technology for Iraq's missile programme.

After the military fair in Baghdad in April and May 1989, I had provided the intelligence service with as much detail as I could find about the Ababel and other missile projects, including technical details and press articles gathered from the *Baghdad Observer*. I also supplied details of Carlos Cardoen's activities at the fair, including the specifications for the thousands of cluster bombs that the Chilean's company was selling Iraq.

In addition, I told the intelligence service about the link between Cardoen and South Africa. Cardoen's fuse technology was South African and his personnel visited the country on a regular basis.

I supplied information about Project 1728, the modification of Scud missiles to give them longer range and better accuracy. I told Balsom that I had learned that 1728 was linked to the manufacture of the Condor missile, the joint project between Iraq, Egypt and Argentina to develop a missile capable of delivering a nuclear warhead.

Along with constant details about the financial set-up at Matrix Churchill, I informed Balsom about the investments in other companies by our parent firm, Technology Development Group (TDG). In West Germany, Safa and his associates had acquired interests in H&H Metalform, TDG/SEG and Neff Pressen. In Switzerland, they had acquired shares in Schmiedemeccanica. They also had signed a letter of intent to enable Matrix Churchill to buy 30 per cent of the shares of Flexible Manufacturing Technology on behalf of TDG.

The Iraqis also were buying technology in an effort to develop their own industries. I described the details and significance of negotiations by Nassr to transfer technology to Iraq. Among the agreements was the plan to manufacture Matrix Churchill CNC lathes and install a hot-die forge shop; the production of small CNC machining centres with Bridgeport Machine Tools; the large machining centres from Flexible Manufacturing; and CNC milling machines from SMW of Germany.

Through Gordon Cooper and other contacts of my own, I was also able to keep British intelligence informed about what the Iraqis were acquiring in America through the Matrix Churchill offices in Cleveland, Ohio. I believe some of those projects had potential uses in the manufacture of nuclear weapons, such as a carbide-tool plant built by an Alabama firm, XYZ Options; a glass-fibre facility under construction by a California company, Glass Incorporated; a centrifugal casting plant by Centrifugal Castings of Oklahoma; and a coil-coating plant set up by a Canadian firm.

Not only did I share all the technical details I could dig up. As with Matrix Churchill, I explained to the intelligence people that many of these American projects were also being financed by Banca Lavoro at preferential rates.

13

Most of us go through life without knowing what we want of it. I was not like that. From the time I walked onto the shop floor at Coventry Gauge and Tool, I knew what I wanted: to be involved with machines that made machines. There was a practical reality to the place that was almost romantic to me.

Over the years, of course, what I wanted had been refined. I had come to believe that the only way to save the company was to own it and run it myself. No one else seemed to care quite as much. The remarkable thing is that I got so close before events that I could not control snatched it away.

It happened in 1990. The year began with great expectations. Most of the machines for the Cardoen and ABA contracts had been sent to Iraq and we were working on a couple of other projects for the Iraqis. Business in Britain was picking up, with a big project for Rover Group and other orders. We'd not ended 1989 quite as profitably as expected, but even so we had earned £2 million and the order book for the new year made 1990 look good. Also, we would soon be ready to start building the prototypes for the new CNC lathes that would carry us into the future. All in all, I thought we'd weather the recession that was beginning to bite.

Then things started to go wrong. In January I was in Baghdad on a routine visit. I was having dinner with Mr Jabbar, the chief of production at Nassr, Jim Bartholomew, our office manager in Baghdad, and Bob Edwards, who was living there while overseeing the transfer of technology project at Nassr.

As the evening progressed and we had a few drinks. Bob started to complain about the lack of support from Matrix Churchill. I told him in no uncertain terms that this was neither the time nor the place to discuss it. He became very angry and I told him that his

178

loyalties were to Matrix Churchill, not Jabbar or Nassr. If he didn't understand that, I said I'd replace him.

Jabbar thought a lot of Bob and had obviously understood the conversation. As we left the restaurant he offered to drive me back to the hotel, which was unusual. When we got into his Toyota Land Cruiser, he took a handgun from the glove compartment. He said it was to protect himself.

'There are many enemies of the state in Iraq,' he said calmly. 'If necessary, I will use this on them.'

I was not sure this was a warning to me, but it reminded me of my worries about the failed attempt to turn Safa.

On 15 March, Farzad Bazoft, the London-based journalist accused of spying, was executed in Baghdad. Wearing a white Arab *dishdasha* gown, he had been hanged after allegedly confessing that he was a spy for Britain and Israel.

Margaret Thatcher's government had pleaded with Saddam Hussein not to execute Bazoft. After the hanging, the corpse was sent to the British embassy for return to Britain. The Iraqi information minister, Latif Nussayyif Jassim, used the opportunity to boast: 'Thatcher wanted him alive. We sent him home in a box.'

Few in the West believed that Bazoft was actually a spy, so the outcry in response to his death was loud and angry. The Prime Minister told the press the hanging was 'an act of barbarism deeply repugnant to all civilised people'. The British ambassador was recalled from Baghdad and there was talk of imposing trade sanctions on Iraq.

The execution had two effects on me. One was professional: a trade embargo would damage the business and cause redundancies. The old threat that the Iraqis might pull out entirely would be there again. However, there might be an opportunity in that. If they were hurried into selling Matrix Churchill, the management might get the chance to buy it cheap and return the company to British ownership.

The other effect was quite personal. I was sitting at the dining-room table at home when I opened the *Daily Telegraph* and read of the execution. The lace cloth on the table beneath the paper was a gift I had brought home for Esther from one of my trips to Baghdad.

I felt sick. For Bazoft and for me. I don't know how long I sat there staring at the newspaper while my coffee got cold. Here was a man hanged after being accused of doing the very thing that I had been doing for two years, spying on the Iraqis. Balsom's repeated warnings about the ruthless nature of the Iraqis. The stories from *Republic of Fear*. The attempt to turn Safa. Jabbar's handgun. It all came rushing back to me.

Be calm, I told myself. There's no reason to be afraid. You've been careful. You've controlled the risk. Bazoft was a journalist who made a mistake trying to get a story. You've been gathering intelligence for nearly twenty years. After a few minutes I collected myself, got in my car and went to the office. I had business to attend to.

A week after Bazoft's execution another death brought back the fear once more. Gerald Bull, the artillery designer, was murdered as he was about to enter his flat in an expensive suburb of Brussels. The press reports said he was shot twice in the back of the head and three times in the body. He was still holding the doorkeys when police found the body. In his pocket was $20,000 in cash. It looked like a professional job. There was speculation in the press the Israelis had stopped Bull because of his work for the Iraqis. That was no comfort for me. If the Israelis would kill Bull to stop his work for Iraq, what might they do to me?

At that time Matrix Churchill was not only working on Iraqi projects and largely owned by the Iraqis; it was also working with Bull's Space Research Corporation to build the fuse factory in Iraq. There was a lot of discussion with Safa and others about whether the project would proceed after Bull was killed. In the end the decision was taken to go ahead. It was business. This attitude continued even after the events of 11 April.

On that day, at Middlesbrough docks, British Customs and Excise officials seized eight steel tubes manufactured by Sheffield Forgemasters.

They were labelled as oil pipes for the Iraqis. But Customs claimed that the tubes were actually part of the barrel for a cannon 156 metres long. They called it the 'supergun' and claimed Bull had designed it the enable the Iraqis to fire nuclear warheads and other projectiles as far as Tel Aviv in Israel.

The press picked up immediately on the name 'supergun'. It was the sort of title that guaranteed front-page stories, particularly when paired with the mysterious death of Gerald Bull a fortnight before.

Two British businessmen were arrested in the supergun case. One was Dr Christopher Cowley, a Bristol-based engineer who had worked on the project for Bull. The other was Peter Mitchell, the managing director of Walter Somers, a foundry in the West Midlands where work had been done on the tubes.

These arrests alarmed me. In June 1988 Sheffield Forgemasters and Walter Somers had asked the DTI if they needed an export licence for the tubes, and were told no licence was necessary. Yet here were a project manager and the managing director of one of the firms involved facing criminal charges.

I'd known that the intelligence service had been interested in the supergun at least since 'Peter' had mentioned it during the safe house debriefing. It had arisen again at a meeting with Balsom on 5 March at the Royal Lancaster Hotel in London.

Balsom had brought a scientist with him who asked me a lot of questions about the ABA contract and what he called Project Babylon. The scientist left me with the understanding that Project Babylon was a huge supergun that Bull was constructing for the Iraqis. He had the impression that the ABA contract was for a projectile to be fired out of the gun. But I tried to explain to him that it was components for a rocket which would be fired from a mobile launcher.

Between Bull's killing and the seizing of the steel tubes, there'd been another action that also raised public anxiety about Iraq. On 28 March six people were arrested in London in what American and British customs officials claimed was an attempt to smuggle nuclear triggers to Iraq. The arrests led to stories about Iraq's attempts to develop a nuclear weapon.

The anti-Iraqi outcry grew louder. In Parliament and the press, the hanging of Bazoft, the supergun and the nuclear trigger cases became lightning rods for political attacks on Iraq. There were calls for a crack-down on all British trade with Baghdad and warnings that Iraq was further ahead in developing nuclear weapons than the West had known. I feared a backlash that could damage Britain's machine-tool industry.

What I had expected to be a year of consolidating the business and moving closer to a management buy-out was turning into a year of turmoil. And it was about to get more unsettling.

I was scheduled to leave on 21 April for a five-day trip to Baghdad. Safa was spending so little time in Britain that board meetings for the parent company were being held in Iraq. Two days before I was to leave I did the normal thing and phoned Balsom to tell him of the trip. He said he wanted to talk to me before I left and on 20 April we met in my office in Coventry.

Balsom appeared to be agitated. At first I put it down to the recent events concerning Iraq. Certainly, as an intelligence man specializing in Iraq, he had been quite busy. But as we chatted he seemed gruffer than usual, his questions more pointed. I got the feeling he didn't believe some of what I told him.

He wanted to discuss a project called K-1000. When he asked me if I'd heard of it, I said I had. But I didn't think it was the kind of thing to interest him.

In 1988 the Iraqis had approached us about about a proposal for machine tools to manufacture components for compressor pumps. The components were intricate and very precise. We had prepared an offer on the basis that we would work with one of three British manufacturers – Compair, Holroyd or Ingersoll Rand – with expertise in this area. Matrix Churchill would provide the machinery and equipment to manufacture the components and the other company would provide the technical know-how. However, nothing ever came of the offer.

A year later we received a pile of drawings of component parts that were listed as the K-1000 project. They came from the Badr General Establishment, a factory west of Baghdad. I had visited Badr General and not seen any military production. This time, however, the Iraqis asked us to manufacture the components because they wanted to make a prototype pump and test it before ordering the machines. So we made another proposal and won the order to manufacture some of the parts. However, other, more precise components were to be produced by a Swiss firm.

'I am sure we have some drawings I can show you,' I told Balsom.

I rang the sales department and asked for the K-1000 file. It was brought over and inside were the drawings for the most intricate parts, the ones that we had not been able to produce on our machines.

'Did you manufacture these parts?' Balsom asked as he examined the drawings of the parts.

'No, we didn't,' I replied. 'We did some work on compressor pumps for the K-1000 project. But these drawings were for components too intricate for our machines. The Iraqis sent them to a Swiss firm.'

Balsom seemed suspicious. For the first time I felt he wasn't being open with me. He asked why we hadn't provided the machine tools for these parts and I explained it again.

I was suspicious, too: of both Balsom and the Iraqis. With the supergun and nuclear triggers cases in the press, why was Balsom asking about compressor pumps? Were they connected with the supergun project? Or worse, with Iraq's work on a nuclear weapon? I began to wonder if maybe the wool had been pulled over our eyes by the Iraqis. Maybe the parts weren't even for compressor pumps. I had no way of knowing, and I told Balsom as much that day.

He didn't divulge anything else, but just asked me to see if I could find out anything more about K-1000 during my trip to Iraq.

Two days later I was sitting across the desk from Safa and Fadel at the Matrix Churchill offices in Baghdad. Safa seemed less friendly than usual. I asked them about K-1000.

'Why do you want to know?' demanded Safa.

I used the excuse of the supergun and nuclear triggers incidents, saying that I wanted to know if K-1000 was connected to either of those matters. Safa assured me it was not and I had the impression that he was telling the truth. However, both Iraqis seemed wary and suspicious of me.

Suddenly Fadel fixed me with a cold stare and asked: 'Why have you had so many meetings with the British Ministry of Defence?'

Since passing through customs at the airport this trip, I had been uneasy. Bazoft had been dead a month. The Iraqis were responding to attacks in the Western press with defiance. Saddam Hussein had gone on television and denounced the British and American governments for trying to intervene in his affairs. He had threatened to use poison gas to destroy half of Israel.

I was now confronted by a very troubling question. I'd only told Safa of one meeting at the MoD, which had been to discuss export licences. Yet here was Fadel asking why I'd had so many meetings. Was he fishing or did he really know? I was worried. I couldn't deny that I'd had meetings with the MoD because I wasn't sure what he did know.

'Dr Safa knows I've had meetings at the Ministry of Defence,' I told him, trying to appear unconcerned. 'You must remember that I told you in my monthly reports that the licences for Iraq were considered by three ministries. I regularly had meetings with all three in order to push the licences through.'

'Ah, I see,' he replied. 'How many meetings have there been?'

'I really don't know. Quite a few.'

Nothing more was said. But as I walked out of his office I could feel their eyes burning into the back of my head.

Perhaps Safa suspected nothing. He always treated me more like an employee when he was back in Iraq. I'd come to realize that, while they could be warm and friendly, the Iraqis managed their businesses in a completely different way from what I was used to.

On one of my earlier trips, for example, I was walking with Jabbar between buildings at Nassr. Outside the heat-treatment plant three or four workers were sitting in the shade. It was a hot, humid day and the lunch hour had just finished. 'They should be working,' Jabbar said, looking at me for agreement.

I didn't respond, thinking that he'd just tell them to get back to work. But he ran over and started shouting fiercely at the men, raising his voice very loud and chastising them for idling. Then he started hitting them hard about the head.

I was stunned by the ruthlessness of it. When Jabbar walked back over to me, still puffing from the exertion, I told him that if something like that happened in Britain we'd have the whole factory walk out on strike and more than likely the manager would be fired. He just shrugged.

'This is Iraq, not England', he said. 'We do things differently.'

After my encounter with Safa and Fadel, I flew back to London on Thursday 26 April. I went directly to the Post House Hotel at Heathrow. Balsom had arranged to meet me there to hear what I'd been able to discover about K-1000. But when I found him in the bar I had other things on my mind.

'How the hell would Fadel know that I had meetings with you and anyone else claiming to be from the Ministry of Defence?' I said to him before we even shook hands, barely keeping my voice below a shout. 'I bloody well never told him. Where did he get this information from?'

'Slow down,' said Balsom. 'What are you talking about, Paul?'

'I'm talking about Fadel accusing me of meeting with MoD people. He asked me in Baghdad why I was having so many meetings with them. I think he knows something.'

'Wait a minute. If he really knew anything, do you think you'd be sitting here? Or would you be in some prison in Baghdad? Let's talk calmly about this.'

Balsom had cautioned me in 1989 about possible leaks of information. He had said he was particularly concerned because MI6 had widened the network that was receiving my information. It had been going to the other ministries; and to the Americans, the CIA. He had assured me I was protected. There was no mention of my name in any of his reports – just a code-name and a number.

But the information was clearly being provided from inside Matrix Churchill. It wouldn't take a very intelligent person to ask: Who is giving the information to MI6? It has to be someone with access to Iraq and a broad range of information. They would suspect the managing director, figuring he has the best access.

I vented my fears to Balsom. He tried to be reassuring, saying there was little chance of a leak. He repeated that I wouldn't have been allowed out of Iraq if they knew anything about my intelligence work.

'Paul, do you want to stop helping us?' he asked finally. 'It would be a bad time, you know. We're very worried about what the Iraqis are up to, what with these nuclear triggers and all.'

'No,' I said. 'I'm concerned about what happened, but I'll go on.'

Driving home, I felt more on the edge than ever before. Where was the line between prudence and foolhardiness? I was beginning to wonder whether I really could control the risks to which I was exposing myself and my family. But, as often happened when I had these doubts, they were soon replaced by worries about the company.

Trade with Iraq was growing more complicated because of political events. In May the Iraqis responded to the British threat of sanctions with a warning of their own.

A senior official at Iraq's Ministry of Industry summoned representatives of British companies in Baghdad to a meeting. Among those who went was Jim Bartholomew, who ran our office there. He later told me that the Iraqi official had angrily denounced the British government for its verbal attacks on Baghdad and for delays in issuing export licences. The official warned that the Iraqis were considering their own trade embargo – against importing any British goods.

The British government was indeed delaying export licences for Iraq. Among the licences being held up was one of ours for the final machines on the ABA contract.

ABA was originally financed by Banca Lavoro in Atlanta. When the American government closed down the office there, the letters of credit were not honoured by the bank. Consequently new financing had to be found, which delayed the process.

When the first delays were encountered in 1989, one of our suppliers, Flexible Manufacturing Technology in Brighton, stopped work on the vertical machining centres they were providing for the order. Work had resumed only when the financing was approved at the end of 1989. By May 1990, Flexible Manufacturing Technology was ready to ship the completed machines to Iraq. Unfortunately, however, the export licence had expired. When we applied to have it validated again, the DTI told us it would have to be reviewed, since the political atmosphere was too volatile. If it leaked to the press that the government was allowing exports of sensitive technology to Iraq, there would be embarrassing questions in the House of Commons.

Behind the scenes at Whitehall there was great reluctance to be caught approving more sales to Iraq. While the ministers acknowledged that there were no security grounds for blocking the exports, even the formerly supportive Alan Clark was advising caution from his position as a minister at the MoD.

'In light of other developments,' he wrote to Trefgarne on 3 May, 'you may wish to give further consideration as to whether this is the right time to approve such applications.'

The indecision was causing even larger problems for other British machine-tool companies. For a change, Matrix Churchill was not in the worst shape because of delays in export licences for Iraq. Bridgeport Machines Limited, a British subsidiary of an American company, had a contract to transfer technology for a series of CNC machining centres. Colchester Lathes also had outstanding contracts. The entire industry needed to know what government policy was regarding the exports and future policy, so a meeting was arranged with Lord Trefgarne.

At 11.30 on the morning of 17 May executives from the largest companies, including myself, walked into Trefgarne's office to present our case and listen to his response. We explained that all the companies had put a lot of investment into the Iraqi market. The indecision was threatening to cause financial problems for the entire industry.

It was Mike Bright, the chairman of Flexible Manufacturing Technology, who put the matter bluntly to Trefgarne. 'We've had the supergun,' he said. 'We've had the nuclear triggers and Bazoft. But the industry has spent considerable time and money promoting its products to Iraq with the support and backing of the British government. What is government policy towards Iraq? We need to know. If you aren't going to issue the licences, then tell us so we can plan accordingly.'

'It's my intention to support you and the approval of the licences,' the minister responded. 'Obviously, recent events have caused problems. But there should be an improvement. The British ambassador will be returning shortly to Baghdad, which will improve relations between the countries. Furthermore, the DTI will be supporting British attendance at the trade fair in November. But on this last point, I would prefer that it not become public knowledge at this point.'

Before we left, the minister asked which licences were the most urgent. He was told they were the ones for Bridgeport, Flexible Manufacturing Technology and Matrix Churchill.

We all left the meeting feeling that Trefgarne would support us. We had never felt any different when we left the DTI, whether it was after a meeting with Trefgarne, Alan Clark or a lower-level official. Never once did I walk out of the DTI and think that I was getting less than 100 per cent support.

Trefgarne did fight for fast approval of the licences. But there was still opposition from the stubborn Waldegrave as well as others. Two weeks after our meeting with Trefgarne, Waldegrave had written to him asking for a three-month delay in issuing any new licences. He made the request even though he said in the letter that there was no 'incontrovertible evidence to suggest that the machinery in question will be used for anything but legitimate civil purposes'.

By the following month, however, Customs and Excise thought they had obtained evidence to the contrary. The source of the information was particularly galling to me.

We were still shipping spare parts and equipment to complete the Cardoen fuse contracts. At Cardoen's request we had shipped them through the Chilean company's forwarding agent in Bremen, where they were combined with some other material that Cardoen were having shipped. West German customs officials had intercepted the shipment and mistaken the Matrix Churchill components for part of some major arms shipment. They had passed on the information to Customs and Excise in Britain.

I believe the West Germans were trying to deflect attention from their own problems. By this time the country's aggressive press was raising questions about the advanced technology that West German firms were selling to Iraq. West German companies had been implicated in the supergun affair and there were reports that they had provided sophisticated machinery for Iraq's nuclear weapons programme. For my part, I also knew that the Iraqis had acquired a 50 per cent interest in H & H Metalform, a West German business which made metal-spinning machines useful in the missile and nuclear industries. The Iraqis also had bought interests in other West German firms.

HM Customs and Excise planned to use the information about Matrix Churchill passed to them by West German customs officials to begin an investigation of the British machine-tool industry, particularly Matrix Churchill.

At the DTI the news generated concern. Officials right up to the Secretary of State for Trade and Industry were worried about the impact on relations with Iraq. They also feared the possibility that the government's long-standing policy of approving exports with military uses might become public at an embarrassing time.

The anxiety was captured in a revealing memo written by a civil servant named Michael Coolican on 14 June. Coolican had just become head of the export control division at the DTI a couple of months earlier. With hindsight, I believe the memo was the first evidence I saw of the government's cover-up.

'Customs have *prima facie* evidence that current machine tool exports from Matrix Churchill and other UK companies under licence are being routed via Chile to Iraq for arms manufacture,' Coolican wrote to Nicholas Ridley, the Secretary of State for Trade and Industry. 'Evidence was available in 1987 to the same effect, but to protect sources ministers took a decision to let the exports go ahead. An investigation will clearly bring all these to light . . . Are the ministers willing to have the 1987 and subsequent decisions exposed and made the subject of court room argument? . . . The dirty washing liable to emerge from the action proposed by Customs will add to the problems posed by the [super] gun. For the DTI, the timing is extraordinarily embarrassing.'

A week later it was Ridley himself who shared the concerns about 'dirty washing' with 10 Downing Street. He did so in a four-page report called 'Trade with Iraq'. It was addressed to the Prime Minister, Margaret Thatcher, and copied to the Cabinet Overseas and Defence Committee, of which John Major was then a member.

Ridley expressed anxiety over the impact of any Customs action on relations with Iraq. While he stressed a desire to 'minimise' involvement in the Iraqi military procurement programme, he warned that further deterioration in relations could jeopardize Iraqi repayment of £1 billion in loans guaranteed by the British government through the export programme.

As Ridley saw things, any investigation into possible violations of export regulations by Matrix Churchill or other companies would alarm the Iraqis even more. Coming alongside the nuclear triggers and supergun cases, it might provoke sanctions on British sales to Baghdad and a default by the Iraqis on the £1 billion in government loans. Rather than a crack-down, Ridley asked for a meeting with the Prime Minister to discuss a relaxation of guidelines on exports to Iraq. The request was too late.

The day Ridley sent his memo to Mrs Thatcher, two Customs and Excise investigators arrived at the Matrix Churchill plant at Fletchamstead Highway. They played innocent for a while on the first day, claiming that it was a low-level visit. They had some questions about our business with Iraq, and said they represented the DTI, which I assume was meant to ease any worries of ours about a possible criminal investigation.

The principal investigator was a man named Christopher Constantine. He had dark, wavy hair and wore glasses. He was in his middle thirties, five foot ten and chubby. Over his suit he wore a green Barbour jacket. He didn't strike me as a very attractive sort of person, and in the following months I came to dislike him.

On 21 June, Constantine and a woman agent examined files of contracts at the plant. They established quickly that the Cardoen contracts were for a fuse plant and told Peter Allen, our sales director, that they believed the contract was a violation of export regulations. As they were leaving the plant that first day, the investigation took a decidedly rougher turn.

Constantine cautioned Peter Allen, Trevor Abraham, who had been Matrix Churchill's commercial manager before moving to a subsidiary, and Richard Seager, who had replaced Steve Brittan as project manager for Cardoen. He told them that they might face criminal charges and suggested that it would be in their interest to have solicitors present when the agents returned the next day.

On Friday 22 June the two officials came back. They didn't stay long, but took away copies of all the Cardoen documents. As they were leaving, Peter Allen stopped them and asked: 'We still have a substantial amount of tooling and spare parts to ship on the Cardoen orders. You've said the sales violate export regulations. What do we do about the remaining goods? And do we withdraw our engineers installing machines in Baghdad?'

'You'll need to talk to the DTI about it,' replied Constantine.

'Surely we should stop sending the machinery,' said Allen.

'Talk to the DTI.'

I had had nothing to do with the investigators over those two days. Most of what I knew, Peter had told me after they had left. But straight away I telephoned and left a message for Balsom at the intelligence number. When he called back he was reassuring, telling me not to worry. The visit was no doubt just routine. I certainly wanted to believe him. I didn't even involve our lawyers at that point. But in the back of my mind was the arrest of the managing director of Walter Somers.

A few days later, I flew out to Baghdad for routine discussions with Safa and some of the engineers there. I had called Safa with the news of the raid soon after it happened, but this trip I reassured him that we apparently had nothing to worry about. It was just routine. That view seemed confirmed around the middle of July. Peter Allen had rung the DTI about the remaining Cardoen equipment. The DTI had no problem with us completing the contract. The ministry confirmed this in writing on 27 July 1990. So we shipped the last of the Cardoen tooling and machine equipment and our engineers went to Iraq to install the machines for the fuse project. This was done with the full knowledge of the DTI. Certainly, I thought to myself, they wouldn't authorize shipping the goods if we had violated export regulations.

Towards the end of July, Balsom rang me several times trying to set up a meeting. I was busy. The plant shuts down for two weeks' annual leave from the first week of August, so it was a very busy time. I had to fly to Spain on business on 30 July. On my return Safa wanted me back in Baghdad on 1 August for a week of meetings. Finally I agreed to meet Balsom at the Post House Hotel at Heathrow when I returned from Spain on Tuesday 31 July.

Balsom had asked me previously to keep my eyes open the next time I was in Iraq. He was interested in any unusual military movements. So I had watched carefully when I was there in late June and early July. I had also questioned some of our engineers who were travelling to the various factories in and around Baghdad.

Now, as we sat in the hotel bar, Balsom was scribbling furiously on a note pad. I was telling him what I had seen on my last trip to Iraq, and what my engineers had described to me.

'A railway line runs along the road from Baghdad to Nassr, almost parallel to it,' I told him. 'Driving up to Nassr on my last visit, I saw fairly heavy train movement travelling south. Particularly tanks and other armoured and tracked vehicles on top of flat cars. I assume they were coming from the military barracks between Baghdad and Nassr. The highway was busier than usual with large trucks.'

By this time we had the threat of the invasion of Kuwait by Saddam's army. Troops were massing on the border. Balsom repeatedly questioned me about what the engineers and I had seen.

'Do you think he'll really invade Kuwait?' I asked.

'No, I don't think he will,' replied Balsom. 'He's basically flexing his muscles, but he won't go into Kuwait. He's got too much to lose.'

The following day was 1 August. I had been scheduled to fly out to Baghdad that night for a week of meetings with Safa. At the last minute he had called and said the trip would have to be delayed for a week. Safa had to leave Iraq himself for a brief trip overseas.

So I was sitting in my office that afternoon when John Nosworthy from the MTTA called. He said that the DTI had cleared all of the remaining licences for British machine tools including Bridgeport Machines, Flexible Manufacturing Technology and the others. All except the remaining Matrix Churchill ones, which included the machines for the ABA contract and five CNC lathes from an American company, Hardinge. We had already shipped five Hardinge machines earlier that year.

'Why would they clear everybody else's and not Matrix Churchill's?' I asked, thinking maybe there was more to the Customs and Excise investigation than I had been led to believe.

'I don't know. That's all the DTI told me,' said Nosworthy. 'I suggest you call them yourself, Paul. The man to talk to is Michael Coolican. He's head of export controls.'

So I phoned Coolican at once and repeated what Nosworthy had just told me.

'No,' said Coolican, 'that's not right. All the licences are cleared. The only one we can't give you clearance on at the moment is the five CNC lathes from America. We need to refer those applications to the Americans. But everything else is cleared, including your ABA machines. I'm just in the process of writing a letter to you and the companies.'

'Great, fine, wonderful,' I said.

I was being pressured by the Iraqis to ship the machines. I immediately sent a telex advising them that I'd spoken to Coolican and that the licences had been cleared. It was just a matter of getting the official letter, and then we would be able to ship.

The next day, 2 August, the world woke up to television images of thousands of Iraqi troops controlling Kuwait City and exchanging gunfire with a last-ditch resistance by a few Kuwaitis. The British, French and American governments condemned the invasion and froze all Iraqi and Kuwaiti assets. Four days later the UN Security Council voted overwhelmingly to impose a worldwide trade embargo on Iraq.

As the world moved towards a possible war I was faced with two serious problems with the business. The first was how to arrange for the return home of the six Matrix Churchill engineers and other employees in Iraq. The second was how to keep the business going in the face of a government-imposed asset freeze that left Matrix Churchill unable to conduct any business. What was going to happen to the 800 people working for Matrix Churchill if the freeze lasted any length of time? We could be forced into receivership in a matter of weeks.

Because of the annual shutdown of the plant, Jim Bartholomew and his family had left Baghdad before the invasion. The other six employees were men there without their families. We expected preferential treatment, as we were an Iraqi-owned company. I had hoped that Safa or some of our other Iraqi contacts would help get them out of Baghdad. But contact with Iraq was almost impossible and I soon learned that I wouldn't be able to count on them for any help.

We tried desperately through the British embassy in Baghdad to arrange for the men to exit through Jordan. Towards the end of August the men were told through the embassy that it would be safe to drive across the desert to Amman, in Jordan. Five of them hired a taxi for a huge sum and set off for the border. One man, Alan Steele, decided not to risk the ride across the desert and preferred to remain behind. The others made it safely to Jordan and back to England, but it would be Christmas before Steele was released from Iraq, along with hundreds of other Westerners held by Saddam as 'human shields'.

Under the UN embargo and a British ban, no company could trade with an Iraqi-owned business. During August the directors and I had worked to try to unfreeze our assets and find a solution to the ban. We knew there would be no further trade with Iraq during the embargo, but we had domestic orders to fill and we were desperate to keep the factory operating once the two-week holiday was over.

Finally we were able to negotiate a deal with the Bank of England and the DTI. Matrix Churchill could trade with companies outside Iraq, but we had to get a special licence for each deal and so did the companies we were doing business with. But some American companies were still refusing to do business with us. And the process itself was so time-consuming and cumbersome that we started to fall behind on our deliveries. New orders were few and far between. On top of that, the Bank of England had refused to release the money in our accounts, arguing that the funds belonged to Iraq and were subject to the government freeze.

It was during this time that I came to believe that drastic action had to be taken to save the company and the jobs. The business was rapidly heading towards bankruptcy. If there was going to be a lifeline for Matrix Churchill, we had to get rid of the Iraqis and make it a wholly owned British company.

On 17 September, Peter Allen and I went to London to meet Coolican and another DTI official, and told them that we were considering a management buy-out to take the company out of Iraqi hands. They agreed that it was a good solution to the problem and encouraged us to proceed. The Bank of England also agreed that a management buy-out could lead to a release of the company's funds.

By this time we had contacted a London-based venture-capital firm, Granville & Company Limited, who had agreed to invest money to finance the management buy-out. They would be paid back over four or five years out of company earnings and eventually the whole business would belong to management.

We had the support of the workforce at Coventry. In early September we had called a meeting of the workforce, and I had addressed them, explaining that we were putting together a management buy-out which would get rid of the Iraqi shareholders and keep the plant open. As part of the deal, they agreed to let us use some of the excess funding in the pension scheme and to work a three-day week to keep the business afloat until the buy-out could be completed. The support was unanimous.

The problem was the Iraqis. I had been negotiating with Adnan, Hana Jon and Robert Koshaba, the financial director of TDG, and of TMG, the holding company for Matrix Churchill stock. I had no contact with Safa or Fadel, but assumed the others were in touch with them. We offered £2 million for the business. We also wanted a parent-company loan of £3.8 million written off. The Iraqis were objecting both to the price and writing off the loan. Their will had been stiffened because of an incident earlier in September and because of what I sensed was a distrust of me by Safa and Fadel.

The Americans had also frozen all Iraqi assets within days of the invasion. But in late August, Gordon Cooper phoned me in a panic. Koshaba had been telephoning him to urge him to authorize the release of $1 million in the accounts of Matrix Churchill Corporation. It was commissions due to TDG. Gordon had contacted the American authorities and been warned that the release of the money could land him in jail.

'I have to go to the national machine-tool exhibition in Chicago early next month,' Gordon had told me. 'I'm afraid that the Iraqis will move the money out of the account while I'm away. You've got to help me out, Paul.'

It required the signatures of two directors for the bank to release the money. The problem Gordon faced was that, while he was out of the office, two of the Iraqi directors could authorize payment. Legally, however, he would remain responsible as the chief executive officer.

The money couldn't be moved into the Matrix Churchill accounts in England. The Americans would think it was a scheme. The critical thing was to move the money out of the US accounts before Gordon left for Chicago. Once he returned, the money could be returned as well.

'Listen,' I said, 'I've got an account in Liechtenstein. It's a numbered account. I've never used it. We could transfer the money there. When you get back from the Chicago show we could then move it back to your accounts. But we've got to keep my name out of it. The Iraqis will be really angry if they find out I am involved.'

I'd opened the numbered account in Liechtenstein shortly after the Iraqis had bought Matrix Churchill. Under the purchase agreement I was actually paid by TMG, not Matrix Churchill. Safa had suggested that it might be beneficial for me to have an account overseas in case they wanted to pay me from one of their overseas accounts for their tax reasons. It was Wadi who had suggested Liechtenstein, but I'd never had occasion to use the account.

To protect us if something went wrong, Cooper cleared the transfer arrangement with Ken Millwood, a lawyer who represented Matrix Churchill Corporation. Gordon's bank manager agreed to accept one signature. However, he would not transfer the money to a numbered account. He insisted that the name of the account holder be shown on the transfer papers. So Gordon reluctantly gave him my name. He figured it was better than facing twelve years in prison for violating US regulations.

I was attending the trade show in Chicago, too, a few days later. When Gordon told me he had used my name, I was angry at first. Then I figured, what would I have done in his place?

However, when I returned to Britain I told Adnan, Hana Jon and Robert Koshaba, TDG's financial director, about the transfer. I said it had been done to protect Gordon Cooper. It seemed better to risk their anger then than take a chance on them discovering it themselves because my name was on the transfer document. A few days later, after Gordon returned to Cleveland, I flew to Zurich, rented a car and drove to Liechtenstein. I had to make the transaction in person. Once there, I transferred the money, with the interest, back to the Matrix Churchill accounts in the USA.

Stopping Safa from getting his $1 million was one of the reasons I believed he was making it so hard on the management in the buy-out negotiations. I'd also angered him earlier in the summer. He wanted to move the company's entire machine production to Jebel Ali, a duty-free zone in the United Arab Emirates. He planned to leave only a sales and marketing operation in Britain. I was completely against this and voiced my opinion strongly.

By early October a price for the management buy-out had been agreed and heads of agreement signed. It would be £2.25 million – a fair price for the business. But as part of the final talks, the Iraqis insisted that I resign as managing director of Matrix Churchill. They believed that I had a conflict of interest, which struck me as a bit odd given the way I'd helped them three years before. I went ahead and resigned, though I continued to work at Matrix Churchill. After all, it was only a matter of days until I resumed the position and became a major shareholder in the business. The final signing was scheduled to take place in Coventry on 17 October.

The roof fell in on 16 October.

Customs and Excise had advised me that they were coming to the plant that day and wanted to see me. They refused to say what it was about, so I had called Balsom.

'Don't worry about it,' Balsom said. 'I know Constantine's boss at Customs and Excise and I'll speak to him.'

On Monday, the fifteenth, Balsom called back. He said it was just another routine visit, a follow-up to gather more information. He told me not to worry.

I was sitting at my desk on Tuesday morning, going over papers relating to the purchase of the business the next day, when Peter Allen walked into my office.

'They're here and they want to see you in the boardroom,' he said.

'OK, fine,' replied. 'Give me a few minutes.'

'Actually,' said Peter, 'it's not fine. They're arresting us.'

'You're pulling my leg.'

'I'm dead serious. They want you immediately.'

In the boardroom were Constantine, Peter Wiltshire, who was his superior, and a customs lawyer. It was Constantine who smiled and said they were officially arresting me for the illegal export of machine tools to Iraq. He cautioned me that I had the right to remain silent and whatever I said could be used against me.

I was in complete shock. Constantine's voice sounded like he was speaking from the bottom of a well. He said they would be searching my office and taking away documents. He said fifteen customs agents had blocked off the entrances and exits and were searching the plant.

I wasn't frightened at this stage; I don't even think I'd become nervous. I was fairly self-contained, but I just couldn't believe it was happening to me. Balsom had told me I had nothing to worry about. Twenty-four hours after he tells me this, they're arresting me, I said to myself in disbelief. I've worked for the intelligence service. I've told them everything. The British government will stop this. It will never come to anything. I've got to go through it, but it will go away.

It was mid-afternoon when they finished tearing apart my office and searching my car. I had been forced to sit and watch as they bundled up my documents, personal and business, and took them away. I even had to have an escort when I went to the toilet. Then they packed me into the back of a grey Ford Sierra and we drove to Coventry police station.

As I sat in the back of the car, shock turned to anger. In all the years I'd travelled and taken risks, only the Russians had detained me. Now it was my own government. I also began to realize that the management buy-out would not succeed if this dragged on more than a few days. And I was concerned about Esther, my family, my eighty-three-year-old mother. How would they react? What was going to happen to Matrix Churchill if the buy-out fell apart?

14

It was near the end of October 1990 when I finally stopped ringing the London number. The same pleasant woman had answered day after day. She had taken the same message each time: Please, ask Mr Balsom to call Paul Henderson. There'd been no return call. I was bitterly disappointed. The fact that I had worked for them for so many years seemed to mean nothing. I'd certainly taken some risks in the latter years and they were dumping me the moment I had a problem.

Yet at the back of my mind I still had this faith that something would be done. The simple truth was that I refused to believe my government could do this. Once Customs and Excise got all the information and were told about my background, this thing would fade into the background. At least, that's what I hoped.

My support in those days came from Esther, David and Sue. They were super. And so were our friends. If the government had dumped me, at least the people who knew me best were sticking by me.

The day of my arrest I was locked in a small cell at the police station in Coventry. The company lawyer didn't do criminal work so he had recommended a local firm. I had called from the Matrix Churchill plant and they'd said someone would be sent immediately to the police station.

The lawyer, David Eyre, arrived about half an hour after I'd been put in the cell. By that time I had agreed to answer questions from Customs and Excise and been moved to an interrogation room. When Eyre came, he took me aside and asked if I wanted to continue the interview. I said I'd nothing to hide.

During the questioning I got my first indication that the Coventry police weren't too happy with Customs and Excise. Eyre asked me if I wanted a cup of tea, and I said I did. He asked a police officer to bring me one.

'I can give you one,' the officer said to me with a smile, 'but I don't have to give these other gentlemen one.' He gestured toward the two customs men and walked out. The officer returned with one cup of tea, for me.

It was 8.30 p.m. before I left the police station. I'd been told to return in the morning for further questions. I was not to talk about the arrest with anyone at the plant or elsewhere. Not even with Esther or the children.

When I got home Esther and Sue were waiting anxiously. I'd managed just a brief call to them earlier. Naturally they were extremely worried. It's impossible not to talk to your wife in a situation like that, so I told Esther everything that had happened. Peter Allen and Trevor Abraham had also been taken into custody, questioned and released. I'd answered all the questions and just hoped the authorities would realize a mistake had been made.

'Esther, the government knew all about what we were doing,' I told her. 'We didn't hide anything from them. Ultimately this case will never go anywhere. I don't want you to worry.'

'I'll be all right,' she said. 'I just can't believe this has happened to you. What will happen to the company? What about the buy-out?'

'Unless this gets resolved very soon I'm afraid the buy-out will be dead.'

I lay awake long past midnight that first night. I kept asking myself, why Matrix Churchill? Why Trevor, Peter and me? There were other machine-tool companies and directors who did as much business with Iraq. Only one answer made sense: they had targeted us because of the Iraqi ownership. Once the UN embargo was imposed on Iraq, Matrix Churchill became a soft target. Customs and Excise felt they were going to get a lot of sympathetic press attention by going after an Iraqi-owned company. And no one would be willing to stand up against them on our behalf.

Charging me was obvious. Trevor was included because, as commercial manager, he had handled the contract negotiations. Peter Allen, who'd only been with us a couple of years, was charged because he had been head of sales. Both he and Trevor were also involved directly in getting the export licences.

I thought about the intelligence service and Balsom. Despite his refusal to return my calls, I couldn't imagine that they would let the case go forward. I'd done too much for them. I'd started to mention the connection to Constantine when he was questioning me at the police station, but then backed off, deciding it might be easier for the intelligence service to protect me if nobody knew about my work for them. They could keep things quiet and make the case go away.

But something darker came to my mind, too. Could they be counting on me to keep silent about my spying? I'd only verbally assented to the Official Secrets Act. But disclosing what I'd done involved other risks. It could put my family and me in grave danger from the Iraqis. And who would believe me? It would be my word against the government's. My silence could protect the intelligence service.

The first key reaction came on 19 October, the Friday after my arrest. I'd driven down to London for a meeting at the MTTA. The arrests at Matrix Churchill had startled the directors of the other companies. John Nosworthy of the association had arranged the meeting so that I could explain what happened and we could assess the possible impact on the industry.

'They started with Matrix Churchill, but what is ultimately going to happen is that all of you sitting around this table have done business with Iraq,' I told them. 'You will be investigated unless the industry uses its political influence and puts a stop to all of this.'

Some of my colleagues from the other companies said nice things, but no one was willing to take any action. They wanted to wait and see what happened to the three of us. They didn't want to attract any more attention to the industry. The message was clear: there would be no help here. John Nosworthy was eager to assist me, but he got no support from the people in the room. Their attitude was to keep their heads below the parapet, hoping the flak wouldn't touch them.

One person at the meeting that day was doing a bit of work on his own. But it wasn't designed to do me any good.

I was trying to keep the buy-out alive. Granville & Company had backed off because of the arrests. So I'd approached Metalexport, the state organization in Poland, with a proposal. They turned out to be quite interested in buying a major stake in Matrix Churchill. The managers would hold the remainder. Before the end of October I had their commitment of £2.25 million. The Iraqis refused to respond to my letters of enquiry. They would not even take my phone calls. What I found out through the grapevine was that they were working to sell the business to Keith Bailey of BSA.

I suspected the Iraqis had been talking to Bailey even earlier. Within a few days of my arrest, he had wound up sitting at my desk, running the company. Now, through his parent company, Automation Investments, he was buying the business out from under me – for less than I was offering.

In the end Bailey bought Matrix Churchill for £1.8 million. The deal did not require him to pay the money for at least two years. Essentially he was getting the company for no money, while I was willing and able to pay £2.25 million cash.

I was worried that Bailey would ruin the company. BSA didn't have a product of its own for the future. Its lathes and other machines were outdated. So the new line that Matrix Churchill was ready to market in 1991, the one I'd overseen for two years, would keep him in business. But I still doubted he had the ability to keep the company going. Furthermore, his plant was about the same size as ours. He would no doubt combine the operations to save money, and that would mean an immediate loss of jobs at Matrix Churchill.

I wanted to stop the deal. When the Iraqis refused to listen to my buy-out offer, I wanted to exercise the veto clause which had been part of the original acquisition agreement with them. But two of the other management shareholders still employed at Matrix Churchill were afraid they'd lose their jobs if we blocked the sale. There turned out to be nothing I could do to stop the sale.

I needed something to occupy my mind. I had to work. So I went back to Hi-Tek and was working with John Belgrove and Mark Gutteridge. Esther had managed our interest in Hi-Tek and she still worked in the office. But I needed something to keep from going crazy. There were no restrictions on my travel, other than having to deposit £25,000 with Customs and Excise to obtain my passport, so I began going back to Eastern Europe, selling the products of other machine-tool manufacturers.

It was 2 December, the day after returning from one of those trips, that the front page of the *Sunday Times* carried the biggest story to date about the Matrix Churchill case. Mark called me at home, asking if I had seen the article.

Under the headline 'How Minister Helped Arm Saddam's Soldiers' was a story saying that the government knew that Iraq was using Matrix Churchill machines to manufacture artillery shells when the export licences were approved. It even quoted from the MTTA's minutes of the meeting with Alan Clark at the DTI in January

1988. Furthermore, an unnamed managing director who attended the meeting was quoted as saying that Clark had given a 'nod and a wink' to the sales. If the government charged the three Matrix Churchill men, the article said, the DTI would be accused of knowingly violating export guidelines.

I read the article a second time. I couldn't believe it. The story was accurate. That was the problem. Where had the information come from? I hadn't talked to the reporters. But I had generally discussed my feelings about the case with Peter Allen and Trevor Abraham after our arrests in October. I'd told them the government knew all along what our machines were being used for. I had described the meeting with Alan Clark at the DTI. I'd said several times that, as far as I was concerned, Clark had given a nod and a wink to the Iraqi sales.

I was annoyed about the story. At this time I was still hopeful that the intelligence service would do something. But those hopes depended on keeping the matter quiet, so that it could be dropped without creating too much attention.

I'd even seen some optimistic news the previous month. In November the government had dropped all charges against the two men arrested in the supergun case, Christopher Cowley and Peter Mitchell. The official explanation was that there was not enough evidence to proceed with formal charges. But the press had speculated that the DTI was too embarrassed to go ahead because it had told the manufacturers that licences were not required. If it could happen in their case, why not in ours? I was also told that the American government, in order to cover up its involvement with the supergun, had put pressure on the British government to drop the case against Cowley and Mitchell. But the *Sunday Times* story did not help. It brought our case into the limelight.

On Monday, Alan Clark was sitting on the government benches when the then Minister for Trade at the DTI, Tim Sainsbury, made the official statement: 'Mr Clark strongly denies the interpretation put on the remarks alleged to have been made to him.' Sainsbury also claimed that the government's restrictions on selling military material to the Iraqis had been 'scrupulously and carefully followed' since they were imposed in October 1985.

I believed Sainsbury had made two misleading statements, though he may not have known the truth. Worse, the government had now said publicly that they didn't know about the uses of our machines. It would be harder for them to back down and drop the case.

Long before the arrest, Esther and I had agreed to meet her sister and brother-in-law for a holiday in Naples, Florida. They had rented a condominium on the beach. Sue and Esther planned to go for month, but because of work, I'd only intended to spend a week. But since the arrest effectively put me out of work, we all went from the middle of December until the middle of January. It was the first long holiday I'd ever had and it turned out to be a relaxing time for all of us. And good preparation for what was to come.

While in Florida, I heard through Gordon Cooper that the American authorities wanted to question us in Atlanta about the Banca Lavoro scandal. They said it was all friendly, and that they were just looking for information about how the bank operated. I still felt we'd nothing to hide, so I agreed.

Gordon phoned back a few days later. He said the Matrix Churchill attorney, Ken Millwood, had advised that we cooperate with the US authorities only if they gave us immunity letters. Such letters, he explained, were promises that we wouldn't be prosecuted. I didn't feel it was required, but agreed with Gordon that it was a sensible precaution. The agreement was reached while I was still in Florida, but the Atlanta people weren't ready to talk to me yet.

Tanned and relaxed, Esther, Sue and I returned to Coventry on Thursday 17 January, the day the air war started in Operation Desert Storm. We turned on the television when we got back to the house and saw the first pictures of air strikes on Baghdad. I felt a sense of patriotism, and hoped none of our boys would be hurt.

Four days later I was on British Airways flight number 227 from Heathrow to Atlanta's Hartsfield Airport. I arrived shortly after five o'clock that afternoon and took a taxi to a hotel.

The federal prosecutor in Atlanta, a frizzy-haired woman named Gale McKenzie, was investigating Christopher Drogoul, Paul Von Wedel and some other former employees of the city's branch of Banco Lavoro. Investigators had discovered that the branch had loaned $5 billion to the Iraqis, often without proper documents. The government believed Drogoul was the mastermind and that he had acted without the knowledge of bank directors in Rome.

I spent a day and a half in a small conference room telling McKenzie and an investigator named Art Wade everything I knew about Banca Lavoro and the contracts the bank had financed for the Iraqis. I also provided them with information about Safa al-Habobi and what I knew about how he and the other Iraqis operated. And I described how Safa had frequently flown to various countries in Europe to meet privately with a woman from the Atlanta bank.

They questioned me about Sadik Taha, an official of the Central Bank of Iraq. I told them that I had met Taha in London, but that he had died in early 1989 after heart surgery at a London hospital. They didn't believe me and kept insisting that he was alive.

Judging from the questions, Drogoul was the real target. I told them Von Wedel was the one who had come to our offices in Coventry. I'd met Drogoul briefly at the Baghdad military fair in the spring of 1989, but had had no real contact with him.

McKenzie and Wade did almost all the questioning, with several other officials coming in and out of the meeting. Two men who had been introduced to me as US Customs agents sat in chairs and were silent. On the second day the two agents began to ask me questions about Carlos Cardoen, and said they had raided Cardoen's offices in Miami, Florida, and discovered documents for the contracts with Matrix Churchill. They said they were investigating Cardoen for supposedly using American technology and material to produce some of the weapons he sold to Iraq.

I told them the contracts were part of the investigation against me in Britain. The agents didn't seem to know too much at that point, but I answered their questions about the financing for the deal and told them what I knew about Cardoen's operation. I had no knowledge that he'd done anything wrong.

On 28 February 1991, about a month after I gave evidence in Atlanta, Drogoul and several other bank employees were charged with making the loans without approval from the bank. Charged with them were Safa al-Habobi and three Iraqi banking officials. I didn't really pay much attention, since my own troubles had increased by then.

Keith Bailey had signed the contract and bought Matrix Churchill on 12 February 1991. After he signed the agreement, Bailey asked my former secretary, Roz Webb, to phone me and ask if Bailey and his wife, Sylvia, could meet Esther and me that afternoon. I wanted to tell him to get stuffed, but I controlled my temper for Hi-Tek represented Matrix Churchill in Eastern Europe.

'Paul, how could you agree to meet that man?' Esther demanded when I told her. 'After all that's happened, you can't go.'

'Esther, we should go and we must be civil,' I explained to her.

We met that afternoon at the Post House Hotel in Coventry. Bailey apologized for the way in which the sale had been handled and the problems caused to Esther and myself. He wanted us to understand that it was the Iraqis to blame, not him. 'If there's anything I can do to help, just let me know, Paul,' he said.

'Thank you,' I said, deciding to give him the benefit of the doubt despite Esther squeezing hard on my knee under the table.

Bailey's promise of help turned out to be empty. I should have known better.

Since the arrest in October I'd been reporting monthly at the police station in Coventry. We had still not been formally charged with any crime; not had we appeared before a judge. And I still held onto the hope that the case would go away quietly. Peter and Trevor followed the same routine of reporting to the police.

On 19 February we were all to report at the police station at ten in the morning – the first time we'd all been requested to attend at the same time. Surprised and worried, I'd asked my solicitor, David Eyre, to check on the reason. He had called back with reassurance, for his impression after talking with Customs and Excise was that we were simply to be questioned. Once again, we would not be charged.

It was a Tuesday, grey and overcast. I hadn't seen sun since my return from Florida. I had a cold feeling that morning when I woke up. I was dead certain the three of us *were* going to be rearrested and charged. I don't really believe in premonitions, but it was a strange feeling that made me nauseous.

'Esther, would you mind running me down to the police station and dropping me off?' I asked, as we stood in the kitchen sipping coffee and looking out over the garden.

'Don't be silly,' she said, more confident than I was. 'There's no need. You'll be all right. Don't worry about it. You'll be finished in the afternoon and home.'

The police station is in the centre of Coventry, in one of the new buildings constructed after the Germans destroyed the heart of the city. I drove myself and went in and found Trevor already there.

'Paul, I heard on the radio driving down,' he said urgently. 'Customs is going to arrest us again and charge us.'

We waited for three-quarters of an hour without seeing anyone from Customs and Excise. David Eyre, who had come to the station, kept assuring me that we would not be arrested. He actually thought they were going to drop the whole matter that morning. The delay was just to work out the details.

Finally Constantine walked out of one of the rooms, and came over to us. His round face showed no emotion. He was stiff and official.

We were taken to separate rooms. I went with Constantine and as the door shut he said: 'You're being arrested again and you will be taken to a magistrate's court in London for the formal charging.'

I shook my head, sorry that my premonition had been spot-on. Eyre was steaming, arguing that he'd been deceived and that there was no reason to take us all the way to London. There is a court right here, he said.

What had caused the delay, we learned, was that the customs officials were arguing with the Coventry police, insisting that we be taken to a magistrate's court in London. The Coventry police were adamant that we were Coventry people and should be taken before the court in the city. I saw it as another example of the local police disliking the high-handed tactics and demeanour of Constantine and his cohorts. In the end a call from senior officials in London packed us off to London for what would turn out to be one of the most humiliating experiences of my life.

As I was being led out the door, Eyre said he wasn't the man to represent me in London. He would have one of the firm's partners in court by the time I got there.

Peter, Trevor and I were put in the back of separate cars for the two-hour drive to London. Constantine was sitting beside me. He said we must stop at my house on the way.

'I suggest you get a bag, just in case you're detained overnight,' he said. 'Also, collect your passports. You'll not be allowed to use them any longer.'

I hadn't had a chance to call Esther, and when I opened the door she came out smiling, thinking it was all over. Then she saw the two officials beside me, Constantine and a woman.

'I've been arrested,' I told her, putting my hands on her shoulders to hold both of us up. 'They're taking me to court in London. I'll be charged and my bail will be set. They say it will be around £50,000. Hopefully, it will be sorted out and I'll be home tonight.'

Constantine had told me that no family member could stand surety. He said that my house, which was paid for and worth far more than £50,000, could not be used. I explained this to Esther and said she should get in touch with John Belgrove and Mark Gutteridge to arrange the bail money.

Esther was shocked. She didn't cry. I was assuring her that I'd be all right and she was more concerned about me than about herself. She handled it exceptionally well. But I could see she was in a state of shock. I told her not to come down to London. David Eyre had promised that one of his partners would come to court. He could drive me home later that night.

We arrived a couple of hours later at Leman Street police station in London's East End. I was handed over to police custody, photographed, fingerprinted and shut in a cell. I sat and waited to go to court, expecting my lawyer to be there with the bail papers.

Not long after I arrived, two policemen came and collected me. I was handcuffed to Trevor and we were stuffed into the back of a tiny Rover Metro for the cramped ride to the Thames Magistrates Court. There, Trevor and I were locked in a cell and told that we'd be up before the judge in a short while. I didn't know what had happened to Peter Allen.

Sitting there, I suddenly realized that this was all really happening, that they intended to proceed with the case. I was very angry. The intelligence people had let me down; they had walked away. I was not going to get any protection from them. The intelligence service was not concerned with what happened to me; it could not care less. I felt almost afraid. At least there was an element of fear in my mind.

It was at this point that I finally faced the truth: I was going to have to fight the case myself. All through my life, things had happened and I had been able to do something about them. I was in control of my life. But here I'd relied on Balsom and other people and they hadn't given a bloody damn. It would be up to me to find a way out of this.

Trevor and I were taken upstairs into the courtroom. Peter was already there. I met David Eyre's partner, Alan Parker, the senior man at the firm. The clerk of the court read the charges. Violations of the Export of Goods Control Orders. Exportation of machines, tools and software programmes specially designed for the manufacture of fuses and of missiles. The language was easy enough to understand, even in my state. They were accusing us of concealing the military purposes of the machines for the Cardoen contracts. The missile part confused me. Then I realized they meant the rockets developed from the ABA contract.

I wanted to shout out that none of it was true. The government knew what those machines were to be used for. Mark Gutteridge and I had both told our intelligence handlers. In January 1988 Alan

Clark at the DTI had told us he knew. He had suggested that we stress the civilian aspect. I said nothing.

Bail was granted with a number of conditions, including two sureties of £25,000 each. Trevor and I were led back down to our cell. Parker came to see me very soon, but he wasn't staying until I was freed on bail. He said everything would be OK, but he had to get back to Coventry. He said Esther was taking care of the bail and he left.

I got a call through to Esther and she said that the bail papers had been taken down to the police station in Coventry. It had taken a bit of time to arrange things through John Belgrove and Mark Gutteridge, but the information was being transferred to London.

A few minutes later Constantine was outside the cell, grinning. 'I forgot one thing,' he said to me. 'I'll be needing your passports.'

I had two passports. Some of the countries I visited did not like to see documents containing visas and stamps from their enemies. I reached into my bag and handed them both through the bars to Constantine.

'Sorry about this,' said Constantine sarcastically. 'I trust you'll be out of here soon.'

Then a policeman came to tell us that the court was closing and we were being transferred to another station. I started to worry that the paperwork from Coventry wouldn't catch up with me. I'd end up that night in jail after all.

Trevor, Peter and I were taken to a big police van. In the back we were each locked into a tiny cell, smaller than a phonebox, and driven across London to Lambeth Street police station. There, we were put into a communal cell and each given a cup of tea. It was the first thing I'd eaten or drunk all day and I was feeling pretty hungry.

Then my name was called out, followed by Peter's. Trevor was detained there and released later that night when his bail came through. I thought we were leaving, but they loaded us back into the van and took us to Wormwood Scrubs, the huge, dark, Victorian prison in West London. I knew the name because of all the IRA prisoners who were kept there. It was a secure, dirty old jail. It was where we'd spend the night.

On our journey between Thames Magistrates Court, Lambeth Street police station and Wormwood Scrubs, we had our legs pulled by a couple of Cockneys. They nicknamed us the 'Supergun Gang', after the police at Thames told them what we had been charged with. Peter and I got chatting to these two guys and I asked them what they had been arrested for. First of all they told us that they were remanded in custody, charged with robbing a travel agent.

'Why aren't you out on bail?' I asked.

'Well, we were caught with a thousand US dollars. But we're not guilty, guv!'

But I still couldn't understand why they were remand prisoners, so I persisted.

'Well, guv, when the coppers got us they didn't just find the money. They found we'd got a couple of sawn-off shotguns with us too. But we were stitched up, guv. We didn't do it.'

I never found out what happened to these two characters, but they certainly kept me and Peter entertained during a very long and difficult two hours.

It was nearly eight o'clock at night when we passed through the huge gates of the prison. The first thing they did was put us in a small room and give us a prison meal of corned beef and mashed potatoes and a lump of dried bread. I ate. Then I was processed into the prison system. They took my name and all of my personal details, including identifying marks or scars. I was given a choice, so I kept my own clothes, but they took my tie and belt and went through my bag and removed my razor and anything else they thought might be dangerous. The staff were courteous and efficient. They gave me a four-digit number and told me not to forget it, since that was how I would be identified in prison.

I was led out of the processing section into the remand section, where they kept prisoners being held for trial. The walls of the prison were old brick, the roof was domed and there were cast-iron stairs between each of the three floors and cells on each side of the long hallway that I was taken down.

I thought perhaps Peter and I would be put in the same cell, but when we came to a cell, the guard stopped and unlocked the door. 'You're in with the "Cleaner",' he said as he locked the cell behind me.

As the guard was opening the door, I heard shuffling sounds coming from inside the cell. I had no idea what had made the noise. When the door slammed shut. I noticed a short, thin man sitting in silence on one of the metal bunks. Finally, I decided I'd better say something if I was going to spend the night with him.

'Hi,' I said. 'My name's Paul.'

'My name's Paul as well,' he said, finally smiling.

We started to chat. I told him what I was in for and he told me. He had been caught stealing stereo equipment and the like from warehouses. Then he had jumped bail and been caught four months later when he was visiting his mother's house to look after her dog while she was on holiday.

'Why do they call you the Cleaner?' I asked.

'I'm the cleaner. My job is to go out there and clean the landings and the toilets.'

'What was all the shuffling when I came in?'

'Oh,' he said with a grin. 'I nearly got caught. I was just preparing myself some hashish. But I had to throw it out the window. I didn't expect a cellmate tonight.'

'You're joking,' I said.

'Not at all. Would you like some?'

I declined, but I asked him how he got the drugs into prison. He showed me some of the dark-brown kernels that he stuck inside a cigarette to smoke and explained how he had come by them.

'My girlfriend brings it in on visiting days. She's searched, but she puts it between the cheeks of her arse and brings it in. Then she goes to the toilet, removes it and passes it to me when she comes out. Sometimes I have to put it in the cheeks of my arse as well to get it up here.'

I was thinking, thank God I don't smoke hashish.

The day had taken its toll of me, so I crawled into bed and slept fairly soundly until about 6.30 the following morning. It was the noises that woke me. It was like being in hospital, with all the early-morning commotion.

Eventually, I went to the communal bathroom and had a wash and later ate breakfast. About eight o'clock one of the guards came up and told me my wife had rung. Bail was in place and she was driving down from Coventry. I'd be leaving in two or three hours. Before then, however, I was to get a crash course in prison life.

The Cleaner and I were sitting in the cell. Outside, several men were washing down the landing. I'd noticed others starting to clean the toilets in the communal room.

'I thought you were supposed to clean up,' I said to my cellmate.

'Yeah, I am. But I've got a couple of guys doing it for me. I provide them with drugs and they do the work.'

Then the guards rounded up the new prisoners and took us to a small room, where we watched a film about contracting AIDS in prison. I counted myself lucky to be leaving in a few hours. Then I went and collected my daily allowance, £1.30. It had to be spent at the prison shop, so I gave it to Paul.

At nine o'clock the Cleaner told me that I was free to walk out into the prison yard and get some exercise. On the way down I passed Peter and told him where I was going. He said he'd catch up with me. In the yard, once you start moving, you have to keep walking. I wasn't allowed to stop and wait for Peter. So I started walking around. I was still wearing a business suit, so I stood out among the prison uniforms.

I was walking along when a character sidled up and started walking close to me. He was a short, stocky guy, with fair hair and a bruised face, a black eye and a cut across his nose. He looked a bit of a thug.

'Why you in a business suit?' he asked. 'What the hell you doin' here?'

I'd seen the films about what happens in prison yards and the warders had warned me to be careful. Just then, Peter walked up and joined us. The thug calmed down and the three of us chatted for a few minutes. It turned out he was in for beating his wife.

While we were walking, the prison loudspeaker crackled, and then a voice said: 'Would Prisoner 1124 please report to the gate.'

That was my number. I was getting out. I felt sorry for Peter. So far, he'd heard nothing about his bail. His surety had been set at £100,000 because he had insisted on keeping his passport. We just figured it was taking longer to raise that much money.

I went to the prison gate and an officer took me into a small room. 'Strip off your shirt,' he said. 'We have to make sure you're Paul Henderson.'

I took off my suit jacket and shirt. Across my back was the scar from my lung operation at sixteen. A few minutes later I was standing in the cold outside Wormwood Scrubs prison, unshaven, holding my overnight bag and feeling like one of those men you see leaving jail in the films.

I saw my car coming down the street, with Sue driving and Esther sitting beside her. Esther was still pretty shaken up, but she seemed to brighten when I climbed into the back of the car.

'Where's Peter?' she asked. 'The administration at the prison said they were expecting his bail to come through.'

We sat and waited for a bit. Then Esther picked up the car phone and called the prison. They said his bail had not come through. Even if it did, it would be late afternoon before he was released, so we decided to return to Coventry. In the end it was nine o'clock that evening before Peter was released.

We had an unplanned party at the house that night. My son, David, had driven up from his job in London. John Belgrove and Mark Gutteridge and their wives had come over, along with my brother and sister-in-law and a few other friends. They just showed up. It was reassuring, especially for Esther.

After everyone had gone and the house was quiet and I was in bed, the feeling of isolation returned that I'd experienced when the cell door slammed shut at Thames Magistrates Court. I felt I'd been deserted. My family and friends would be there. But they could only support me – not fight this battle for me.

My whole life had just shattered. I was coming to grips with the criminal charges. I was fifty-two. The trial would take place in a couple of years. If I lost and went to prison for seven years, I'd be about sixty. My family and their well-being were in jeopardy. We were not rich by any means, but we had worked and we'd got certain things. The children had been educated privately and Sue had gone on to university. We had a nice home and a comfortable life. All of a sudden it seemed to me that all this was going to disappear. Lying there, I realized something that was terribly important: if I'm going to win this, I'm going to have to do it myself.

That was when I started to think about how prepared I was to reveal my intelligence work. What could I do to put pressure on the government to get this case dropped? How was I going to get any documents to prove what I was saying? And what about Mark Gutteridge? Mark could provide critical help. He could explain how he had been doing the same thing. He wouldn't be someone trying to save himself by making it up. But I didn't know how far I was prepared to go in exposing my intelligence role. I certainly had no idea what Mark would be willing to do. It wasn't time to ask him yet. What if he said no?

In March 1991 Christopher Cowley, the engineer of supergun fame, telephoned Peter Allen. He said he had seen the *Sunday Times* article in December about the Matrix Churchill case. 'There's a lot I can do to help you guys,' Cowley had told Peter. 'You should get the other two and come down to my house.'

I wasn't sure it was going to be beneficial to us, but I figured there was nothing to lose and I joined Peter and Trevor for the drive to Hot Wells, a nice part of Bristol where Cowley had a tall house at the bottom of a steep hill.

We arrived late in the afternoon and spent the next several hours listening to Chris, a good-looking, middle-aged man with hair that was silver-grey like mine. He described how his lawyer had threatened to confront the government with numerous cases in which the DTI knew military material and even weapons were exported to Iraq. To prove the case, they had promised they would demand testimony by Nicholas Ridley, the Secretary of State for Trade and Industry, and Alan Clark, his former Minister for Trade. Chris offered to share all of his information with us and our lawyers.

'Have you got good solicitors?' Chris asked

Peter and Trevor indicated that they were satisfied with theirs. But I was not particularly comfortable with mine: I'd had great difficulty getting appointments with Alan Parker since my release from prison.

'My problem is I can't get to see my damn solicitor,' I complained. 'I want to talk to him because I'd like to try and understand more about this case.'

'Well,' said Chris, shaking his head, 'there's one guy I can recommend to you and that's Kevin Robinson of Irwin Mitchell in Sheffield. He did a hell of a job for me.'

Before we left, Chris handed us a photocopy of an unusual Christmas card. A man's body was lying on the ground with a knife sticking out of his back. At the top of the card it said: 'Happy Christmas Wishes.' Across the bottom, it said the card was from the government, the DTI, the MoD and the Attorney-General to 'All Operation Bertha Staff'. Operation Bertha, Chris explained, was the code-name at Customs and Excise for the case involving the supergun, a reference to the Second World War cannon known as Big Bertha.

'Customs was mighty angry when the case against me was dropped,' said Chris, who declined to tell us how he had come by the card. 'They felt they'd been stabbed in the back.'

It occurred to me that the charges against us were revenge by Customs and Excise against those same agencies. By convicting us, customs would redeem its record. If the government told the truth and the charges were dropped, it would become clear that customs had been kept in the dark about the real policy toward Iraq. It was a theory that I kept to myself for a long time, but one to which later events would lend a ring of truth.

Driving back to Coventry, I discussed the idea of changing solicitors with the others. While they were fairly satisfied, we all agreed it would be worth going to see Kevin Robinson in Sheffield. I said I'd phone him and set up an appointment.

I called Robinson early the next morning, explained who I was and asked if my colleagues and I could come up and see him. 'Why not tomorrow?' he said. 'I have to be in court all day, but I'll see you at five o'clock.' I agreed without hesitation. After weeks of not getting to see my own lawyer, here was a solicitor who was prepared to see me immediately. It was only one of the ways that I'd learn Kevin Robinson was far from a typical lawyer.

On 28 March Peter, Trevor and I drove up the M1 to Sheffield, arriving at Irwin Mitchell's quaint offices near the city centre shortly before five. Kevin Robinson saw us straight away. We chatted a bit and then described our case to Kevin, who listened intently, interrupting only to clarify a point or ask a good question. After we'd finished, he started.

He described his background. He'd taken a job as a prosecutor in Sheffield after qualifying as a lawyer, but after a few months he'd gone to Irwin Mitchell. It was a medium-sized firm, but the lawyers were expert and experienced. However, he said it would be necessary to find the right QC. Solicitors would develop the overall strategy, prepare the facts and gather evidence for the defence. The case would be presented in Crown Court by a barrister since solicitors were not allowed to appear in the higher courts.

'You do realize that you are fighting the establishment, don't you?' Kevin asked. 'There are some QCs who are just not prepared to fight the establishment. You need someone who will take on the government. You need a man like Geoffrey Robertson.'

A QC with a reputation for working outside the government, Robertson had strong ties with the international human rights movement and had won acquittals for a number of political defendants in cases that had embarrassed the government.

Kevin's comments about taking on the establishment showed me that he already had a grasp of the case. He was a thinking man, and was developing a strategy for the case that fitted in with my idea of how to go forward. But Kevin had gone a step further already. I knew there would be no help from the government. But I thought my fight was with the justice system. I hadn't realized until I sat in his office that the battle was against the government itself. I had to have somebody prepared to go after the whole establishment.

In addition, Kevin knew the situation with Iraq. Working with Chris Cowley, he had a grasp of the real government policy on dealing with Baghdad. In fact, he later told me his theory about the dismissal of the supergun prosecution. He believed the American and British governments had conspired to kill the case and avoid revealing the extent of their assistance to Saddam Hussein before his invasion of Kuwait. Chris had told him the US State Department knew of the supergun and had even helped win approval for export licences for its design. It seemed perfectly credible that the White House could call Downing Street and put the lid on a case that threatened to expose their secret policies during the run-up to the Gulf War.

I took an instant liking to Kevin Robinson. He was in his late thirties, but seemed almost boyish in his enthusiasm and keen intelligence. He also seemed down to earth, honest and trustworthy.

I was struck by one of his remarks particularly. Trevor said he understood that this offence carried a maximum sentence of seven years. Kevin replied quickly: 'So does stealing a Mars bar.'

After about an hour and a half Peter, Trevor and I left the offices of Irwin Mitchell and went down the road to a corner pub. I asked Peter and Trevor what they thought about hiring Kevin. They were uncertain. Neither wanted to rush into changing his solicitor. Because of my experience with mine, I decided straight away I wasn't going to waste any more time. I told them I was going to use Kevin.

The next morning, I telephoned Kevin first thing.

'Would you represent me?' I asked.

'Yes, I'd be happy to do it,' Kevin said. 'I was hoping you'd call.'

He told me we had to do it properly. Since I already had a solicitor, I would have to tell him I was switching to another firm. He said I should write a polite letter immediately to inform Alan Parker of my decision.

By the end of the day the message had been conveyed. I had a new solicitor, and finally some hope. I wouldn't have to win this battle by myself after all.

15

Two weeks later, on 12 April 1991, Mark Gutteridge and I were driving back to Prague from a small town in southern Czechoslovakia. We'd been there on business for Hi-Tek, trying to sell machine tools to a company that manufactured cutting tools for the textile industry. It was Mark who started to discuss my situation and the way the government was treating me.

'It's grossly unfair after all the work we did for the intelligence service,' he said. 'They put you out in the cold.'

'I'm hoping to find some way to use it to help,' I told him. 'My new solicitor says we've got to fight the government. The intelligence service is the ace up our sleeve. The problem is how to prove it.'

Kevin Robinson and I had discussed my intelligence work briefly. I hadn't gone into detail yet, but he clearly saw its significance. Every step of the way I had been telling a government agency what I was doing with Iraq. Now, the same government was prosecuting me for concealing it.

'It's all very interesting,' Kevin had said. 'It will be the main thrust of the case. But it's useless unless we can prove it, Paul. You can't just say it.'

I'd been gathering papers that might help. I had copies of the gate records from Matrix Churchill. They showed John Balsom of the DTI signing in. But it wasn't his real name and he didn't work at the DTI. I had a few mentions of his name in my business diary and on my secretary's calendar. It was just bits and pieces. Nothing substantive. Nothing a jury would believe.

Mark puts a lot of thought into things. He is not impulsive. As we sat in the car in silence. I could guess what he was considering. But I didn't want to ask.

'I'll talk to your solicitor and see what can be done,' he said after several minutes. 'I'll help you.'

'It's a risk for you,' I said.

'I'll tell him what I know and what I've done. But Paul, I'd like to stay in the background. I don't want to testify in court, if I can avoid it.'

'I understand.'

I knew generally what Mark had given the intelligence service in recent years. But as we talked he surprised me. Michael Ford from MI5 had told Mark he had prepared a report on the British machine-tool industry's involvement with Iraq that was seen by Margaret Thatcher when she was Prime Minister. I was shocked. By this time she had left office, but her successor, John Major, I believed had been a close confidant of hers. Was it possible the cover-up extended all the way to 10 Downing Street?

Early the next morning we were sitting in the coffee shop at the Hotel Esplanade in Prague when the waiter said I had a telephone call. It was David Leppard of the *Sunday Times*, who told me the paper was running an article on Sunday about John Balsom and my contacts with the intelligence service. He said they had copies of the gate records from Matrix Churchill which showed Balsom claiming to be from the DTI and having signed in to visit me.

I was angry. I was sure that only Peter or Trevor could have provided this story, for they were the only ones who would have access to the gate records. They knew nothing about my contacts with MI6, so they could only be guessing. But they were playing a dangerous game with other people's lives. I hadn't yet decided whether I could risk disclosing my intelligence links because of the possible danger to my family. I hadn't even got around to explaining it all to Kevin Robinson. And now it was going to be featured in the *Sunday Times*.

'I'm not prepared to comment,' I told him. 'As far as I'm concerned, forget it.'

'I'm sorry, Mr Henderson,' he said, 'but I can't forget it.'

'If you link me to the intelligence service, I'm going to take legal advice,' I warned.

Leppard tried to persuade me to make a comment, but I refused. After I got home on Saturday night he telephoned again. Again I refused to comment. In the end, the article did not directly associate me with the intelligence service. For that much, I was grateful. But it clearly alerted Customs and Excise that they might have a problem later on.

The press was often maddening and always interesting on such days. On 1 April I received a call from a reporter who told me the American government had placed me on a blacklist. They claimed I was an agent of the Iraqi government. At first I thought it was an April Fool's joke. I realized by the third or fourth press call that it was not.

I had had a long business relationship with the USA, and I had many friends there as well. I was rebuilding my personal and business life and I saw America playing a big part in that rebuilding. Gordon Cooper and I had talked about a partnership. But the blacklist meant no American company could do business with me. So it was a hell of a shock, and even more so since I'd been out there in January to help the authorities in Atlanta and been told that no one was investigating me. They had even given me immunity against prosecution.

Mark Gutteridge was troubled as well. Since his promise to help me, we had driven up to Sheffield and met Kevin briefly. But Mark had not told him any details of his intelligence work. Clearly he was torn between his own fears and a keen desire to save a friend he had known for thirty years. He also feared putting his wife and children in jeopardy from the Iraqis if his intelligence work became known. I had no choice. I had to be willing to disclose my intelligence activities to save myself and my family. Mark had a choice, and it was a difficult one.

Mark sought advice from what I consider an unlikely source, his current intelligence contact. It was a man who called himself Ian Eacott. Mark had to ring him three days running before Eacott returned his call on the morning of 1 May. When Mark said he was considering talking to a defence lawyer in the Matrix Churchill case, Eacott urged him to come to London immediately. They arranged to meet at four-thirty at Euston that very day.

Eacott telephoned Customs and Excise and reported that one of their contacts had been approached by the defence in the Matrix Churchill case. He was coming in for a meeting. Of course, the customs people wanted to hear what was happening.

From the station in London, Mark and Eacott took a taxi to Bouverie Street, near Fleet Street. They went into Harmsworth House, the headquarters of Customs and Excise, and met Cedric Andrew, a lawyer for that department. The three men spent an hour in Andrew's office. The discussion started out stiff and cautious. At one point, when Andrew said he was choosing his words carefully, Mark responded by saying that he thought they were all on the same side.

Mark said he was certain the intelligence work he and I had done would come up at the trial. I'd asked him to discuss his activities with my solicitor, he said. He shocked Eacott when he said he was the one who had recommended me to the intelligence service as a contact when he left Matrix Churchill in 1988.

Andrew, the lawyer, was the one who told Mark he was free to answer defence questions if he saw fit. Mark pressed him to tell him what would happen if he were called as a witness. He said he feared his business livelihood would be ruined if his espionage activities were disclosed. And he was worried about his family. Could his testimony be held *in camera*, before the judge and jury but not the press and public?

No, Andrew said. But there was a more effective way to stop the defence lawyers from asking Mark publicly in the witness box if he had worked for the intelligence service. Ministers could sign documents, known as Public Interest Immunity Certificates, which could prohibit disclosure of any intelligence evidence, including whether Mark or anyone else had connections with MI5 or MI6.

'If the judge accepted this, it would preclude any such question being asked of you in open court,' explained Andrew.

There was another factor. 'In previous cases, in order to protect sources, Customs and Excise has dropped proceedings altogether when the judge declined to accept such a certificate,' said Andrew.

After the meeting, Eacott and Mark went to a pub. Eacott claimed in a later report that he wanted to soothe Mark's nerves. They were standing at the bar when Mark pulled out a lighter for his cigarette, and put it down on the bar. On the lighter's side were the words 'Matrix Churchill'. Eacott turned it over, hiding the inscription.

'It is better that our contact now becomes historical,' he told Mark.

It was the end of Mark's contact with the intelligence service. His calls were never returned again. When he described the meeting with Eacott and Andrew and the scene in the pub to me the following day, he said: 'You know, Paul, I've been shut out in the cold just as you have.'

That was a costly mistake by the intelligence service. They might have been able to persuade Mark not to cooperate with Kevin and me. But they backed away, leaving him little choice but to go ahead with his instinct to help a friend.

Later in May, Mark and I drove up to Sheffield for a much longer session with Kevin, who was anxious to get a statement about Mark's involvement with the intelligence service.

When we sat down in Kevin's office, Mark surprised Kevin by saying he'd already been interviewed at length by the prosecution. In a sense, they'd signed him up for their side. We still had a right to interview him, but Kevin said propriety required him to inform Customs and Excise.

'This case is an iceberg,' he explained. 'We don't know how much lies below the surface. But we do know that there can be no suggestion of impropriety from our side.'

While we sat there Kevin rang up Chris Constantine. He told him that I'd brought Mark Gutteridge up to his office, and that he wanted to interview Mark. Kevin was smiling. Constantine said he had no objection.

For a couple of hours Mark outlined his meetings with Michael Ford from MI5. He told Kevin he had kept Ford up to date on the Iraqi acquisition of the business. He had given him hundreds of pages of documents to photograph. He had provided information about machines from Matrix Churchill, Colchester, BSA, Wickman Bennett and the German and Swiss companies that were installed at Nassr and Al Hutteen to manufacture parts for artillery shells. There weren't a lot of details yet, but there was the promise of more.

'I've got my diaries,' said Mark. 'I wrote down the time, date and place of every meeting with Ford and Eacott. It was against the rules, but you never know when it might come in handy. I'll come back up and we'll go over them.'

This was critical corroboration of my story. Kevin was quite pleased. But he warned me not to become too excited. There was still a long way to go.

'We need documents,' Kevin explained. 'With the dates and information that you and Mark are giving me, we can make a request for specific records of these meetings. If we can get these documents, we'll nail them.'

Mark had mentioned what he had been told about the possibility of the prosecution seeking Public Interest Immunity Certificates to block the release of the documents. He also said he'd been told about the possibility of dropping the case if a judge refused to keep the papers secret.

Kevin saw danger in the certificates. The government seemed prepared to use all its powers to try to suppress evidence about the intelligence aspects of the case. It was, he said, a highly unusual action in a criminal case. The government was rarely allowed to withhold information that could jeopardize a person's liberty.

On the other hand, if the judge refused the request, Customs and Excise might drop the prosecution. While I found encouragement in this, Kevin was more cautious. 'We can't think that way,' he said. 'We have to think that this case is going to trial, and I'm telling you it will go to trial. What we've got to do is develop a strategy to win this case. And win it we will. With or without the papers.'

Our strategy had two elements. First, prove the government was completely aware of what Matrix Churchill was doing because of information provided to the intelligence services by Mark Gutteridge and me. Here, it would depend heavily on the documents. But there also was the testimony of Mark and me. Secondly, show that, because of the information, the government knew Matrix Churchill machines were being used by Iraq for munitions production and nevertheless permitted the sales as part of its policy. This would be established largely through evidence from the DTI officials and ministers.

Kevin had contacted Geoffrey Robertson, who had confirmed that he would take the case as the QC. Assisting Robertson would be Ken MacDonald, a high-flying young London barrister. We'd secured the best legal representation possible. Now it was a question of really hard work.

And that work involved me. Peter Allen and Trevor Abraham were not spending as much time with their lawyers. They seemed to prefer to let the professionals take care of it. I'm not one to sit back and let things happen to me. I'd go up to Sheffield and spend two or three days at a time there. Kevin would pick a subject and we'd go right through it. I'd remember all I could about a contract or a meeting with the government. He'd write everything down in blue books. Then he'd ask more questions. When you're thinking back and stretching your mind and your memory, by the end of the day you feel tired. But Kevin would always turn around and look at me with a funny smile and say: 'It's fun this, isn't it?'

He was good-humoured and filled with optimism. It wasn't going to be easy, and sometimes it even seemed too hard, as if we'd never win against the whole government. Yet Kevin's enthusiasm was infectious, and so was his confidence. He never even hinted that we'd do anything but win.

The next encounter with the government was scheduled for November 1991. A committal hearing would be held at Thames Magistrates Court before a magistrate, not a jury. The prosecution was required to convince the magistrate that there was enough evidence to put the three of us on trial. Often these hearings are short: the defence agrees that the evidence is sufficient and a trial date is set. But Kevin was preparing for a full fight.

'We're not going to lie down and let them walk over us,' he explained to me one day in early summer as we sat in his office. 'We're going to make it tough on them. We're going to show them that we're going to win this case. We're going to fight it all the way down the line.'

It wasn't a matter of winning at this stage. There'd be little chance of that in front of a magistrate, unless someone stood up in the witness box and confessed that the government knew all along. But the hearing would let us test the prosecution case and look for weaknesses.

The prosecution would put on its best witnesses. Government officials would give witness statements in advance, which Kevin would use to cross-examine them at the hearing. The government version of what happened would be on record. It would give us a view of the case that the prosecution would present at trial a year or so later.

The witness statements began coming into Kevin's office in the middle of the summer. To me, the pattern was clear straight away: the government officials were claiming that they did not know the machines were for military purposes. They said Peter, Trevor and I had deceived them. It was rubbish. They knew. We had to prove they knew.

A critical part of our defence was the meeting on 20 January 1988 between the MTTA and Alan Clark, the Minister for Trade at the DTI. It was there that Clark had indicated that he knew what the machines were being used for. He had advised us to stress civilian uses to ensure approval of future export licences and to move quickly.

But, in his two-page witness statement, Clark denied any knowledge of the military purposes of the machinery. 'The advice I gave to the MTTA was based upon the assumption that the exports were intended for civil applications,' he said.

John Balsom's witness statement ran to three pages. The story in the *Sunday Times* in April and Mark Gutteridge's session with Ian Eacott and Cedric Andrew in May had alerted the prosecution to our strategy. Balsom's statement was carefully worded to undermine my credibility. He distanced himself and the intelligence service from me. He minimized my information and ignored the risks I'd taken. It was a kick in the teeth.

Kevin said it would be important to show my history with the intelligence service. We didn't want to leave the impression that I had just started working for them to win favourable treatment on the licences for Iraq. By establishing a relationship extending back years, it would be clear that my motives were patriotic, not self-serving. But Balsom said he had reviewed my files from the seventies and found I had provided 'low-level information'.

As far as my dealings with him were concerned Balsom was wrong about when we first met, and he withheld other important facts. He said he'd first met me in April 1989, six months after we'd sat together at the Inn on the Park in London. He claimed that I'd never discussed specific contracts involving Matrix Churchill and the Iraqis. He acknowledged that I'd given him the ABA drawings, but claimed I'd never said Matrix Churchill was involved. He claimed I'd never mentioned that we were working with Carlos Cardoen. And he made no mention of the meeting in the safe house in September 1989.

'During the period up until July 1990 Henderson provided a certain amount of useful though generally not high-level information on Iraqi policy, operational activity and a few technical snippets relating to this field,' the intelligence agent said.

'A few technical snippets.' I was steaming. Balsom had portrayed me as a deceiver, someone who withheld the most important information. I wondered if even my own solicitor would begin to doubt me. It seemed to me that the government cover-up was being put into place, but I never expected Balsom to lie. I wondered just how far the government would go. Kevin was calm. His faith in me and my innocence was never affected by the government's lies. The trick, he explained as we reviewed Balsom's statement, was showing that the intelligence service, like the other members of the government who were involved, knew more than they were admitting.

Kevin decided that he would do the cross-examination of witnesses at Thames Magistrates Court. He had the best feel for the case by that time. Neither Geoffrey Robertson nor Ken MacDonald had been involved up to that point.

I was a bit frightened as the date for my court appearance drew near. For the first time, I'd sit in the dock and listen to the prosecution and its witnesses accuse me of betraying my country.

Thames Magistrates Court is a modern building in what is not an upmarket area of East London. The courtroom itself had high ceilings and terrible acoustics. The spectators were separated from the rest of the court by a glass screen, the dock for the defendants was at the back of the courtroom, and the magistrate sat behind a raised section at the front.

Shortly before ten o'clock on the morning of 18 November, Peter Allen, Trevor Abraham and I were led into the dock by a court official. The lock on the door closed behind us and we sat down on a hard wooden bench behind a waist-high rail. It was an odd and disorientating experience. For the next nine days I would spend most of every day sitting there, listening to government lies and to Kevin fighting to save me.

The prosecution was represented by Alan Moses, a QC with a reputation for a keen intellect and an ability to handle complicated cases. Earlier in the year he had prosecuted the nuclear triggers case for Customs and Excise. There had been a five-year sentence for Ali Daghir, the Iraqi businessman who was convicted of importing the triggers into Britain and planning to re-export them to Iraq.

The evidence varied little from the statements we had seen. It was not the truth as I knew it. I was angered by what seemed to be the prosecution's strategy of putting up only witnesses who had something bad to say about us. It wasn't the full facts, but a confusion of fact and fiction.

Not until Kevin began cross-examining Anthony Steadman did I get a glimmer of hope. Steadman had been a director in the export licencing unit at the DTI. As early as 1987, he admitted to Kevin, there were suspicions within Whitehall that British machine tools were being used by Iraq for military purposes. Some of the information had come, he said, from a 'delicate source'. The Iran–Iraq war was still going on, but Steadman acknowledged that export licences for Matrix Churchill and other companies were approved after a brief delay despite the suspicions.

Eric Beston, Steadman's superior, also admitted there were wide suspicions as early as 1987. He also testified that Whitehall were concerned about the Iraqi ownership of Matrix Churchill, which he acknowledged was suspected of being part of the procurement network. Nevertheless, he claimed there had been no direct knowledge of the military uses of British machinery.

Walking out of the courtroom after cross-examining Steadman and Beston, Kevin was buoyant. 'Wasn't that beautiful,' he said eagerly to me. 'We've got them now.'

The testimony had established that the government suspected Matrix Churchill machines were used for military purposes. It was more than they'd admitted before. If they suspected it, why didn't they ever ask the obvious, direct question?

'Because,' Kevin said happily in answer to his own question as we walked down the steps, 'there was no need. They already knew.'

Kevin told me a joke during the lunch break that summed up the attitude of the DTI. A man was out walking his Yorkshire terrier when he decided to go into a pub for a drink. 'I'm sorry, sir, dogs aren't allowed in the pub,' said the barman. The man, being a quick thinker, responded: 'I'm blind. He's my guide dog.'

'Oh come on, sir. Guide dogs are big, like labradors,' said the barman.

The man, thinking quickly again, exclaimed, 'What have they given me, then?'

I was learning the strategy of a trial. A court hearing is a game of increments. Small disclosures provide a foundation for an entire case. For his part, Kevin compared cross-examination to fishing. Gently draw the fish in and don't frighten it away until it is hooked. That was the way he handled another important witness.

In November 1990, after my first arrest, I had attended the annual Machine Tool Technologies Association dinner at Grosvenor House in London. During cocktails I was chatting with Joseph Wickham, a director of Flexible Manufacturing Technology, the firm which had supplied the vertical machining centres for the ABA contract. He told me about a conversation he'd had about the contract with an official at the British embassy in Baghdad in May 1990.

Wickham had gone to Iraq for technical discussions on the ABA contract. At that time we were trying to get the ABA export licence renewed. Wickham already knew the contract was for munitions, and during a visit to the Nassr factory he saw a mock-up of the ABA rocket. The following day he was at the embassy talking with an acquaintance in the commercial section. He had mentioned the efforts to revalidate the export licence and the missile, and the embassy man, Martin Hall, replied that he knew all about it.

'They knew about the ABA contract and they knew that it was defence-related,' Wickham told me at the dinner. This was a vital piece of evidence. When Kevin began to question Wickham at the magistrate's hearing, he walked on eggshells. He didn't want to scare him away from recalling the meeting at the embassy. Instead, he led him along, asking about his visit to Iraq that May, the model of the rocket, his trip to the embassy. But he mentioned nothing about his conversation with Hall.

After Wickham acknowledged these facts, then Kevin questioned him about the conversation with me at the machine-tool convention. When he recalled that conversation Kevin had him repeat the one he had with Martin Hall, which disclosed that the embassy officer knew in 1990 that the contract was for defence products.

We'd decided not to require Alan Clark or Balsom at the magistrate's hearing. Kevin didn't want to cross-examine them at a hearing where the outcome was inevitable.

I would have loved to have walked away from that court a free man, but on Tuesday 26 November the magistrate found there was enough evidence to remand us for a full criminal trial at the Old Bailey.

But we felt the magistrate's hearing was a success, for Kevin was confident we had found some weakness in the prosecution case. Even so, the last thing I wanted to do was wait another year for the trial.

The Christmas holidays after the hearing at Thames Magistrates Court were a difficult time. I'd known I was unemployable in the industry since the arrest. We weren't badly off, and I was doing some work for Hi-Tek on commission. Esther and the children, as well as our close friends, had been supportive from the start. And in recent months I'd discovered that neighbours and other people who didn't know me as well believed what was happening was unfair.

Until the magistrate's hearing I'd still held onto the idea that the government would drop the case and I wouldn't have to reveal my intelligence work. Now, facing a full trial, with my future at stake, I understood that I would have to disclose it publicly. Doing so could put my family at risk.

I wasn't so worried about the Soviets or the Eastern Europeans.

They had done their share of spying, and the political scene there was changing rapidly. It would be of no consequence to them. In any case, I had learned from my contacts in Poland and Czechoslovakia since the demise of communism that my name, together with those of Mark Gutteridge and John Belgrove, had been in their secret state files as political enemies of the government.

I was concerned about the Iraqis, however. Who knew what they might do? It would have been difficult to live with my conscience if anything happened to Esther, David or Sue. But I didn't see that there was any choice. Without disclosing my intelligence work, I seemed likely to go to prison. There would be no help from MI6.

In early 1992 David was home from his job in London and Sue was at home with Esther. The four of us sat down and I described to them some of the detail of my activities on behalf of the intelligence service. I told them I planned to disclose these activities at the trial unless they objected. They were not shocked, although there might have been an element of surprise. But I'd always been a risk taker, so it was no bombshell that I'd been a spy. Esther, it turned out, had had her suspicions. She is a very intelligent person. She'd twigged that I was doing a little more than selling machines.

My family supported me in my decision. David, who had been with the Coldstream Guards in the army and served in Northern Ireland, was enthusiastic. There seemed a bit of pride in him that I'd been a spy. 'Go for it, Dad,' he said.

Through the early months of 1992 Kevin Robinson and I met almost weekly, often for two or three days at a time. Usually I drove up to Sheffield and sometimes I went to Kevin's house, where I met his wife Louise and their lovely daughters, Emma and Alice. Sometimes, he came down to Coventry.

There was a major flaw in the prosecution case. They were claiming that the Matrix Churchill machines were 'specially designed' for military use in Iraq. This was rubbish. The machines could be used for military purposes. They had been used for military purposes. But they were not designed specially for military purposes. They were dual-use technology, with as many civil applications as military ones. It was a technical point, but an important one.

It had become clear at the magistrate's hearing that the prosecution did not have a good technical grasp of the machine-tool business. Some days before the hearing Customs and Excise had called a journalist named John Dunn of the publication *Engineer* and asked a question that betrayed their ignorance: 'Have you got a definition of a CNC lathe?'

Kevin said we'd got to find an expert witness who would derail the prosecution's argument that these were specially designed for the munitions industry. After considerable searching, Kevin came up with Dr Roger Hannam, a lecturer at the University of Manchester's Institute of Science and Technology. Dr Hannam had also spent time in the industry, including some work for TI Group many years earlier, and knew the business thoroughly.

After looking at the prosecution papers on the case and examining the data on the machines sent to Iraq, he told us flatly: 'It's nonsense. Not only were these machines not specially designed for military uses – even the tooling and fixtures were not.'

Dr Hannam prepared a paper for us discrediting the prosecution's contention. He also would prove invaluable during the trial itself. In Kevin's view this in itself was enough to defeat the prosecution. They had claimed that the machines were specially designed for military uses, but we had an expert who would testify that they were not. The prosecution had acted out of ignorance.

'This is a 100 per cent, cast-iron defence,' Kevin told me one day. 'It's perfectly valid, Paul. But it's technical, a play on words which may be unattractive to a jury. The real defence, which will win this case, is the political one.'

The trial was due to start on 5 October at the Old Bailey. Beforehand, there would be a series of hearings to resolve matters before trial. The first hearing was in June 1992. Before that I met Geoffrey Robertson and Ken MacDonald, the other key members of the defence team.

'Hello, Paul, it's nice to meet you,' Robertson said when I walked into his chambers in Doughty Street that Saturday morning. 'This is a disgraceful case. You should never have been prosecuted.'

The first thing that struck me was that he was not an establishment man. Because of the stature of a QC, I had been expecting someone in extremely conservative clothes and with a formal manner. I had turned up in a collar and tie myself. But here was Geoffrey Robertson calling the case disgraceful and wearing very sporty summer clothes. He was about six feet tall, in his early forties, with a fair amount of bushy, wavy grey hair.

Kevin had prepared the case in a dozen thick volumes and sent them to Robertson. The QC questioned me all day, and I was impressed at how he had understood every aspect of the case. His memory for detail was fantastic and his questioning was thorough and accurate.

Ken MacDonald, the barrister assisting Robertson, showed up a bit later in the day. He was wearing a suit and had come from a cocktail party, but he was equally engaging and down-to-earth.

The strategy we developed was simple. We had to get the intelligence documents and the internal government memos. They would prove that the government knew what the machines were for.

It was clear that the prosecution intended to call Balsom as a witness at the trial. It would be the first time a British intelligence officer had given evidence in open court. He would be used to serve as a counterweight to my evidence about my intelligence work, to minimize what I'd say. If we could get Balsom's reports it would be far harder for him to play down my information. If not, it would be my word against his.

We set about getting those documents, memos and reports. Ken MacDonald prepared a formal request to the prosecution for all of the documents. The material we sought was in six basic categories. There were minutes of meetings by the Inter-Departmental Committee on export licences. Written communications between senior officials of the DTI and Foreign Office on export applications. Minutes of the January 1988 meeting with Alan Clark and the September 1989 meeting with Lord Trefgarne, as well as briefing papers prepared before and after those meetings. Reports and other written material prepared by intelligence officers using the names Michael Ford and Ian Eacott regarding meetings with Mark Gutteridge. The specific report prepared by Ford and seen by Mrs Thatcher. And finally, all records of meetings between the intelligence services and me since 1973.

The first hearing was held at the Old Bailey on 19 June 1992. It was before Judge Brian Smedley, who was so trusted by the establishment that he'd recently been appointed judge for the British military base in Cyprus. He would be the one to decide whether we got access to the government papers and the intelligence documents.

The hearing was only for administrative issues, setting dates for the prosecution's handing over material to the defence and similar matters. At the start of the hearing Geoffrey Robertson gave the court and the prosecution copies of our request for documents, which was dated 16 June 1992. Moses and his assistant, Gibson Grenfell, kept their poker faces in court, but afterwards we learned that the extensive demand had caused considerable alarm in government circles.

Judge Smedley set a deadline of 2 September for the prosecution to supply the documents or to argue the case for non-disclosure. But the prosecution signalled its intention to fight us well before then. At a hearing in late July it was Grenfell who told the court it was likely that several ministers would sign Public Interest Immunity Certificates to prevent disclosure of most of the material we had called for. Geoffrey Robertson indicated that he would oppose the procedure. The prosecution asked for more time to prepare. So the judge set a hearing on it for the end of September, just days before the trial was scheduled to begin.

There was no certainty that we'd ever get the documents. We had to prepare for a trial without the papers. If they came at the last minute it would be a welcome victory. If not, we had to find another way to win the case.

In the spring and early summer of 1992 there had been a number of stories in the American press about US policy towards Saddam Hussein in the years before Operation Desert Storm. It was clear from the cuttings that American reporters had access to CIA documents and other intelligence records about the Iraq policy. One of the stories mentioned a 1989 CIA report about the Iraqi arms-buying network. Among the companies named was Matrix Churchill Limited.

'Press stories aren't enough for court,' Kevin explained to me as he showed me the cuttings. 'We need the actual documents. With them, we'll show that the Americans knew what the Iraqis were up to. And that they knew about Matrix Churchill's involvement. Yet both countries were still approving sales to Iraq. It is common knowledge that the Americans and British share intelligence information. So we can show this way that the British government knew what was going on. Any intelligent person is going to believe that.'

Through contacts with lawyers and others in America, Geoffrey and Kevin began to get the actual documents. One of the first ones he received was a top-secret order signed by President Bush in October 1989. It spelled out an American policy towards Iraq that was a clone of the British policy.

'We should pursue, and seek to facilitate, opportunities for US firms to participate in the reconstruction of the Iraqi economy,' the President wrote in the order, called National Security Directive 26. 'Also, as a means of developing access and influence with the Iraqi defense establishment, the United States should consider sales of non-lethal forms of military assistance . . . on a case by case basis.'

Even closer to the target was the CIA's analysis, dated 6 November 1989, which identified Matrix Churchill as part of the Iraqi arms procurement network, along with firms such as TDG and Gerald Bull's Space Research Corporation.

What Kevin needed was evidence that demonstrated the common knowledge that the CIA shared intelligence information with its British counterparts. He once compared preparing a defence to archaeology: a bit of bone, a piece of skull and eventually the skeleton is completed.

Late that summer, Kevin found a big bone. He was examining hundreds of pages of hearings and documents from the government commission appointed to investigate the supergun case. A member of the commission, apparently in an unguarded moment, had referred in a session to 'our joint intelligence operation with the Americans'. It was slim, but Kevin thought it would be enough to enable us to use the CIA records in the trial.

But it may not have been enough to win my freedom. That chance was resting heavily in the hands of Judge Smedley. How would he respond to the ministers' demands that he suppress the information? As summer gave way to autumn and the hearing on that issue approached, a little bit of fear was creeping into my mind.

The government was not prepared to release the documents that I believed proved my innocence. I was beginning to fear the power of the government more and more. Kevin was telling me we'd win the argument. But it hit me hard that the government was so powerful that it could just refuse to release the documents that would determine how my family and I spent the rest of our lives.

16

I found it difficult to sit silently. I wanted to shout: 'Stop this rubbish.' Alan Moses, the prosecuting QC, was making statements to the court which, to me, could not be true. But he kept repeating them. The government papers the defence had demanded were not relevant, he claimed. There was no reason to hand them over.

'I have read these documents,' Moses said loudly as he stood, in robes and wig, before Judge Smedley. 'So has my learned junior. We do not consider they assist the defence in relation to any foreseeable issue.'

I shook my head in stark wonder. Had Moses actually read the documents? If so, had the papers themselves been altered? Or had the ministers instructed him to make this argument? Moses could not stand there and say the documents were not relevant if they were the true story of what had happened. Yet here he was trying to convince the judge – and us – that they contained nothing of relevance. I listened in growing amazement as he continued trying to justify what I viewed as a massive cover-up.

'These documents do not assist in any way the defence. And it is for these reasons that your Lordship should not order their disclosure.'

It was the morning of Wednesday 30 September when I sat in Court 15 at the Old Bailey listening to Moses. By then, it was clear that the government were prepared to go to great lengths to stop us getting the documents.

By the end of the previous day we had received six Public Interest Immunity Certificates, signed by four different ministers. Invoking the privilege of the Crown, the ministers claimed that lives might be lost and intelligence operations threatened if the court ordered disclosure of the documents.

Two certificates were signed by Kenneth Clarke, the Home Secretary, who was responsible for MI5. He said disclosure of its documents 'is likely to prejudice national security' and disclose matters to people 'whose actions in the past have shown that they are willing to kill innocent civilians'.

Along with the hyperbole, a curious thing about Clarke's certificates was the date he had signed the first one: 16 June 1992. That was the day the defence letter demanding the documents had been written. But it was three days *before* the letter was handed over to the prosecution and the court. My lawyers thought the government had prepared the certificate before ever receiving our letter and then dated it the day of the request.

It was another indication of what we felt we were up against. When you challenge the full power of government, there is a tendency to get a bit paranoid. But several occurrences in recent weeks had left all of us wondering if the government had the defence under surveillance.

For example, Geoffrey Robertson had picked up strange static on telephone lines in his chambers a few weeks earlier. His father-in-law, an electronics expert, checked the line and told him there was a listening tap on it. There also had been several instances in which we appeared to be under physical surveillance.

I'd seen the first time I met him that Kevin Robinson was down-to-earth. But he took the possibility we were under surveillance quite seriously. It was entirely likely, he said, that the secret services had put bugs on all our phone lines. Christopher Cowley had become convinced during the supergun case that his phones were tapped. He had even complained to the police that it was government agents who had burgled his home.

As a result of these suspicions the date on Clarke's first Public Interest Immunity Certificate added to our concerns. The other such certificates took the same basic position. They were signed by Malcolm Rifkind, the Defence Secretary, Michael Heseltine, the new President of the Board of Trade, and two were signed by Tristan Garel-Jones, a minister at the Foreign Office. Garel-Jones was the most infuriating.

MI6 reported to the Foreign and Commonwealth Office, and revealing anything from the MI6 documents, claimed Garel-Jones, would 'substantially impair' the ability of the agency to protect Britain from foreign threats. 'Human sources' expected to have their identities kept secret. Exposing them would place informants in 'grave danger'.

What about the danger that I was in? I thought to myself when I read Garel-Jones's words. What about the threats that Mark and I would be living under for the rest of our lives because the government was forcing us to reveal our work as informants in order to save me from prison? What hit me once again after reading the certificates was the power of the government.

Geoffrey Robertson determined right from the start that we had to attack the certificates head on. Later events proved how right he was. But while we were waiting for the hearing to begin that Wednesday morning, I was approached by Gilbert Gray, who was Trevor Abraham's QC, and James Hunt, the QC for Peter Allen, who said they were less confident that anything material would emerge and were troubled that if documents did not help it would be more damaging.

I suppose their reasoning was that we'd score some points with the jury if we could refer to material we weren't allowed to see. But I knew the significance of those documents. I knew what should be in them. I was speechless at the proposal. I turned and walked away from the two QCs. When I told Geoffrey and Kevin about it a few minutes later, Geoffrey just laughed.

In his argument to the judge, Alan Moses said the concept that the government could suppress documents was well established in civil cases. He described three other criminal cases where it had happened, and he said there was no difference between the way the law applied in civil and criminal matters. In fact, he claimed, the ministers had a legal 'duty' to keep certain material secret to protect the public interest.

Geoffrey accepted none of the reasoning. The very idea that ministers could keep evidence out of a criminal case was an affront to the concept of a fair trial.

'One of the mistakes my learned friend has made is in advising these ministers that they have a duty to claim PII,' he told the judge. 'It is simply not so.'

As a compromise, Moses had suggested that the documents be turned over to Judge Smedley. He could read them and see for himself that they were of no relevance to the matters at trial. Robertson again was opposed completely. He argued that there was no way the judge could determine what evidence was relevant to the defence case. Only the defence could determine what was relevant in the documents. 'It is a meaningless exercise,' he told the judge. 'You have no idea what the defence case is.'

However, Gilbert Gray then rose and spoke in favour of Moses's idea of letting the judge read the material and decide the issue. With that bit of help from the defence itself, Judge Smedley could not resist. He said he would read the documents and decide whether the balance tipped in favour of the prosecution or the defence.

Moses made a great show of the secrecy and gravity of the documents. He told the judge that security people would be stationed outside his chambers the entire time he possessed the documents. The material would then be returned to the MI5 and MI6 vaults at night.

The arguments over the documents had covered nearly three days. It was Friday before they were delivered to the judge's rooms so that he could examine them over the weekend. The material from the Foreign Office, DTI and MoD came in fat bundles. But there was great drama attached to the MI5 and MI6 documents, which were transported to the judge's rooms in sealed containers by security personnel. A guard was stationed outside the judge's rooms. It all served to highlight the prosecution's argument about the gravity of these documents being disclosed.

The prosecution had divided the documents into three categories. There was Category A, which apparently contained very few documents. They were all said to deal with information about Matrix Churchill provided by another confidential source, neither Mark nor me. Category B was supposedly the ministerial documents from the DTI, FO and MoD about the exports by Matrix Churchill and other British machine-tool companies: internal memos, meeting minutes, briefing papers, export applications and the like. The MI5 and MI6 papers were in Category C.

On Monday morning, after spending the weekend examining the material, Judge Smedley came to court with his decision.

Category A, which was described as a letter from an informant and a memo about it, would remain secret. It didn't matter, and Geoffrey would not object.

Then Smedley shocked the prosecution. He granted the release of the Category B documents. These were to include references to actions on export licences from other companies. Finally, there would be a look behind the scenes at Whitehall's secret policy towards Iraq.

'Henderson's case is that, although the terms in which applications were made might have been misleading to the casual reader, that was done with the complicity of the department concerned for its own policy reasons,' he said in a lengthy statement from the bench. 'To prevent access to those documents may well result in a miscarriage of justice in an important criminal case.'

As far as I was concerned, the judge had seen that Moses's argument was rubbish. The documents were indeed relevant to the defence. His ruling was a big victory for us. But it was followed by a serious set-back.

Judge Smedley then turned to Category C, the intelligence material. As he continued with his statement it became clear that he had been influenced heavily by the Public Interest Immunity Certificates from the four ministers. He said only the Home Secretary and the Foreign Secretary could judge the effect of disclosing the MI5 and MI6 material. He called their arguments in favour of suppression 'powerful and weighty'.

With regard to the documents about my meetings with the intelligence service, the judge said that John Balsom wold testify about his recollections of those sessions. He could examine the documents to refresh his memory. 'If Mr Henderson wishes to give evidence about those meetings, then he can do so,' he said. 'The evidence may be unchallenged. If there is any advantage to him in seeing these records, which I doubt, it does not outweigh the objections put forward in the certificate.'

There it was: my word against Balsom's. It was a dismal defeat. Followed by another, for Smedley dismissed the request for Mark Gutteridge's records, saying: 'I can only regard this as a fishing expedition.' He said he saw no relevance to the defence in disclosing the MI5 material concerning Mark's activities.

I left the Old Bailey that afternoon with a feeling of relief and concern. Some documents would be released, but important ones were being kept secret. If there were documents that proved my innocence, why the hell couldn't I have them?

Later that evening I was with my lawyers in Geoffrey's chambers when a set of the Category B documents was delivered to us. Geoffrey, Ken MacDonald, Kevin and I had been joined by Peter Weatherby, a promising young lawyer who was working with Ken.

As we began to go over them it became obvious to all of us that the ministries knew some of the machines had gone for military purposes. It was clear that Whitehall was aware of the military nature of some of the applications as early as 8 January 1988. Minutes of an inter-ministry committee recorded Item 15: 'SECRET UK EYES

ONLY . . . MACHINE TOOLS FOR IRAQ. MoD and SIS reported that machine tools sent to Iraq were for use in the manufacture of munitions. The IDC would watch out for licence applications.'

In the alphabet soup of government, SIS was the Secret Intelligence Service, also known as MI6. IDC was the Inter-Departmental Committee, which reviewed sensitive export licences. In plain language, the minutes meant that the information Mark Gutteridge had supplied to Michael Ford had been passed on to MI6 and then distributed within the government.

Correspondence between the various ministers and officials also referred to intelligence sources regarding Matrix Churchill machines. One of the documents showed that the intelligence services had argued for approving licences to keep information flowing from a source within the company.

It became all the more important to obtain the intelligence files dealing with Mark and me. They would link up neatly with the other documents, showing that the government was aware that Matrix Churchill machines were for military uses before approving either the Cardoen or ABA licences, the contracts over which we were charged.

Geoffrey, Ken and Kevin discussed the matter well into the night. They came to an unprecedented decision: they would reveal part of the defence strategy in the hope of forcing Judge Smedley to change his mind and release the Category C documents. The material from Category B was important, perhaps even sufficient for victory. But we'd win for sure if we could get the intelligence material. The documents were more important than the secrecy of our defence.

During the informal discussions at court, there had been hints that the prosecution might be willing to discuss a plea bargain. There was the possibility that we could plead guilty to a lesser charge in exchange for the certainty of not going to prison.

Even if Peter and Trevor had said yes, my view was that I'd still fight my case on my own. I was prepared to take the risk of going to prison, but the world would know my story. I wanted to go in the witness-box and tell it, even if we didn't get the intelligence documents. In the end, it came to nothing.

On Tuesday morning we were back in court for the showdown over the all-important intelligence papers.

'I invite your Lordship to reconsider your ruling in relation to

Category C in view of the disclosure I intend to make in relation to Mr Henderson's defence,' Geoffrey told Judge Smedley.

Then, in precise language, he outlined the case against me and the essential value of the intelligence papers. I was accused of deliberate deception and distorting the truth about the uses of the machines sent to Iraq under the Cardoen and ABA contracts.

Yet, he continued, 'Paul Henderson believed that the information that he and Mr Gutteridge were supplying to the intelligence service was being transmitted to the DTI and to ministers. This belief was based upon information that was given to him by members of the security service and, indeed, by Mark Gutteridge.'

The records of those meetings with Balsom and all the others would confirm my belief. They would demonstrate that I had not deceived the DTI or anyone else, and that the machines had been approved knowingly and as part of British government policy. Mark's records were as essential in establishing this as were mine.

With the defence strategy as naked as Lady Godiva, even Alan Moses could no longer justify concealment of the papers. 'We can well see how the balance tips clearly in favour of the defence seeing the records of those meetings,' he told the court.

This time, Judge Smedley did not even retire to his rooms to consider the matter. He ruled at once, saying: 'It seems to me now that, contrary to what I said yesterday, these accused could not be fairly tried if I were to uphold the class objection to the Category C documents . . . I shall order their disclosure.'

It was four o'clock on Thursday 8 October before the prosecution sent over the bundles of MI5 and MI6 documents. The manner in which they arrived would have been funny had it not been such a serious matter. The documents that had been given to the judge in sealed containers and guarded by security personnel came round to the Doughty Street chambers on the back of a motorbike. A commercial bike messenger was carrying these top-secret papers that could jeopardize lives and topple the government.

Peter Weatherby stayed up most of the night, copying and sorting the files into chronological order. It was a hard wait, but I wouldn't see them until Friday morning when we all gathered again at the chambers.

My sense of relief was total. Reading through my set of documents, I could see they proved what I had said. This was Paul Henderson's vindication, so to speak. The last two years of work with Kevin, scouring my memory for meetings and information I'd provided to Balsom – there it was. My recall, Kevin would later say, had been better than 90 per cent accurate.

Not only was I vindicated in my own eyes, but the documents showed Kevin, Geoffrey and Ken that I hadn't led them down the garden path. I had told them the truth. Even James Hunt QC would later walk up to me, shake my hand and apologize for doubting the relevance of the documents.

The reaction of my own lawyers was pure delight. As they read through the documents on Friday morning, occasionally someone would call out: 'Here's a good one' or 'This is dynamite'. The atmosphere was like a party.

The government had blacked out large portions of the reports prepared by John Balsom and Michael Ford on their meetings with Mark and me. But the remaining sections clearly showed that we had told them everything we knew about the uses of our machines in Iraq. And we had told them early and often.

It was there in the first report prepared by Ford that mentioned Iraq. Mark was still working for Matrix Churchill and the company was owned by TI. Dated 6 May 1987, the document was headed 'SECRET' and called 'Contact Note'. Much was blacked out about a meeting between Ford and Mark in a hotel room. Untouched was paragraph 12, which said: 'Lastly, and much as an afterthought, (G) told of TI Matrix dealings with a London-based Iraqi company. This company is buying milling machines specifically tooled up for arms production. He was concerned that we should not interfere with this business since it is of high value and will be taken up by the West Germans if TI Matrix withdraw.' In such documents the intelligence people had inserted 'G' and 'H' within brackets to indicate Gutteridge and Henderson, respectively.

One of Balsom's reports identified me only as a 'British business-man' and told how, in early 1990, I had described 'sensitive Iraqi military projects'. Among them, he noted, were the fuse project with Gerald Bull's SRC and Project ABA, which involved 'long-range artillery rockets'.

Some of the information was inaccurate and confused. Some meetings, such as the one in the safe house in September 1989, were not disclosed. But again and again the reports showed how Mark and I kept the intelligence services informed on our dealings with the Iraqis.

Kevin, who months ago had become a close friend as well as my trusted lawyer, was smiling widely when he got up from the conference table and walked over to me. He clapped me on the back and said: 'There's no way we can lose now, Paul. No way. I'm not sure the prosecution will even go ahead with the trial now that we've got these.'

The arguments over the documents had delayed the start of the trial. It was to begin on the morning of Monday 12 October. I took a set of documents home to Coventry with me and spent the weekend making notes about them for the lawyers. It was a nerve-racking time. I wanted to be free, so I hoped the prosecution would drop the case. Yet Customs and Excise had taken the last two years of my life, robbed me of my lifelong ambition of owning Matrix Churchill. Only in the last few days, the business had gone into receivership, with the loss of all but a handful of jobs. I wanted the world to know my story, so I hoped for the opportunity to go ahead with the trial. I'd find out on Monday morning.

17

At ten o'clock on Monday 12 October 1992 I sat in the dock at the Old Bailey with Trevor Abraham and Peter Allen. I glanced over at Esther and Sue, who were in the public gallery, and we smiled our mutual support.

The television cameras and photographers had been waiting outside when I arrived. The case had been well covered in the press, but although the papers had heard that the intelligence services were going to be involved, court rules had not allowed them to report it. They filmed and photographed me as I walked towards the Old Bailey, and then they were gone as I passed through the tight security. An attendant directed me to Court 16; the case had been moved to the largest court because of the expected crowd.

I shook hands with Geoffrey, Kevin and Ken. It was all 'Don't worry' and 'We'll win', but I was getting nervous. It was odd how polite everyone was. Alan Moses and the other members of the prosecution smiled and said good morning to all of us. It all seemed a bit unreal. After all, Moses was trying to send me to prison for seven years.

The court was rather a fascinating scene for its pageantry and formality: the judge, QCs and barristers wore robes and wigs, and the judge was seated up high at the far end of the room. Facing the judge on the left-hand side of the court was the press box, adjacent to it was where the jury would sit, and to the right of the judge was the witness-box. In front of him were three rows of tables for the prosecution and the defence. The QCs sat in the front row, the barristers in the second and the solicitors in the third. The dock, where Trevor, Peter and I would sit, was at the back of the court.

First came the selection of the jury. About sixty people were called in as a group. They stood under the public gallery, to our right, and listened as the judge read out some facts about the case. The trial would probably last about ten weeks, and any prospective jurors who couldn't commit that much time could stand down. If they worked for the intelligence service or the ministries involved, they were ineligible to serve in this case. When their names had been read, the judge questioned them individually, and eventually twelve jurors were picked, sworn in and seated.

Trevor, Peter and I were told to stand. We listened as the charges against us were read out, and were required to respond individually. It was unnerving. I had not spoken at the preliminary hearing in Thames Magistrates Court, and it was the first time I had ever uttered a word in court. But I answered in as loud a voice as I could muster: 'Not guilty.'

As I spoke the words I reflected on my situation. How far would the government go to cover up the policies arrived at behind closed doors? Government officials had hidden the truth in their witness statements. Balsom wasn't telling all that he knew, and had even tried to discredit me.

When he opposed the release of the documents, Moses had repeatedly said that there was nothing in them of relevance to our defence. He'd told Gilbert Gray that they were not helpful to us. Four Ministers of the Crown had put their signatures on Public Interest Immunity Certificates to prevent disclosure of the papers. Judge Smedley had forced Geoffrey to disclose part of my defence in order to obtain the Category C documents, and this gave the prosecution an advantage which they immediately used by preparing to put Michael Ford in the witness-box to discredit Mark Gutteridge before he gave evidence.

We'd been told that Category C contained only material relating to meetings Mark and I had had with our intelligence controllers. In truth, Category C also contained other material vital to our defence, such as minutes of inter-agency meetings. We didn't even know the full extent of what the material said, because sections of many, many pages had been blacked out.

Why was the prosecution continuing? The documents proved our innocence. What else did they have up their sleeve? How far would they go? Obviously, all the way. They were prepared to send three innocent men to prison. Why?

In order to prove my innocence I was going to have to reveal a part of my life that I would have preferred to keep secret for ever.

Mark would be doing the same on my behalf. Moreover, both of us could be placing our families at risk.

I thought to myself, my fate is in the hands of twelve strangers. At the end of this ordeal I'd either walk out the way I came in or be led through the door at the other side, the one that led to the cells and prison for up to seven years.

Alan Moses read his opening statement to the court. It was long and detailed to the point of being boring. He described how the three of us were charged with violating export laws and deceiving the Department of Trade and Industry about the true nature of the machines we had sold to Iraq. These, he said, helped Iraq to produce fuses for artillery and to develop missiles.

The prosecution, Moses went on, would prove three things: that the machines required export licences under the military list, not the industrial list we'd used; that the three of us had helped export them to Iraq; and that we'd deceived the government and evaded licensing requirements by lying about their uses. Repeatedly Moses referred to the Matrix Churchill machines as 'specially designed' for military production. Every time he said it I flinched.

By lunchtime Moses had completed his statement. But when we returned after lunch a problem had developed. During the break a juror had said that he was a Jew and didn't think that he could be fair in deciding on a case involving Iraqi missiles. He was dismissed and a new juror sworn in. Moses repeated his statement word for word.

The trial began with less attention from the press than we had hoped for. For me, telling my story in public was part of my vindication. From Britain, only Richard Norton-Taylor from the *Guardian*, Mark Lloyd from Channel 4 and a reporter from the *Financial Times* were there. I had also been introduced to Dean Baquet, a *New York Times* reporter who was very friendly with Bobby Lee Cook, an American lawyer who represented Christopher Drogoul, the former manager of the Atlanta branch of Banca Lavoro. The lawyer had come over to sit in on the trial.

Cook and Kevin Robinson had been comparing strategy and evidence all summer. In Atlanta Cook had just won a major victory for Drogoul and riveted American attention on what was called 'Iraqgate'.

Drogoul had pleaded guilty to the charge of defrauding his bank by loaning $5 billion to the Iraqis. He had admitted that his superiors in Rome were not aware of the loans, but then Cook had turned up intelligence material indicating that the CIA and others thought Rome did know. In fact bank officials in Rome and Italy's ambassador to the USA had tried to keep the Americans from fully investigating the scandal because of potential embarrassment to the Italian government.

In the end the prosecution had been forced to allow Drogoul to withdraw his guilty plea and plan for his trial. The judge then issued a stern public order accusing the CIA and the government of President Bush of trying to influence the investigation of the bank loans. He said the evidence showed that the American government had been trying to conceal its true policy of assisting Saddam Hussein in the years leading up to Operation Desert Storm. It had a familiar ring to it.

The opening prosecution witnesses at the Old Bailey were former employees of Matrix Churchill. All were men I knew well, and from where I sat none seemed particularly helpful to the prosecution's case. They testified that the use of our machines was 'general engineering', as described on the export licence applications.

John Adams identified the blueprints for the ABA contract, which I had supplied to Balsom in 1989. He confirmed that he'd prepared the drawings and given them to Steve Brittan, the ABA project manager, before my meeting at the safe house. Steve had told Adams that the drawings were for me and that I would be passing them on to a government ministry.

With Dr Roger Hannam, the university lecturer, providing expert advice, Geoffrey asked excellent technical questions that disputed the notion that the machines had been specially designed for military production.

It was one of those Matrix Churchill witnesses, in answer to a single question, whose testimony touched me deeply. What he said seemed to symbolize the folly and unfairness of the whole process. Barry Tomalin, a man in his forties, had been an engineer with the company who had worked on some of the Iraqi contracts, and Moses had called him to establish the special design of the machine tooling. When Moses asked, Tomalin said that he'd worked at Matrix Churchill for many years. The next question was a routine one too.

'And what is your present position?' asked the prosecution QC.

'I have no employment,' Tomalin said with feeling. 'I haven't been in work since this case was brought.'

Keith Bailey had failed to make a go of Matrix Churchill. He had even wound up charged with illegal exportation to the Iraqis when he was at BSA. As I sat in the dock listening to Barry Tomalin, the company that I had helped to rebuild to the brink of great success was employing a dozen or so people. It was a catastrophe for good men and women, for their jobs would never be restored, no matter how my trial ended.

On Wednesday, towards the end of the day, the few reporters in the press box were starting to leave as Geoffrey stood to begin his cross-examination of Ron Ash, the former head of defence projects at Matrix Churchill. Not long into the questioning, Geoffrey confronted Ash with the stunner: 'Did you know that throughout 1987 and 1988 Mark Gutteridge was working as an agent for British intelligence?'

Ash seemed to be in shock. Finally he shook his head and uttered a faint no.

With that carefully planned question the defence strategy revealed with reluctance in the pre-trial debate had gone public. It made front-page headlines the next day, even in the *New York Times*. From that point on, the crowd in the press box grew steadily.

In the public gallery another scene was being played out. People entering the gallery, including Esther and Sue, had to explain why they were attending the trial, and give their names and addresses. Each person was allocated a number, which they had to quote on subsequent visits. 'It's just in case we have to contact you in future,' they were told.

But it was intimidation, an attempt to limit attendance. There was even a notice on the door that said the trial was closed to the general public. Why? This was a public trial. Was this another facet of the government's cover-up?

The gallery also had some unusual visitors. A woman from the Jordanian embassy took voluminous notes. At the time the Jordanians were looking after Iraqi interests in Britain as diplomatic relations between London and Baghdad had been broken with the Gulf War. Another visitor was Ali Daghir of nuclear triggers fame. He had been released on bail pending an appeal against his conviction after a report by UN inspectors suggested that the capacitors he'd sent to Iraq were not for nuclear use at all.

I'd become friendly with some of the court personnel, including a lady usher who told me that she usually made up her mind about the innocence or guilt of defendants a couple of weeks into a trial. So at the two-week mark Peter Allen asked her what her verdict was. She pointed to the area beneath the public gallery where the Customs and Excise people were sitting and said: 'They should be the ones in the dock.'

By 30 October the prosecution had presented a batch of lower-ranking civil servants, mostly from the DTI. But that Friday there were preparations for a different type of government employee to testify.

Police officers were taping brown paper over the windows of the court. Special screens were installed around the witness-box. The press were ordered to sit at the back of the room, out of viewing range. Only the jury, the judge and the lawyers would be able to see the witness. Trevor, Peter and I were allowed to sit with our barristers, so we could watch the face of Michael Ford of MI5.

The release to the defence of Ford's reports on his meetings with Mark had forced the prosecution to call him to testify. They needed the intelligence agent to discount what they knew Mark would say for the defence in its portion of the case.

My first reaction was, God, he doesn't look the part. Mark had described Ford to me as overweight, but I was not prepared for a man who must have weighed twenty stone. He wore round, bull's-eye glasses and the bit of hair he had on the sides of his head was combed over the bald crown.

Despite Geoffrey's objection, Ford was identified in court only as 'Officer B'. He described how intelligence worked. He gave evidence about how his reports were filed with desk officers and sometimes were sent to 'Box 500', where MI6 picked them up. He said he'd not been particularly interested when Mark Gutteridge first started talking about Iraq. But then MI6 had got involved and he'd questioned Mark extensively about the Iraqis and the technology they were acquiring through Matrix Churchill and others.

Mark had told Kevin that Ford had said one of his reports was seen by Margaret Thatcher. The report was among many documents missing from the material given to the defence. But Geoffrey wanted to ask Ford about it anyway. It was important for the jury to see the value of Mark's intelligence material.

'Do you recall telling Mr Gutteridge that your report was going to be seen by the Prime Minister,' he asked.

'I may well have done that, sir,' answered Ford.

When Geoffrey read to the court from one of Ford's reports after problems developed with Matrix Churchill's licence applications, he

246

forced the MI5 man to make an embarrassing admission. Ford had written that he'd tried to assure Mark that his information had had no effect on the licences 'with my nose growing ever longer'.

'That being a reference to Pinocchio?' asked Geoffrey.

'Correct, sir,' came the reply.

Ford admitted that Mark had provided him with a considerable amount of information. But he refused to say that Mark had ever mentioned the Cardoen contract. This was important because we needed to establish that the government knew about it, since it was one of the specific charges against us.

The closest we got was a 'Source Report' filed by Ford in July 1988 in which he wrote that Mark had told him that the company 'had dealings with Chileans through their office in Miami. An agreement has been signed for a large consignment of fuses to be sent to Iraq.' Another such report stated that the Cardoen contract was known in Matrix Churchill as the 'Chilean contract'.

The testimony set the stage for 'Officer A', the man from MI6 I knew as John Balsom. At that point he was the most important witness in the case.

Each day after we finished in court I would go back with Kevin and the rest of the team to discuss our strategy for the following day. In preparation for Balsom's evidence, we felt it would be easier to meet in a public place, so we went to a café. Even then we felt we were being watched and listened to by a man who sat down alone at a nearby table in a room full of empty tables.

The night before Balsom was to testify I sensed Geoffrey was slightly nervous. He had earned my respect for his intellect and the cool, calculating way he cross-examined witnesses. But Balsom was a critical figure.

We knew that the prosecution would have rehearsed him in a dummy court. A barrister playing Geoffrey would have adopted his mannerisms and style so that Balsom would know what to expect. Concerns of this kind were heightened for us because we knew our phones were tapped and assumed that even Geoffrey's chambers had been bugged. Balsom would be a formidable witness, and he would probably know everything we planned. As it turned out, one answer he gave convinced all of us that our private conversations had been monitored. When something I had said to only Geoffrey was put to

Balsom in the witness-box, he seemed to slip and replied: 'I am aware of that.'

It was Tuesday 3 November when John Balsom took the seat behind the screens. His appearance had changed. He wore glasses, something I'd never seen him do. I thought they looked like plain glass. His hair, usually parted on one side, was parted down the middle. We made eye contact almost immediately. He never avoided it; somehow he could still look me in the eye.

Under questioning by Moses, 'Officer A' acknowledged that we had discussed Matrix Churchill business. He was talkative and intelligent, particularly compared with the stiff and formal Ford. He admitted that our discussions covered export licences as well as my annoyance at the delays. He said his relationship with me was 'a good one and important'.

Balsom refused to say that I'd given him information about the Cardoen and ABA contracts. Yet he did not seem hostile to me while giving his evidence, and occasionally glanced over at me. Under cross-examination by Geoffrey he remembered giving me a copy of *Republic of Fear*, saying it had been to warn me of the brutal regime of Saddam Hussein.

'Your warnings to him were re-emphasized after the arrest and execution of the journalist Mr Bazoft?' Geoffrey asked.

'They were,' Balsom replied, 'because obviously that was an appalling crime Saddam Hussein carried out against an innocent journalist.'

Geoffrey then reminded him that I had continued to provide information after the execution, including information on Iraqi military movements just before the invasion of Kuwait. It led to one of those moments when you could honestly have heard a pin drop.

'Mr Henderson was a very brave man,' said Balsom, glancing from me to the jury and then back to Geoffrey. 'Together with all the problems, the pressures on his business from the media coverage, financial pressures, to take this extra risk, he was extremely brave. There are very few people I have met who would take such risks and take them so much in their stride, with all the pressures on him.'

I felt myself going red in the face. I was embarrassed. I was flattered. This had been said in open court, in front of a lot of people. I looked down at the table in my embarrassment. I had never thought of myself in the words that Balsom had just used.

I thought, this man is trying to help me. He is not prepared to openly admit about ABA and Cardoen. His superiors probably won't let him. But he is trying to help me in a different way for the times I helped him. My respect was restored for John Balsom in those moments. He'd done his best.

Geoffrey continued questioning him about the information I'd provided on the Iraqis.

'He was telling you not only about their commercial dealings, but about their personal lives?'

'Yes. That is true.'

'And personal weaknesses they have. Was that a matter you asked him about?'

Before Balsom could answer, Alan Moses rose and objected. Such matters, he said, were a breach of security.

'We will leave that,' said Geoffrey. 'The things he saw and the people he met on his trips to Iraq.'

'Yes.'

'In doing that, you accept that he was running personal risks?'

'Absolutely,' replied Balsom, 'I mean, our relationship was voluntary. But as I say, he was a very, very brave man who, on top of all the other pressures on top of him, took these extra risks.'

Leaving court that afternoon, Ken MacDonald was beaming as he threw an arm around my shoulder. 'We're not just going to win this case,' he said. 'We're going to win it in style.'

Kevin agreed. Balsom had tried to help and done it. 'The jury's thinking that they've got a national hero in the dock,' he said. 'He nearly sanctified you.'

But there was still a good way to go. From long conversations with Kevin, I had learned that nothing dare be left to chance in a jury trial. No one can tell what will matter when twelve people close the door and begin to deliberate on whether a defendant should be set free or go to prison.

In August an article had appeared in the *Sunday Telegraph* about the Matrix Churchill case. It quoted Alan Clark as saying that he had given the machine-tool industry the go-ahead to export machinery to Iraq that was for military purposes. The potential for the case was enormous. It gave us brief hope. The prosecution promised that they would stop the case if the claim were true. But Customs and Excise put out a statement saying that Clark had been misquoted. 'It is balls I would have said that,' they claimed Clark had told them.

Kevin had rung up the reporter, Graham Turner, who stood by

the quotes. And I certainly knew it was the truth. But Turner, who was reluctant to say anything, had said he did not tape-record the conversation. All he had was notes, and even if we could force him to produce them, they were of no evidential value.

Alan Clark is a wealthy aristocrat who had been regarded as one of the brightest of the Thatcherites. When it came to his role in the government, my lawyers viewed him as someone with a cynical disregard for everything except the political objective. It was an attitude that had allowed him to quietly encourage me to sell machines for munitions to Iraq because it furthered government policy. And an attitude that allowed him to deny doing so.

It was Wednesday 4 November when Alan Clark entered the witness-box. Under the prodding of Moses, he reviewed the minutes prepared by Anthony Steadman of the critical meeting with the machine-tool makers on 20 January 1988. They were, he maintained, 'completely accurate'. When asked about the significance of the purpose of the machines when export licensing was considered, he said: 'Well, it was important that the specification should be of a nature that the peaceful use of tooling was the principal element in considering their eligibility.'

Moses questioned him about autumn 1989, when he had discussed relaxing restrictions on sales to Iraq with William Waldegrave and Lord Trefgarne.

'If you had known that machine tools were going to be exported with tooling, fixtures and part programmes to machine parts for fuses for military ordnance, what would your attitude have been then in relation to the granting of licences?' asked Moses.

'My attitude would have been that they would have fallen irredeemably within the guidelines, even though the guidelines had been relaxed.'

Judge Smedley interrupted to clarify the answer, asking: 'You mean their export would be a breach of the guidelines?'

'Yes, exactly,' replied Clark.

It was highly damaging evidence. Export licences for the Cardoen contract had been granted after the meeting of the ministers on 1 November 1989. Minutes after eliciting the statement he needed, Moses sat down. The examination of Clark had taken only an hour. Geoffrey Robertson's dismantling of him would go on considerably longer.

I cannot recall ever hearing Geoffrey say he was going to destroy a witness or take him apart. His strategy with Clark would not be to confront him at all.

'I am going to win him over to our side,' Geoffrey told me the night before Clark's appearance. 'I'll handle him with kid gloves and make him feel good. He'll want to help us by the time I ask the important questions.'

Clark had certain personality traits that the defence lawyers felt could be exploited. He was a bit of a rogue, ostentatious in his lifestyle and willing to speak his mind. He was not a typical establishment man, and he was intellectually aloof. Geoffrey's strategy was that, the more respect he showed Clark, the more malleable he would become.

Throughout the evidence of the lower-ranking civil servants Geoffrey had set the scene for the appearances of Clark and then Lord Trefgarne. Men such as Anthony Steadman and Eric Beston had each given evidence under cross-examination that the ultimate decisions had been made by the ministers. Now, the jury would be poised for Clark and Trefgarne to give them the final answer. Did the government know about the real purpose of the Matrix Churchill machines?

Geoffrey started politely, asking general questions about the nature of the guidelines for sales to Iraq from 1987 to early 1989, when Clark left the DTI for the MoD. He probed the ways they had been eased after the end of the Iran–Iraq war in the summer of 1988.

Then he showed him a memo written by Stephen Lillie of the Foreign Office on 1 February 1989. It had supported the decision by the ministers to approve the licence for the ABA contract.

'Does it assist you to recall the basis for this decision?' asked the QC. 'Although they "may be used for munitions manufacture", the ceasefire had held for long enough to make that not a sufficient reason under the new guidelines to stop them?'

'Yes,' said Clark.

'The third reason you see is the attraction of allowing them to be sent "rather than losing an intelligence access" to the Iraqi procurement network that was in Matrix Churchill?'

'Yes,' said Clark. 'I think the anxiety by now had started to shift towards Iraq's nuclear and chemical capability, and this rather pedestrian technology was no longer a matter of very great concern to us.'

Clark had made a distinction of significance. The government was concerned with nuclear-weapons technology and similar weapons of mass destruction. But even the prosecution had never linked our machines to such matters.

By late afternoon Clark seemed tired of the process and eager to get out of the witness-box. Geoffrey had remained steadfastly polite and respectful. They had gone over the debate with Whitehall concerning Iraq policy and sales of defence goods to Saddam Hussein. Clark had admitted that he favoured sales. As Minister of Trade at the DTI, it was his job, he said, to 'maximize' trade. Whenever Clark's memory seemed to fail, he had been reminded gently with a document.

The following day, by the time Geoffrey brought up the meeting in January 1988 where I had argued for releasing the hold on our licences, he had Clark precisely where he wanted him.

'You knew by that stage, 20 January, that the exports had been frozen because of the discovery they were going to munitions factories?' he asked.

'Yes,' said Clark.

'Was the purpose of that meeting to consider whether they could be unfrozen?'

'Yes.'

'And do you recall congratulating them on getting the order?'

'I expect, I hope I would have done. It would be uncivil if I did not.'

Using the minutes prepared by Steadman and the set prepared by John Nosworthy for the MTTA, Geoffrey led Clark through the meeting ever so slowly and carefully. Sitting in the dock, I had a vision of my life boiling down to these few minutes.

The licence applications said the machines would be used for 'general engineering purposes'. But, asked Geoffrey, didn't Clark know at the time that they were for military purposes?

'I do not see that the fact that they are using them, were they using them for munitions, excludes them using them for general engineering purposes,' responded Clark.

'But here, the writer of this minute is attributing to you a statement: "The Iraqis will be using the current order for general engineering purposes." Which cannot be correct to your knowledge?'

'Well,' said Clark with a thin smile, 'it's our old friend "being economical", isn't it?'

'With the truth?' Geoffrey asked.

'With the *actualité*,' said Clark. 'There was nothing misleading or dishonest to make a formal or introductory comment that the Iraqis would be using the current orders for "general engineering purposes". All I didn't say was "and for making munitions". If I thought that they were going to be doing that. It simply would not have been appropriate, at a meeting of this kind, to widen it any further than the rather stilted and formal language which I used.'

There it was. The admission. He knew they were for military purposes. Yet he had not said so in 1988 because it would have been 'inappropriate'. It was the 'nod and a wink' I had long been describing.

Geoffrey continued with his willing subject.

'You didn't want to let anyone know that, at this stage, these machines and their follow-up orders were going to munitions factories to make munitions?'

'No,' said Clark.

'And the emphasis on "peaceful purposes" and "general engineering" and so on would help keep the matter confidential?'

'I do not think it was principally a matter for public awareness. I think it was a matter for Whitehall cosmetics.'

'A matter for Whitehall cosmetics, to keep the records ambiguous?'

'Yes, yes.'

'So the signal you are sending to these people is, "I am the minister. I will help you get these orders and the follow-up orders through the rather loose guidelines and the rather Byzantine ways of Whitehall. Help me by keeping your mouth shut firmly about military use"?'

'I think that is too imaginative an interpretation. I think it was more at arm's length than that.'

'But in any event, it was how they would help you, by not making the Whitehall cosmetics run, rather by keeping quiet, stating "nothing military"?'

'Yes,' said Clark. 'I do not think they needed that advice from me but . . .'

'But they got it?'

'Not quite in so many words. I do not think I said "nothing military".'

'They got it by implication?'

'Yes,' agreed Clark. 'By implication is different. By implication they got it.'

Geoffrey Robertson sat down. There was a silence, then a buzz of whispers as the court adjourned for a short while. As Judge Smedley left the bench he was overheard saying to a clerk: 'Can you believe what you have just heard?'

Certainly I could believe it, though I had never expected to hear it in open court.

After the break Judge Smedley returned and Gilbert Gray stood to begin his cross-examination of Clark. I do not recall much of the detail of his questioning nor of James Hunt's, which followed. I think I was still considering the implications of what Clark had already admitted. But I do remember thinking that they were both more antagonistic in their approach than Geoffrey had been.

However, one question and answer really stick in my mind. Gray had been building up a picture of Clark's privileged background and public-school education, followed by his studying history at university.

'Where did you read history?' Gray asked.

Alan Clark, who maybe felt he was being patronized, replied sarcastically: 'In an armchair.'

This answer sent a ripple of laughter around the court, which helped to ease the tension slightly.

Gray and Hunt were both brief, and Moses, perhaps feeling that had left him an opening, got up to re-examine his witness. Unfortunately for him Clark simply reaffirmed what he'd told Geoffrey earlier, so Moses was quick to halt the proceedings, requesting an adjournment until the next day to consider his position.

Esther and Sue drove back to Coventry that evening. With them was Rosaline, Esther's sister, who had come over from the USA two weeks earlier both for a visit and to offer moral support. She'd been staying with us in the flat I'd rented in Canary Wharf for the duration of the trial.

I returned to Doughty Street with Geoffrey and Ken. Poor Kevin had missed the dramatic confession. He had had to return to Sheffield that night for a school function for one of his daughters. Back at the chambers, another QC, Helena Kennedy, rushed up to me and gave me a kiss. 'I've just heard. I've just heard. Congratulations.' Geoffrey said: 'It's not all over until the fat lady sings.'

On Friday we were back in court, and Kevin had returned from

Sheffield. Moses requested another adjournment, until Monday, as he needed to consult with others.

We were convinced that Moses had stopped the proceedings so that he could talk to his superiors about dropping the prosecution. We thought the matter would have to go all the way to 10 Downing Street because of the high profile the case had developed in the press. But it was a bit early for a final celebration. There was, Geoffrey warned us, a chance that the prosecution might be compelled to go on to escape the embarrassment of withdrawing. But he said it as though he didn't really believe it could happen.

I took the train home to Coventry on Friday afternoon. The uncertainty made the weekend tense for all of us. However, my youngest nephew, Neil, was getting married on the Saturday, and the wedding took my mind off the trial. Kevin phoned me a couple of times just to ease my mind. He was, as ever, optimistic. He said they'd let me know as soon as they heard from the prosecution what would be in store for us on Monday.

I had my doubts that the prosecution would give in. They'd gone on after we thought they would drop the case when the documents were released. The fact that they had brought the case at all always reminded me that logic wasn't something to apply to government decisions.

Esther, Sue and Rosaline drove down with me to Canary Wharf on Sunday night. We didn't want to take a chance on traffic making us late for court on Monday. Kevin phoned early that morning.

'I think you're going to be pleased today, Paul,' he told me.

'Have you heard?' I asked anxiously.

'No,' he said. 'But Geoffrey has heard on the grapevine that Judge Smedley is taking a case in Cornwall next week. That means our case is over.'

The street outside the Old Bailey was swarming with photographers and camera crews, and the press box inside was full. They expected the case to be dropped. It was Ken MacDonald who walked up to me when I entered court, and shook my hand.

'Congratulations,' he said. 'We won. It's done. We're finished. They've just told us they are dropping the case.'

I was in the dock when Judge Smedley entered the court and took his seat. Then Alan Moses announced that the prosecution was dropping the charges and the case, in the light of Alan Clark's testimony. The judge refused to allow Geoffrey to say a word, however. He just said that it was his duty to instruct the jury to return verdicts of not guilty on all three of us on all the charges.

The foreman of the jury stood as the clerk read the counts. After each, the foreman said: 'Not guilty.'

Epilogue

An the day my trial collapsed I was wearing a Remembrance Day poppy, as I do every year. Someone who saw me on television wrote a letter to the Matrix Churchill offices which eventually found its way to me.

'What right did Paul Henderson have to wear a Remembrance Day poppy?' asked the writer, who of course didn't sign the letter.

I was upset. I felt that I had every right to wear a poppy. I believed I'd served my country pretty well – not just in terms of the intelligence service, but in spending half my working life overseas promoting the sale of our products and generating work and employment in Britain.

I look back and realize that I was obviously taking risks, although I never thought of my intelligence activities as brave always knew that there was an element of risk in what I was doing, yet I saw it as a calculated risk. I thought I could always stop if I was going too far and others were becoming suspicious of me. I thought I was in control. At the same time I believed I was helping my own country, to which I felt very loyal, but my own government let me down.

I have no problem with the fact that we sell machine tools that will make munitions components. That is a consequence of the machine-tool industry and an inescapable fact of industrialization. Nor do I think there is a single machine-tool manufacturer who can put his hand on his heart and say: 'I've never supplied a machine to the defence industry.'

In selling machines tools to Iraq I was abiding by the policy of my government. I was not trading with the enemy, since Iraq was not the enemy then. And I was telling the government not only what Matrix Churchill was doing, but what many other British and foreign companies were doing. So it knew we were supplying equipment for manufacturing munitions parts. Right up until the day before the invasion of Kuwait, the British government was releasing licences for the export of our machine tools to Iraq.

It was the government who let me down by not being honest. Ministers should have stood up very early on and said: 'This is an injustice. We knew that those machine tools were supplied for making munitions parts and these men should not be put on trial.' But they were more concerned with their reputation than they were with three innocent people going to prison.

The result of the government's refusal to be honest was a major cover-up. As far back as 1 May 1991, when Cedric Andrew, the Customs and Excise lawyer, and Ian Eacott, from MI6, met Mark Gutteridge, the cover-up was being planned. Ministers signed Public Interest Immunity Certificates to keep documents from us that proved my innocence. It was flagrantly dishonest. It was my personal belief that the knowledge of what was happening went all the way to the top. The Matrix Churchill case was too sensitive and the profile in the press too high for 10 Downing Street not to have been involved.

From where I sat in the dock at the Old Bailey, I could see that the dishonesty had spread to the prosecution. Otherwise, how could Alan Moses have stood up in court and told the judge no fewer than seven times that there was nothing relevant to my case in the government papers? How could he have argued to keep secret the very documents that demonstrated government knowledge of what Matrix Churchill's machines were for?

If the documents had not been released, things might well have turned out differently. It was Alan Clark's admission that he knew the machines were for military purposes that forced the prosecution to end the charade. But without the intelligence service documents proving that Mark Gutteridge and I had told our controllers about the uses of the machines from 1987 onwards, Geoffrey Robertson might not have been able to drag the truth out of Clark.

Not only could Trevor Abraham, Peter Allen and I have gone to prison; so might others have done. Even the charges against Keith Bailey for selling to Iraq were dropped after our trial collapsed in its monumental splash of publicity and embarrassment for the government.

The prosecution undeniably behaved poorly. Alan Moses must have known over that last weekend that the charges would be dropped on Monday morning, but he lacked the basic decency to tell us. Instead we three defendants and our families were forced to endure two more days of uncertainty.

Judge Smedley has been praised for ordering the release of the documents. To my mind, he did so only after being forced by Geoffrey Robertson. Without Geoffrey's legal argument and his decision to reveal our defence, the judge allowed himself to be misled by the distortion within the Public Interest Immunity Certificates. His attitude showed on that last day, too. He refused to let Geoffrey speak out in court, deprived him of the chance to declare on the record that a travesty of justice had nearly occurred. Smedley never even pronounced us free men. I believe we deserved at least that much.

Although the government let me down, the people did not. Esther, Dave and Sue never wavered in their belief in my innocence. The support they gave me was incredible. You try to convince yourself not to worry, and that it will all go away eventually. But the fear is never far from the surface. My wife and children were always there to help me cope with it. We came through those two years a much stronger family.

I always knew my family would stick by me. But I was overwhelmed by the support of all my other friends. Especially John Belgrove and Mark Gutteridge, who provided between them the £50,000 surety needed for my bail, and took me back into the business at Hi-Tek. They helped me rebuild my business confidence at a time when everything else seemed to be crumbling.

Mark, of course, did much more than that. I was left with no choice when it came to revealing my intelligence work. He had a choice – and he chose to support me. He put himself at personal risk by coming forward and telling the truth. I don't know how you ever really thank someone for something like that.

After the verdict that Monday morning in November 1992 Trevor Abraham, Peter Allen, myself and our families posed for photographs outside the Old Bailey, glasses held high. That celebration might never have occurred without a simple miscommunication between my first solicitor and me.

In the days after the formal charging in February 1991, Alan Parker was too busy to see me. I thought he wasn't concerned about my case, so, thanks to Chris Cowley, I ended up appointing another solicitor. Only later did I learn that it was because Parker's mother was seriously ill. I've no doubt that he would have made a fine job of defending me. But I do not believe any solicitor could have represented me the way that Kevin Robinson did.

Right from the start Kevin recognized that we'd only win by taking on the establishment and challenging the government at every step. He assembled a brilliant team with Geoffrey Robertson and Ken MacDonald. They were not against the government, but they were outside it and believed in justice. Their position enabled them to see beyond the prosecution's lies and to confront the government.

As for Kevin, a special bond developed between us over the two years we worked together on this case. I developed a tremendous respect for him while we prepared for the hearing at Thames Magistrates Court. He is a fighter, a thinker and a man who believes in fairness in the law.

Our relationship grew into real friendship. There were times when I'd get depressed; I didn't see how we could fight the whole government. But Kevin was always able to restore my confidence. He was convinced there was no way we could lose and, as in all things to do with this case, he was right. I shall always be grateful for that.

Despite the victory in court, my loss is immeasurable. The damage to my reputation is incalculable. But the loss that hurts more than everything else is the death of my dream of rebuilding Matrix Churchill to the status and profitability of the old Coventry Gauge and Tool Company, where I started learning my trade as a fifteen-year-old apprentice.

Before I was arrested in October 1990, I'd reached my objective of becoming managing director. I was within one day of owning a large share in the business and having the control necessary to steer the company along the path the other managers and I had prepared so carefully in the previous three years. Our workforce was superb: skilled and intelligent people, with years of experience. Together we would have made it work. And it was taken away – not just from me but from all of them. I am sorry for them it went wrong.

Several months after the trial I was asked to attend a meeting at the Coventry branch of the Transport and General Workers Union. The former employees of Matrix Churchill were trying to get compensation from Keith Bailey or the government for the loss of their jobs. They believed they had been treated unfairly by Bailey and they had asked for my help. Ray Lissamann, General Secretary of the AEEU, told me that he had headed up a meeting of about 300 former Matrix Churchill employees the previous Saturday. He said they'd told him something that I found both uplifting and terribly sad. Had Paul Henderson not been arrested, they said, had he been able to buy the business, there'd still be a Matrix Churchill operating and we would still have jobs.

I believe that the government was more concerned with the possibility of continuing the Iraqi connection through my acquisition of the business than with my purchase of it. It was more than a coincidence that I was arrested the day before I was due to conclude an agreement to buy Matrix Churchill.

Matrix Churchill no longer exists. The factory is still there at Fletchamstead Highway. The lights still burn in a few windows at night, just to keep the vandals away. The business is gone, as are the skills and traditions of all who worked there. Those workers are the final victims of the government's tragic failure to be honest with its people.

Appendix of Key Documents

The following documents are a tiny percentage of those made available to the defence in the Matrix Churchill trial. Judge Smedley examined all the documents before their release and agreed to the deletions seen here. The annotations 'G' and 'H' – standing for Gutteridge and Henderson and replacing what are probably code-names – were added by intelligence service officers before the documents were released.

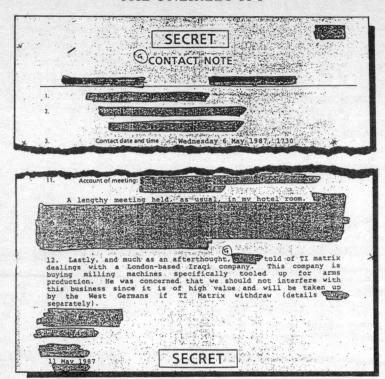

SECRET

CONTACT NOTE

1.

2.

3.   Contact date and time   Wednesday 6 May 1987. 1730

11.   Account of meeting:

A lengthy meeting held, as usual, in my hotel room.

12. Lastly, and much as an afterthought, ████ told of TI matrix dealings with a London-based Iraqi company. This company is buying milling machines specifically tooled up for arms production. He was concerned that we should not interfere with this business since it is of high value and will be taken up by the West Germans if TI Matrix withdraw (details separately).

11 May 1987

SECRET

6 May 1987 First time MI5, in the person of Michael Ford, was told of Iraqi procurement activities, by Mark Gutteridge.

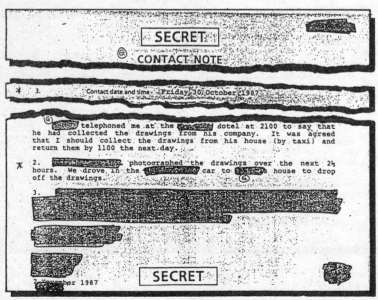

SECRET

CONTACT NOTE

3.   Contact date and time   Friday 30 October 1987

████ telephoned me at the ████ hotel at 2100 to say that he had collected the drawings from his company. It was agreed that I should collect the drawings from his house (by taxi) and return them by 1100 the next day.

2. ████ photographed the drawings over the next 2½ hours. We drove in the ████ car to ████'s house to drop off the drawings.

3.

2 November 1987

SECRET

30 October 1987 Photographing of drawings by MI5 at request of Ford.

SECRET

SOURCE REPORT

Date Report from Source
Obtained from Source
8.12.87

SUBJECT: HUTTEEN General Establishment

A small group of UK businessmen recently visited the HUTTEEN General Establishment for Mechanical Industries in Iraq.

3. The visitors were shown the 130mm shell and mortar shop. Within the shop were some 50 GEORGE FISHER CNC lathes from Switzerland. These machines were linked with a conveyor system. The machines were installed in 1983 and use CNC technology equal to the best available in the UK.

5. HUTTEEN staff said that other sizes of shells, cartridges, anti-personal and anti-tank mines were also manufactured. These were filled elsewhere on the site.

5. Both during the visit to NASSIR and briefings in London by WADI, yearly production targets were mentioned. These were:

    a.   122 missile. 10,000 per year

    b.   130 shells 150,000 per year.

    c.   Mortar shells (60,82,120 mm) 100,000 per year total

    d.   Fin stablised 155 mm shells (similar to those produced by PRB in Belguim) 1000 per 8 hour shift at 85% efficiency (300,000 shells per year). These shells were judged by Iraq to be the latest type not available in UK. The objective is for main production in 12 months with full production in 18 months.

    e.   Large numbers of 122 mm, 130 mm and 155 mm shhlls at the HUTTEEN factory.

8 December 1987 Details of armaments production at Al Hutteen acquired on visit by Mark Gutteridge and Ron Ash.

dti
the department for Enterprise
EXPORT LICENSING BRANCH

CONFIDENTIAL

Mr A Barratt
DESS2/MOD
Room 0206
MOD Main Building
Whitehall

Department of
Trade and Industry

Millbank Tower
Millbank
London SW1P 4QU
Switchboard
01-211 3000

13 January 1988

Dear Allan

I refer to last Friday's emergency IDC meeting concerning the report that the Nassr Establishment for Mechanical Industries and the Hateen Establishment for Technical Industries in Iraq were heavily engaged in a munitions production programme. We established that licences had been issued to 3 British machine tool manufacturers to supply CNC machine tools which the report said were being used in that programme worth a total of £37m to the companies involved. We agreed that before submitting to Ministers we needed to know the extent to which the licences had been used, the contractual relationship between the supplier and importer and any further points relevant to Ministers' consideration of the problem.

I have spoken to all 3 UK companies involved. BSA Tools Limited, Wickman Bennett Machine Tool Company Limited and TI Machine Tools Limited. The following is the position for each :

· TI MACHINE TOOLS LIMITED

Export licences 3M/2732/87 - 3M/2734/87 issued 2/12/87, 141 machine tools/ presses, value £19m.

Letter following with details. No shipments yet on ELs 3M/2732/87 and 3M/2734/87. Thirteen lathes sent on EL 3M/2733/87 (balance £3.8m remaining).

Contract has a "force majeure" clause covering such things as frustration of contract by trade embargo. Iraqis have placed 29 per cent downpayment. Company has to train Iraqis and commission equipment. Cancellation of contract would be regarded as terminal for the company resulting in loss of 1000 jobs. Machines could not be readily be sold elsewhere.

Mr Paul Henderson, M.D., has contacted John Butcher's private office (Mr Butcher is the company's MP and Minister for Industry). He has also organised a meeting of the UK companies involved at MTTA on Thursday. I warned Mr Abraham, Commercial Manager of the company that publicity would not necessarily help and may hinder their cause. Mr Abraham suggested that not all of the machines would be used on the Middle East which is what the company thought was behind the development. He also confirmed that the Italians and, he thought, German manufacturers were heavily committed.

COMMENTS

We have a situation where all 3 companies are heavily committed to fairly substantial contracts : the consequences of cancellation in each case, even if there were no legal Iraqi penalties, would be catastrophic for the companies involved. Export licences were issued before the knowledge of the consignees' activities became known to Departments.

The Iraqi policy of self sufficiency could be said to have a prolonging effect on the conflict, but against this it is in effect a substitute for Soviet supplies. Its significance may not therefore be as great as at first it would seem. The machine tools in themselves are not defence equipment, they are used in a variety of general engineering purposes and some may in fact be so. They do not therefore fall precisely within the Iran/Iraq guidelines, though that is not to say we should not consider the implications of a use such as that which has now come to light.

The guidelines also allow for the overriding consideration that we should attempt to fulfil existing contracts. Since the evidence was not available to us prior to the issue of licences it should not be too difficult presentationally to defend a line which does nothing about the existing contracts, especially bearing in mind the implications for the companies concerned, but say that we are not prepared to consider further applications for either of the consignees

dti
the department for Enterprise

involved for the time being. All three companies said they were interested in further business in Iraq. To revoke the existing licences for further shipments under these contracts to these consignees would virtually kill off any hope of other non-sensitive business in this market for these and possibly other UK firms, and let in foreign competition. My view is therefore that there is scope for the balanced approach of allowing existing commitments but refusing for the present future licence applications for munitions or other military programmes from the consignees.

I am copying this letter to Bill Patey and Eric Beston.

Yours sincerely

A D STEADMAN

13 January 1988 Memo from A.D. Steadman, Head of Export Licensing Branch at Department of Trade and Industry, to A. Barratt of the Ministry of Defence before Matrix Churchill's meeting with Alan Clark, Minister for Trade. Steadman had been told by Abraham that not all the machines in question would be used for munitions production.

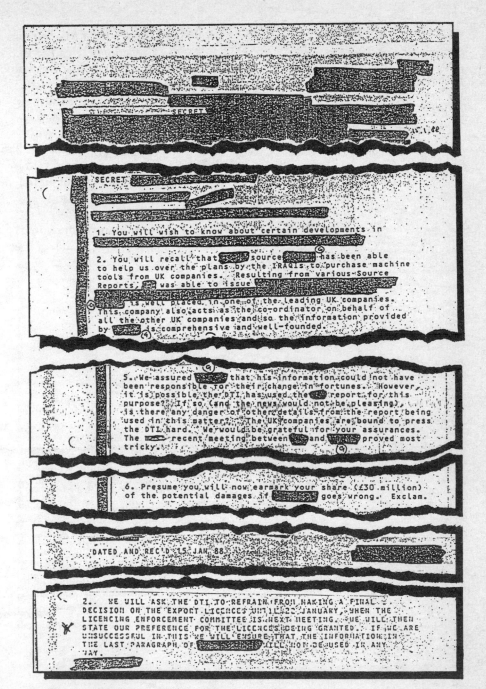

SECRET

SECRET

1. You will wish to know about certain developments in

2. You will recall that ▓▓▓ source ▓▓▓ has been able to help us over the plans by the IRAQIs to purchase machine tools from UK companies. Resulting from various Source Reports, ▓▓ was able to issue ▓▓▓▓▓▓▓▓▓▓▓▓▓▓▓ ▓▓▓ is well placed in one of the leading UK companies. This company also acts as the co-ordinator on behalf of all the other UK companies and so the information provided by ▓▓▓ is comprehensive and well-founded.

5. We assured ▓▓▓ that his information could not have been responsible for their change in fortunes. However, it is possible the DTI has used the ▓▓ report for this purpose? If so (and the news would not be pleasing), is there any danger of other details from the report being used in this matter? The UK companies are bound to press the DTI hard. We would be grateful for your assurances. The ▓▓▓ recent meeting between ▓▓ and ▓▓▓ proved most tricky.

6. Presume you will now earmark your share (£30 million) of the potential damages if ▓▓▓▓▓ goes wrong. Exclam.

DATED AND REC'D 15 JAN 88

2. WE WILL ASK THE DTI TO REFRAIN FROM MAKING A FINAL DECISION ON THE EXPORT LICENCES UNTIL 25 JANUARY, WHEN THE LICENCING ENFORCEMENT COMMITTEE IS NEXT MEETING. WE WILL THEN STATE OUR PREFERENCE FOR THE LICENCES BEING GRANTED. IF WE ARE UNSUCCESSFUL IN THIS WE WILL ENSURE THAT THE INFORMATION IN THE LAST PARAGRAPH OF ▓▓▓▓▓▓ WILL NOT BE USED IN ANY WAY.

15 January 1988 Internal intelligence service document sent before our meeting with Clark.

SECRET   Reference..

TO: cc M
PS/MINISTER FOR TRADE

FROM:
ERIC BESTON
OT2/3
V301:215 5242

18 January 1988

MFT's MEETING ON 20 JANUARY WITH MMTA : EXPORT LICENCES TO IRAQ

Mr Steadman's minute of today's date sets out the general background to
this meeting and suggests a line to take with which I entirely agree. Before
submission however I deleted a paragraph drawn from the intelligence report
which seems better placed in this more restricted minute. The providers of
the intelligence are most anxious that their source should not inadvertently
put at risk by anyone referring to the detailed information provided in, say,
a meeting with the companies. For this reason, they, like DTI and other
officials, would favour allowing the present contracts to be completed and
export licences refused only for any future suspect business. If we need their
backing for this line they will weigh in with others in Whitehall.

The intelligence report, from a reliable source, names UK machine tool firms
engaged in the supply of CNC machine tools to the Nassir Establishment for
Mechanical Industries and the Hateen Establishment for Technical Industries
in Iraq. Both are said to be engaged in a substantial munitions manufacturing
programme to enable Iraq to become less dependent on Soviet supplies. Among
other things the report lists yearly production targets for shells and missiles.

E W BESTON

18 January 1988 Final memo from E. Beston of the DTI, Steadman's boss,
to Clark's personal secretary, two days before our meeting with the latter,
confirms DTI knew machines were to be used for munitions production.

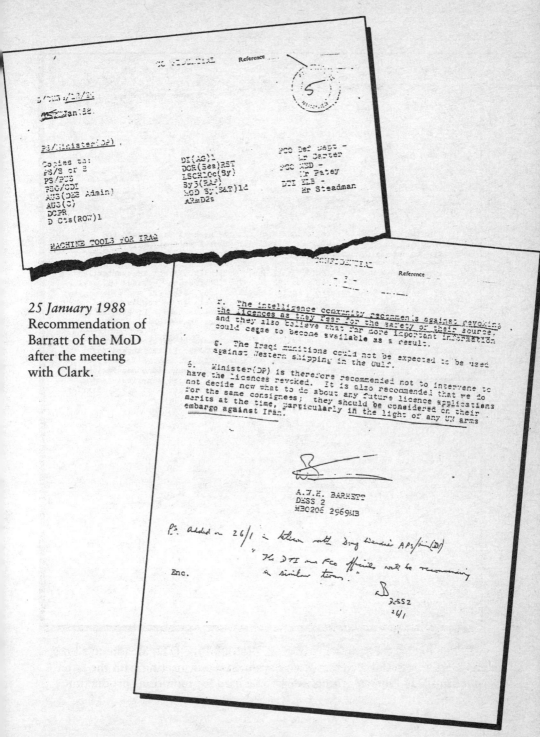

25 January 1988
Recommendation of
Barratt of the MoD
after the meeting
with Clark.

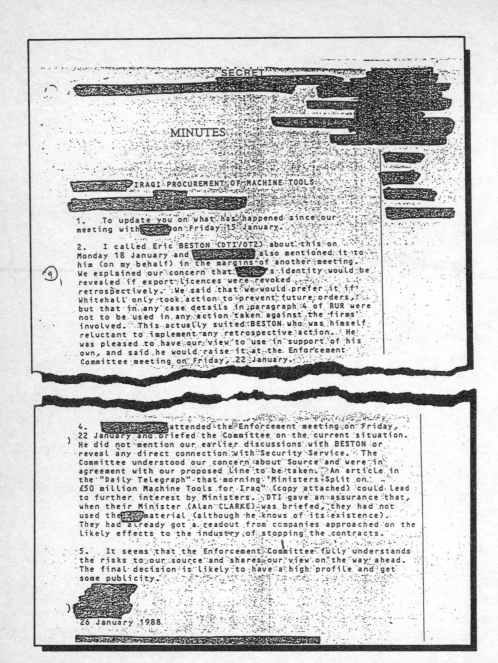

SECRET

MINUTES

IRAQI PROCUREMENT OF MACHINE TOOLS

1.   To update you on what has happened since our meeting with ████ on Friday 15 January.

2.   I called Eric BESTON (DTI/OT2) about this on Monday 18 January and ████████ also mentioned it to him (on my behalf) in the margins of another meeting. We explained our concern that ████ 's identity would be revealed if export licences were revoked retrospectively. We said that we would prefer it if Whitehall only took action to prevent future orders, but that in any case details in paragraph 4 of RUR were not to be used in any action taken against the firms involved. This actually suited BESTON who was himself reluctant to implement any retrospective action. He was pleased to have our view to use in support of his own, and said he would raise it at the Enforcement Committee meeting on Friday, 22 January.

4.   ████████ attended the Enforcement meeting on Friday, 22 January and briefed the Committee on the current situation. He did not mention our earlier discussions with BESTON or reveal any direct connection with Security Service. The Committee understood our concern about Source and were in agreement with our proposed Line to be taken. An article in the "Daily Telegraph" that morning 'Ministers Split on £50 million Machine Tools for Iraq' (copy attached) could lead to further interest by Ministers. DTI gave an assurance that, when their Minister (Alan CLARKE) was briefed, they had not used the ████ material (although he knows of its existence). They had already got a readout from companies approached on the likely effects to the industry of stopping the contracts.

5.   It seems that the Enforcement Committee fully understands the risks to our source and shares our view on the way ahead. The final decision is likely to have a high profile and get some publicity.

26 January 1988

26 January 1988 Intelligence service minutes following Clark's meeting with Machine Tool Technologies Association.

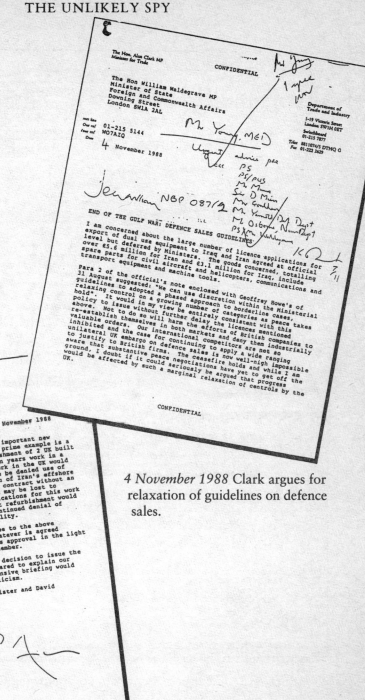

4 November 1988 Clark argues for relaxation of guidelines on defence sales.

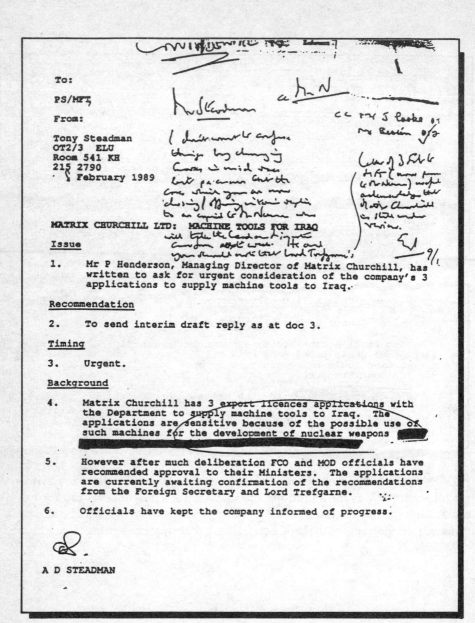

To:

PS/MFT,

From:

Tony Steadman
OT2/3 ELU
Room 541 KH
215 2790
8 February 1989

MATRIX CHURCHILL LTD: MACHINE TOOLS FOR IRAQ

Issue

1.   Mr P Henderson, Managing Director of Matrix Churchill, has
      written to ask for urgent consideration of the company's 3
      applications to supply machine tools to Iraq.

Recommendation

2.   To send interim draft reply as at doc 3.

Timing

3.   Urgent.

Background

4.   Matrix Churchill has 3 export licences applications with
      the Department to supply machine tools to Iraq. The
      applications are sensitive because of the possible use of
      such machines for the development of nuclear weapons

5.   However after much deliberation FCO and MOD officials have
      recommended approval to their Ministers. The applications
      are currently awaiting confirmation of the recommendations
      from the Foreign Secretary and Lord Trefgarne.

6.   Officials have kept the company informed of progress.

A D STEADMAN

8 February 1989 DTI, MoD and Foreign and Commonwealth Office
continued to support granting of export licences to Matrix Churchill.

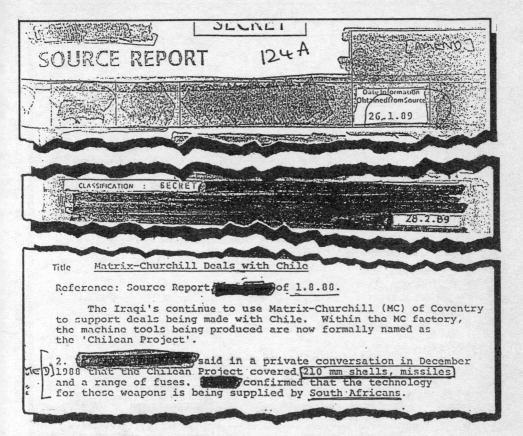

SECRET

SOURCE REPORT   124A

Date Information
Obtained from Source
26.1.89

CLASSIFICATION : SECRET

28.2.89

Title   Matrix-Churchill Deals with Chile

Reference: Source Report ▨▨▨▨▨ of 1.8.88.

The Iraqi's continue to use Matrix-Churchill (MC) of Coventry to support deals being made with Chile. Within the MC factory, the machine tools being produced are now formally named as the 'Chilean Project'.

2. ▨▨▨▨▨▨▨▨▨▨▨ said in a private conversation in December 1988 that the Chilean Project covered 210 mm shells, missiles and a range of fuses. ▨▨▨▨ confirmed that the technology for these weapons is being supplied by South Africans.

28 February 1989 Intelligence service knew in August 1988 that the Cardoen Chile contract was for munitions and that Matrix Churchill was producing machines for this contract. Mark Gutteridge's controller, Michael Ford, and mine, John Balsom, both denied under oath that they knew this.

SECRET

SUMMARY RECORD OF THE INTER-DEPARTMENTAL COMMITTEE ON DEFENCE SALES
TO IRAN AND IRAQ: 14 MARCH 1989

1.   The IDC discussed the implications for its work of the Rushdie
affair. The Committee agreed that a distinction should be drawn
between our policy towards the situation in the Gulf and the present
crisis in UK/Iran relations. The guidelines had been drawn up, and
were kept under review in the light of the conflict and, now, the
ceasefire. The possibility of imposing a defence sales embargo
against Iran in retaliation for its action over Rushdie was a matter
for the MISC 118 committee, and the IDC should not pre-empt any
decision reached in MISC 118.

2.   However the IDC agreed that in the present uncertain
circumstances the more flexible implementation of the guidelines
which Ministers had decided to take since the ceasefire would no
longer be appropriate for Iran. The exact nature of the new
guidelines for Iran would have to be agreed once it was known where
the downward spiral in bilateral relations began to level out.   In
the meantime, the IDC agreed to recommend that decisions on all

83

4.   The IDC agreed that we should not penalise Iraq for the crisis
with Iran, and so should continue to use the more flexible
interpretation with Iraqi applications. We had already used
differing interpretations for the two countries during the conflict,
and the 1985 guidelines were sufficiently broad to cover this.

5.   The IDC therefore recommended that Mr Waldegrave should write to
Lord Trefgarne and Mr Clark to propose this approach. FCO would
submit a draft letter for Mr Waldegrave which could be sent out in
time for the next IDC on 23 March.

14 March 1989 Inter-Departmental Committee favoured Iraq over Iran in matter
of defence sales.

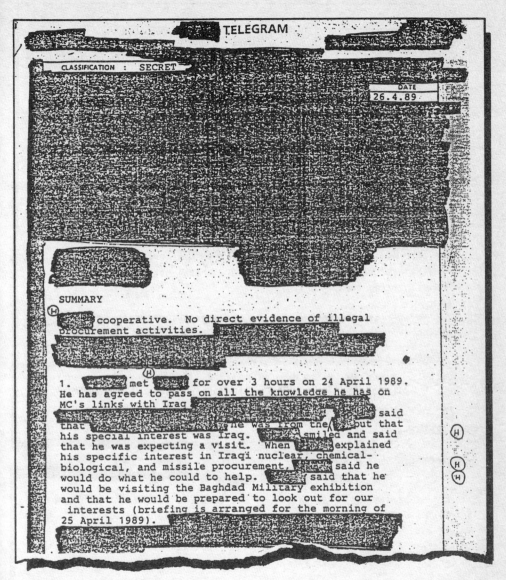

TELEGRAM

CLASSIFICATION : SECRET

DATE
26.4.89

SUMMARY

cooperative. No direct evidence of illegal
procurement activities.

1.   met   for over 3 hours on 24 April 1989.
He has agreed to pass on all the knowledge he has on
MC's links with Iraq   said
that   he was from the   but that
his special interest was Iraq.   smiled and said
that he was expecting a visit. When   explained
his specific interest in Iraqi nuclear, chemical-
biological, and missile procurement,   said he
would do what he could to help.   said that he
would be visiting the Baghdad Military exhibition
and that he would be prepared to look out for our
interests (briefing is arranged for the morning of
25 April 1989).

26 April 1989 Intelligence service report on meeting with me.

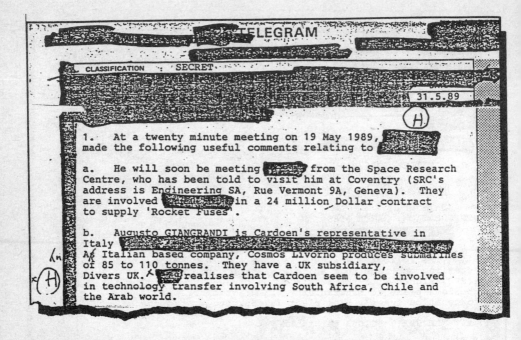

1. At a twenty minute meeting on 19 May 1989, ▓▓▓▓ made the following useful comments relating to ▓▓▓▓▓▓

a. He will soon be meeting ▓▓▓▓ from the Space Research Centre, who has been told to visit him at Coventry (SRC's address is Engineering SA, Rue Vermont 9A, Geneva). They are involved ▓▓▓▓▓▓ in a 24 million Dollar contract to supply 'Rocket Fuses'.

b. Augusto GIANGRANDI is Cardoen's representative in Italy ▓▓▓▓▓▓▓▓▓▓▓▓ An Italian based company, Cosmos Livorno produces submarines of 85 to 110 tonnes. They have a UK subsidiary, Divers UK. ▓▓▓▓ realises that Cardoen seem to be involved in technology transfer involving South Africa, Chile and the Arab world.

d. ▓▓▓▓ asked to visit project 1728, but this was refused. It is situated on the way back from the NASR establishment at TAJI, about 8 kilometres from BAGHDAD.

e. Naturally we will be going into further detail with ▓▓▓▓ after he has met Michel from SRC.

31 May 1989 Intelligence service report on meeting with me confirms Space Research Corporation's fuse contract, Cardoen's involvement in Italy and links with South Africa, and existence of Project 1728, for the modification of Scud missiles.

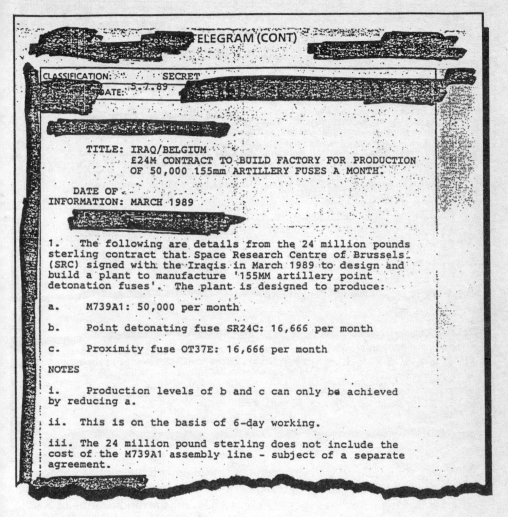

TELEGRAM (CONT)

CLASSIFICATION: SECRET
DATE: 5.7.89

TITLE: IRAQ/BELGIUM
       £24M CONTRACT TO BUILD FACTORY FOR PRODUCTION
       OF 50,000 155mm ARTILLERY FUSES A MONTH.

DATE OF
INFORMATION: MARCH 1989

1.   The following are details from the 24 million pounds
sterling contract that Space Research Centre of Brussels
(SRC) signed with the Iraqis in March 1989 to design and
build a plant to manufacture '155MM artillery point
detonation fuses'. The plant is designed to produce:

a.   M739A1: 50,000 per month

b.   Point detonating fuse SR24C: 16,666 per month

c.   Proximity fuse OT37E: 16,666 per month

NOTES

i.   Production levels of b and c can only be achieved
by reducing a.

ii.   This is on the basis of 6-day working.

iii. The 24 million pound sterling does not include the
cost of the M739A1 assembly line - subject of a separate
agreement.

5 July 1989 Information obtained by intelligence service from copy of fuse
contract that I provided.

CLASSIFICATION: SECRET

DATE: 23.8.89

c.   We think that your idea of a long session with ▮▮▮ in London, ▮▮▮▮▮▮▮▮▮▮▮▮▮▮▮▮▮▮▮is a good one. We have provisionally arranged this with ▮▮▮▮for the first week in September (after the visit of the Director Generals). We would get much more ▮▮▮▮ information out of him if we had at this meeting ▮▮▮ of where we suspect sensitive research establishments are and an organogram of the establishments, so that he can fill in the gaps from his own personal knowledge.

23 August 1989 Confirms setting up of meeting between me and intelligence service at safe house.

SECRET

000261

4

To:

1. Mr Boston
2. PS/MFT

From:

Tony Steadman
OT2/3 ELU
R.541 KH
215 2790
25 September 1989

cc PS/S of S
    PS/MFT
    PS/Sir P Gregson
    Mr Dell
    Mr Meadway   OT2
    Mr Muir   OT4
    Mr Petter   OT4/1
    Mr Gallaher   OT4/1
    Mr Morgan   EM2
    Mr Nunn   OT2/3

MATRIX CHURCHILL LTD: EXPORT LICENCE APPLICATIONS FOR IRAQ

ISSUE

CONCLUSION

16.   When balanced against these arguments the FCO line is
        unconvincing. We would have difficulty defending a refus
        under the guidelines and, as previously accepted by FCO,
        the supply of Matrix Churchill machine tools is not
        critical to Iraqi's nuclear development programme. A
        refusal would be seen as presentational in the face of
        recent press publicity about the Iraqi procurement netwo
        and the fact that Matrix Churchill is largely Iraqi owne
        However this could be turned against us, the implication
        being that we were wrong to approve the previous
        applications and are now only reacting to press reports.

17.   A refusal of general purpose equipment to Iraq would hav
        serious implications for UK machine tool sales into an
        important market and is likely to have repercussions
        generally for our expanding trade with Iraq.

A D STEADMAN

25 September 1989 DTI support for issue of export licences, including Cardoen
licences.

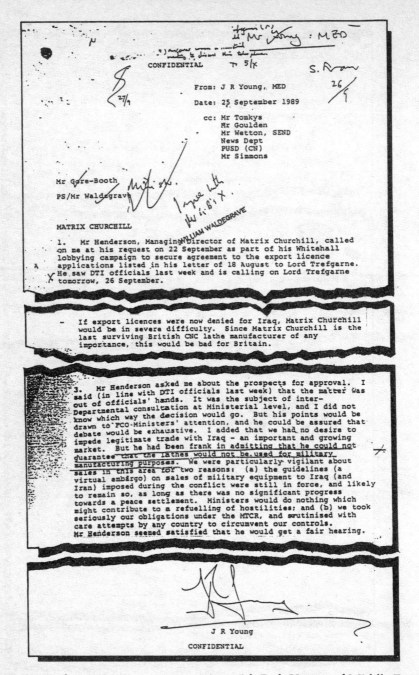

CONFIDENTIAL

From: J R Young, MED

Date: 25 September 1989

cc: Mr Tomkys
Mr Goulden
Mr Wetton, SEND
News Dept
PUSD (CN)
Mr Simmons

Mr Gore-Booth
PS/Mr Waldegrave

WILLIAM WALDEGRAVE

MATRIX CHURCHILL

1. Mr Henderson, Managing Director of Matrix Churchill, called on me at his request on 22 September as part of his Whitehall lobbying campaign to secure agreement to the export licence applications listed in his letter of 18 August to Lord Trefgarne. He saw DTI officials last week and is calling on Lord Trefgarne tomorrow, 26 September.

- If export licences were now denied for Iraq, Matrix Churchill would be in severe difficulty. Since Matrix Churchill is the last surviving British CNC lathe manufacturer of any importance, this would be bad for Britain.

3. Mr Henderson asked me about the prospects for approval. I said (in line with DTI officials last week) that the matter was out of officials' hands. It was the subject of inter-Departmental consultation at Ministerial level, and I did not know which way the decision would go. But his points would be drawn to FCO Ministers' attention, and he could be assured that debate would be exhaustive. I added that we had no desire to impede legitimate trade with Iraq - an important and growing market. But he had been frank in admitting that he could not guarantee that the lathes would not be used for military manufacturing purposes. We were particularly vigilant about sales in this area for two reasons: (a) the guidelines (a virtual embargo) on sales of military equipment to Iraq (and Iran) imposed during the conflict were still in force, and likely to remain so, as long as there was no significant progress towards a peace settlement. Ministers would do nothing which might contribute to a refuelling of hostilities; and (b) we took seriously our obligations under the MTCR, and scrutinised with care attempts by any country to circumvent our controls. Mr Henderson seemed satisfied that he would get a fair hearing.

J R Young

CONFIDENTIAL

25 September 1989 Report on meeting with Rob Young of Middle East Department of FCO before Ministers approved Cardoen licences. Note underlined sentence.

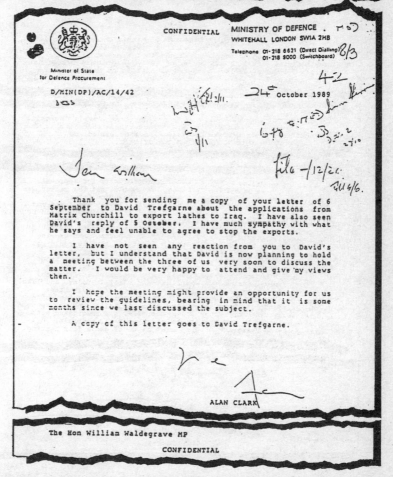

24 October 1989 Compare draft letter prepared for Alan Clark, by now Minister for Defence Procurement, about issue of Cardoen licences, with letter he actually sent to William Waldegrave.

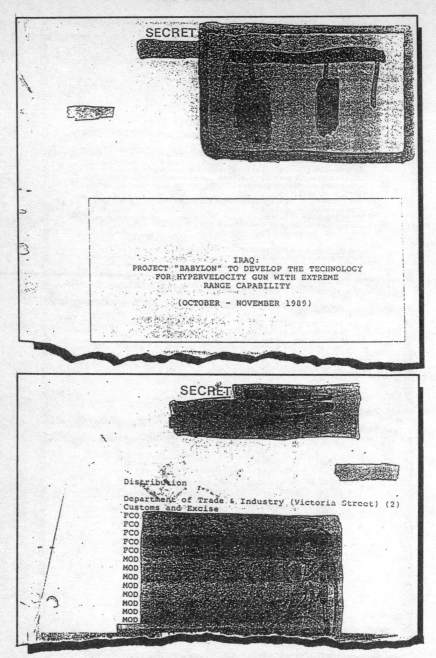

SECRET

IRAQ:
PROJECT "BABYLON" TO DEVELOP THE TECHNOLOGY
FOR HYPERVELOCITY GUN WITH EXTREME
RANGE CAPABILITY

(OCTOBER - NOVEMBER 1989)

SECRET

Distribution

Department of Trade & Industry (Victoria Street) (2)
Customs and Excise
FCO
FCO
FCO
FCO
FCO
MOD
MOD
MOD
MOD
MOD
MOD
MOD
MOD

October-November 1989 Intelligence service report compiled from information and drawings I provided at our meeting at the safe house confirms they knew of the 'supergun' at that time.

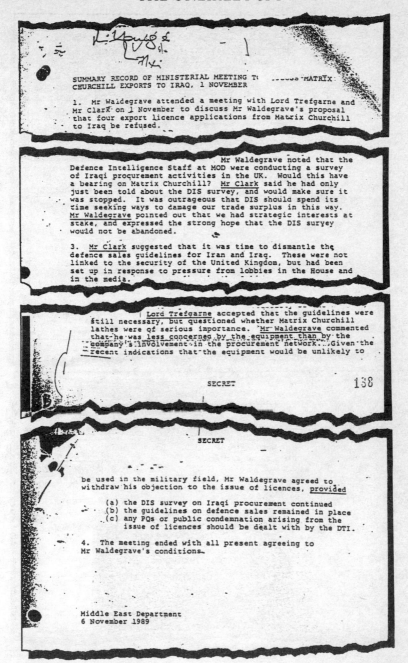

SUMMARY RECORD OF MINISTERIAL MEETING T̶ ̶.̶.̶.̶.̶.̶ MATRIX
CHURCHILL EXPORTS TO IRAQ, 1 NOVEMBER

1. Mr Waldegrave attended a meeting with Lord Trefgarne and
Mr Clark on 1 November to discuss Mr Waldegrave's proposal
that four export licence applications from Matrix Churchill
to Iraq be refused.

Mr Waldegrave noted that the
Defence Intelligence Staff at MOD were conducting a survey
of Iraqi procurement activities in the UK. Would this have
a bearing on Matrix Churchill? Mr Clark said he had only
just been told about the DIS survey, and would make sure it
was stopped. It was outrageous that DIS should spend its
time seeking ways to damage our trade surplus in this way.
Mr Waldegrave pointed out that we had strategic interests at
stake, and expressed the strong hope that the DIS survey
would not be abandoned.

3. Mr Clark suggested that it was time to dismantle the
defence sales guidelines for Iran and Iraq. These were not
linked to the security of the United Kingdom, but had been
set up in response to pressure from lobbies in the House and
in the media.

Lord Trefgarne accepted that the guidelines were
still necessary, but questioned whether Matrix Churchill
lathes were of serious importance. Mr Waldegrave commented
that he was less concerned by the equipment than by the
company's involvement in the procurement network. Given the
recent indications that the equipment would be unlikely to

SECRET   138

SECRET

be used in the military field, Mr Waldegrave agreed to
withdraw his objection to the issue of licences, provided

(a) the DIS survey on Iraqi procurement continued
(b) the guidelines on defence sales remained in place
(c) any PQs or public condemnation arising from the
    issue of licences should be dealt with by the DTI.

4. The meeting ended with all present agreeing to
Mr Waldegrave's conditions.

Middle East Department
6 November 1989

6 November 1989 Record of meeting at which Cardoen licences were approved.

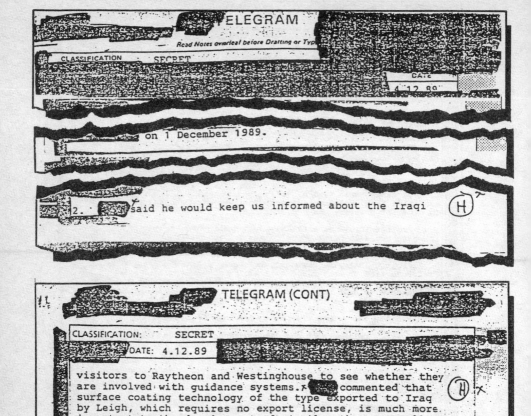

4 December 1989 Shows cooperation between British and US intelligence services since I was being asked to obtain information on American companies Raytheon and Westinghouse.

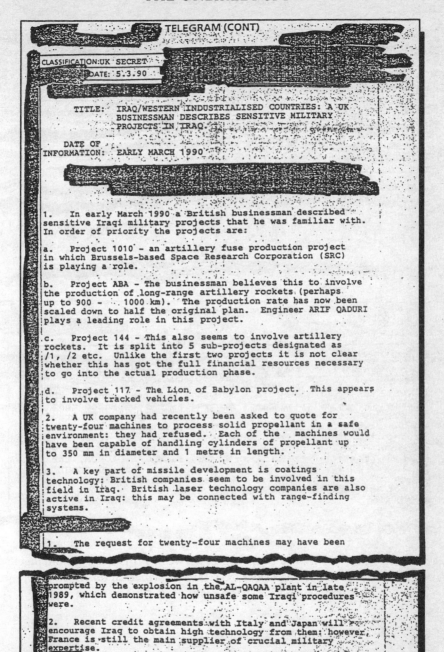

TELEGRAM (CONT)

CLASSIFICATION:UK SECRET
DATE: 5.3.90

TITLE: IRAQ/WESTERN INDUSTRIALISED COUNTRIES: A UK
         BUSINESSMAN DESCRIBES SENSITIVE MILITARY
         PROJECTS IN IRAQ.

DATE OF
INFORMATION: EARLY MARCH 1990

1.   In early March 1990 a British businessman described
sensitive Iraqi military projects that he was familiar with.
In order of priority the projects are:

a.   Project 1010 - an artillery fuse production project
in which Brussels-based Space Research Corporation (SRC)
is playing a role.

b.   Project ABA - The businessman believes this to involve
the production of long-range artillery rockets (perhaps
up to 900 - 1000 km). The production rate has now been
scaled down to half the original plan. Engineer ARIF QADURI
plays a leading role in this project.

c.   Project 144 - This also seems to involve artillery
rockets. It is split into 5 sub-projects designated as
/1, /2 etc. Unlike the first two projects it is not clear
whether this has got the full financial resources necessary
to go into the actual production phase.

d.   Project 117 - The Lion of Babylon project. This appears
to involve tracked vehicles.

2.   A UK company had recently been asked to quote for
twenty-four machines to process solid propellant in a safe
environment: they had refused. Each of the machines would
have been capable of handling cylinders of propellant up
to 350 mm in diameter and 1 metre in length.

3.   A key part of missile development is coatings
technology: British companies seem to be involved in this
field in Iraq. British laser technology companies are also
active in Iraq: this may be connected with range-finding
systems.

1.   The request for twenty-four machines may have been

prompted by the explosion in the AL-QAQAA plant in late
1989, which demonstrated how unsafe some Iraqi procedures
were.

2.   Recent credit agreements with Italy and Japan will
encourage Iraq to obtain high technology from them: however
France is still the main supplier of crucial military
expertise.

Early March 1990 Partial list of Iraqi projects I compiled for intelligence
service.

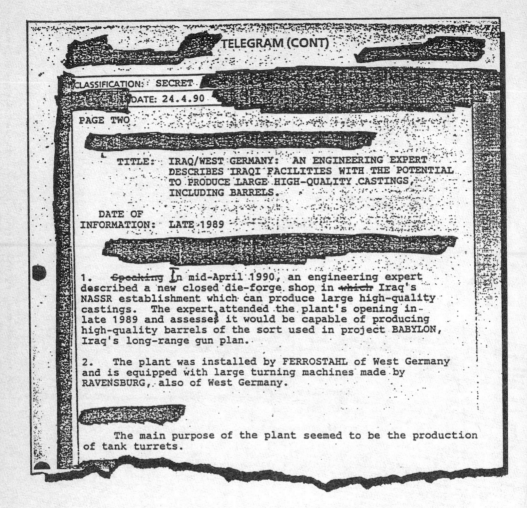

TELEGRAM (CONT)

CLASSIFICATION: SECRET
DATE: 24.4.90
PAGE TWO

    TITLE: IRAQ/WEST GERMANY: AN ENGINEERING EXPERT
    DESCRIBES IRAQI FACILITIES WITH THE POTENTIAL
    TO PRODUCE LARGE HIGH-QUALITY CASTINGS
    INCLUDING BARRELS.

DATE OF
INFORMATION: LATE 1989

1. Speaking In mid-April 1990, an engineering expert
described a new closed die-forge shop in which Iraq's
NASSR establishment which can produce large high-quality
castings. The expert attended the plant's opening in
late 1989 and assesses it would be capable of producing
high-quality barrels of the sort used in project BABYLON,
Iraq's long-range gun plan.

2. The plant was installed by FERROSTAHL of West Germany
and is equipped with large turning machines made by
RAVENSBURG, also of West Germany.

    The main purpose of the plant seemed to be the production
of tank turrets.

24 April 1990 Confirms I supplied details of supergun to intelligence service in 1989.

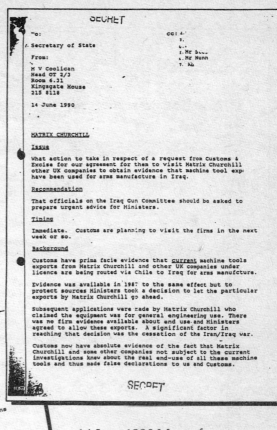

An investigation will clearly bring all these cases to light.

Most of the machine tools in question will be removed from any export control following the recent COCOM meeting unless a decision is taken now to retain control to all or selected destinations.

Argument

There are three issues to be addressed:

(1) are Ministers willing to have the 1987 and subsequent decisions exposed and made the subject of courtroom argument?

(2) are Ministers willing to face a worsening in our relations with Iraq?

(3) if the answers to (1) & (2) are affirmative should we retain controls on machine tools despite the COCOM relaxation and if so to what destinations?

Given the fact that all machine tools can be used for manufacture of arms a decision in principle is now needed on whether the UK should licence such exports to countries subject to a UK arms embargo. (Currently Syria, Libya, Iran, Iraq, S. Africa, Burma, China and Taiwan). While a stout defence of not doing so can be mounted any such decision would contrast sharply with the very far-reaching interpretation currently placed on the embargo (eg not supplying parts or spares for aircraft which could be converted for in-flight refuelling). Presentationally such a decision would sit uncomfortably with the concern over the super-gun.

Iraq is already very huffy about recent successful attempts to break-up their arms procurement activities and a move against Matrix-Churchill which is Iraqi owned will only add to the problem. To the extent that other companies are involved the current line - that if people break our laws they must expect punishment, and that we are not picking on Iraq - can be sustained. But UK trade interests in Iraq will no doubt suffer (and possibly some unfortunate people also).

The dirty washing liable to emerge from the action proposed by Customs & Excise will add to the problems posed by the gun. For DTI the timing is extraordinarily embarrassing given recent correspondence between ourselves, MoD and FCO. Needless to say we were not aware of Customs knowledge and activity when we briefed MFT on this issue. This underlines the need for our formal inter-departmental forum for exchanging this sort of information to be looked at - this is currently in hand.

Conclusion

I expect you will wish to discuss this and Mr Steadman and I are ready for this.

M V COOLICAN

SECRET

14 June 1990 Memo from
M.V. Coolican, Head of Overseas
Trade, reveals panic setting in and
cover-up already being prepared.

TELEGRAM

CLASSIFICATION   SECRET

DATE
2.7.90

1.   For the record, the following is ▓▓▓▓ first person
record of his contacts with ▓▓▓ before and after the
Customs' visit to his company during 19 - 22 June.

2.   As I had been tipped off, first by ▓▓▓ and then
▓▓▓▓▓ before the visit I knew in advance and managed
to speak to Peter Wiltshire in Customs, who is aware that
we have a source in Matrix Churchill Ltd (MCL). Both then
and since Peter WILTSHIRE has been very helpful in keeping
me informed on the general thrust of the investigation
and detailed points about it.

           he describes the case as sensitive and
political not because of our interest but because of the
relevant matters involved export licence applications,
with the companies sending large amounts of documentation,
including component drawings, to the DTI. Therefore, any
prosecution would risk a large amount of potentially
damaging Government documentation being produced in court.

3.   Perhaps the most significant indication of whether
my relationship with ▓▓▓ will have any bearing on this
case is that ▓▓▓ did not ring me until Thursday, 21 June
three to four days after he knew the Customs were going
to make enquiries. Naturally, he was worried by the
investigation and both for himself and for his staff.
The cautioning of one of the members of staff and
suggesting that we seek legal advice worried him further.
However, he was reassured to some extent by the low-key
nature of the Customs' interviews (at no time did they
interview him) and he says that in the particular case
involved, the 'Cardoen' connection MCL have copies of the

large number of component drawings that they sent to the
DTI.

4.   Speaking to both Wiltshire and ▓▓▓ I got the feeling
that on balance they seemed to feel that prosecutions are
less likely not only because any contraventions of the
law might be described as technical as DTI have large
amounts of information and because the companies concerned
feel that they were being encouraged to expand their trade
in Iraq by the Government: also nearly all of the equipment
concerned will not be licencable after 1 July, and
retrospective prosecutions are less likely.

2 July 1990 Report by Balsom, formerly my controller, summarizing situation
after first Customs and Excise visit to Matrix Churchill. Intelligence service
already recognized potential embarrassment to government.

the department for Enterprise

Mr C A Weakford
Matrix Churchill Limited
PO Box 39
Fletchampsted Highway
Coventry
CV4 9QA

Department of
Trade and Industry

Kingsgate House
66-74 Victoria Street
London SW1E 6SW

Enquiries
071-215 5000

Telex 930069 DTIKH G
Fax 071-931 0397

Direct line 071 215 8102
Our ref MATRIX CHURCHILL
Your ref PFA/IF/471
Date 29th July 1990

Dear Mr Weakford

EXPORT LICENCE ENQUIRY

I am responding to your letters dated 5th and 23rd July 1990
addressed to myself and my colleague Mr Steadman respectively in
respect of the export licensing position of:

1)   one-case of parts required to modify Swarf Conveyors

2)   one case of shortages

3)   one side of garages

I am able to inform you that following assessment by our Technical
Adviser the above equipment do not require an export licence under
the current Export of Goods (Control) Order 1989.

You should note that the above assessment only applies to Group 3
of the above mentioned Order. Group 1 (Military goods) and
Group 2 (Atomic Energy and Nuclear goods) in the Order should be
consulted if appropriate.

The foregoing assessment has been made on the information given in
your letters dated 5th and 23rd July 1990.

Notice of changes to the export regulations are published in
'Lloyds List' available on subscription from Lloyds of London
Press telephone number 0206-772277.

Yours sincerely

PETER MAYNE

KHT15THUR.43

29 July 1990 Clearance from DTI, following Customs and Excise visit, for
Matrix Churchill to ship more equipment to Iraq to fulfil the Cardoen contract
for fuse parts.

31 October 1990 Intelligence service report made after my arrest reveals among other things the belief that I would keep quiet about my involvement with it.

Index

291